THE CORPORATE GUIDE TO THE MALCOLM BALDRIGE NATIONAL QUALITY AWARD

PROVEN STRATEGIES FOR BUILDING QUALITY INTO YOUR ORGANIZATION

The Malcolm Baldrige National Quality Award Series

*The Small Business Guide to the
Malcolm Baldrige National Quality Award*

*The Manufacturer's Guide to the
Malcolm Baldrige National Quality Award*

*The Service Industry's Guide to the
Malcolm Baldrige National Quality Award*

THE CORPORATE GUIDE TO THE MALCOLM BALDRIGE NATIONAL QUALITY AWARD

PROVEN STRATEGIES FOR BUILDING QUALITY INTO YOUR ORGANIZATION

SECOND EDITION

Marion Mills Steeples

ASQC QUALITY PRESS
Milwaukee, Wisconsin 53201-3005

BUSINESS ONE IRWIN
Homewood, Illinois 60430

This publication is designed to provide accurate and
authoritative information in regard to the subject matter
covered. It is sold with the understanding that neither the
author nor the publisher is engaged in rendering legal, accounting,
or other professional service. If legal advice or other expert
assistance is required, the services of a competent
professional should be sought.

From a Declaration of Principles jointly adopted by a Committee
of the American Bar Association and a Committee of Publishers.

ASQC Quality Press acquisitions assistant: Deborah Dunlap
ASQC Quality Press production editor: Mary Beth Nilles
Sponsoring editor: Jean Marie Geracie
Project editor: Jean Roberts
Production manager: Diane Palmer
Jacket designer: Image House, Inc.
Compositor: Impressions, a Division of Edwards Brothers, Inc.
Typeface: 11/13 Electra
Printer: R. R. Donnelley & Sons Company

Library of Congress Cataloging-in-Publication Data

Steeples, Marion Mills.
    The corporate guide to the Malcolm Baldrige National Quality Award
    : proven strategies for building quality into your organization /
    Marion Mills Steeples. — 2nd ed.
        p.   cm.   (The Malcolm Baldrige National Quality Award series)
        ISBN 1-55623-957-2
        1. Total quality management.   2. Malcolm Baldrige National Quality
    Award.   I. Title.   II. Series.
    HD62.15.S74   1993
    658.5'62—dc20   92-26216

Printed in the United States of America
1 2 3 4 5 6 7 8 9 0 DOC 9 8 7 6 5 4 3 2

For John Mills and Victoria Joy

FOREWORD

The Corporate Guide to the Malcolm Baldrige National Quality Award meets the challenge of being both an eminently readable book about the principles of quality and an immensely valuable reference to the Baldrige Quality process.

If you are considering whether to make the investment of time to read this book, keep in mind that quality is no longer an optional concern for corporate America.

While it might seem implausible, a little more than a decade ago consciousness of the importance of quality and customer satisfaction was relatively low in the United States. At that time, we subscribed to certain "truths" about quality, such as better quality costs more, quality requires extra time to produce, and quality programs best fit manufacturing. Today, thanks in considerable measure to the total quality movement and the Malcolm Baldrige National Quality Award, leaders in quality have dispelled the old myths. New truths have emerged. We now know that raising quality doesn't raise costs, it lowers them; that quality doesn't take time, it saves it; and that service organizations need quality most urgently.

The recurring question in our society is "How do you become more competitive?" A good surrogate question is "What are you doing about quality?" The fundamental answer is that we must become competitive one person at a time. Quality is a personal responsibility. Quality is achieved through personal excellence, with an expectation of perfection. Human beings can operate to that standard, and they thrill at operating to that standard. And the aggregation of all of us working on quality ultimately holds the potential to substantially affect our country's future.

The Baldrige process does, indeed, have a national consequence. If every institution in the United States—service, manufacturing, and public—would embrace the philosophy of meeting the standards of the Baldrige

Award, and would commit to them with genuine enthusiasm, there would be a tremendous leveraging effect on our country as a whole. My instinctive calculation is that the economic multipliers that would be engaged in for quality improvement (which include more research and development, the acquisition and employment of new equipment, and the deployment of better processes) would raise the seedbed of our economy. The Gross Domestic Product would go up a minimum of one percentage point, from a growth rate of typically two-and-a-half or three to a typical growth rate of three-and-a-half or four. The whole economy would flourish, we would serve our customers more, and the cycle would reinforce itself.

Our destiny is in our hands. We have the privilege of expecting perfection and when we present perfection to our customers we will do more business, increase the wealth of this nation, and improve the choices and freedom of our republic.

Whether your organization is motivated to reach for the Baldrige Award or simply aspires to elevate its quality level, the two subjects usefully converge in this unique dual-purpose text. Marion Steeples here outlines the quality strategies that have worked at Baldrige-winning companies and makes information accessible so that you can better understand and implement total quality.

Robert W. Galvin
Chairman of the Executive Committee, Motorola Inc.
Chairman of the Board of Overseers,
Malcolm Baldrige National Quality Award
1989–1991

ABOUT THIS BOOK

Everybody hates to take tests.

All the same, since the Malcolm Baldrige National Quality Award was created in 1987, hundreds of companies have applied and gone through the close scrutiny of its examination process. More significantly, over 500,000 copies of the Application Guidelines have been requested by companies eager to improve their quality efforts. The numbers and range of interested companies grow each year. This despite the fact that it is the country's most thoroughly rigorous prize.

All this activity is driven by a great urgency in the United States to improve quality. Those companies that have embraced quality will most often say that, for them, it was a matter of corporate survival. The Malcolm Baldrige Award is the manifestation of the growing opinion that quality is also a matter of national survival.

In response to the growing national interest in quality, there has been a profusion of quality-related publications. These range from condensed how-to manuals to massive reference volumes. Much of the information available is good, useful stuff, and any company that is serious about quality will end up with its own library of favorites.

To date, most of the information that is available falls into two distinct categories: The first group is highly technical, written chiefly for degreed quality practitioners, and weighted heavily toward quality implementation in the manufacturing sector. The second group is a sizable library of primers geared toward business leaders who know little about continuous quality except that they would like their companies to practice it. These books typically offer a set of quality principles espoused by the author or the author's mentor.

What has been missing is a complete department-by-department, goal-by-goal, area-by-area outline of what total quality management encompasses. That outline became available with the creation of the Baldrige Award. The Baldrige criteria are a complete and one might say "nondenominational" framework of what it takes to be a quality company. Designed with the help of our nation's leading quality experts, the Applications Guidelines are an objective yardstick by which to measure a total quality process.

The rapid acceptance of the Malcolm Baldrige National Quality Award as the national standard of excellence is in large part due to the fundamental value the Guidelines provide in laying out a blueprint for quality, while at the same time allowing each organization to develop its own quality system appropriate to its situation.

Unfortunately, the Guidelines can tell you more about where you want to be than how to get there.

As more and more companies become interested in Baldrige, the challenge becomes finding sources of information on how to utilize the Guidelines to integrate a total system of quality management. While seminars and consultants proliferate, to date there has been no comprehensive reference providing background information to help companies benchmark their quality efforts against those of the winning companies.

That's where this book comes in. Together with the Baldrige Guidelines, it is designed to be a practical and affordable resource for those interested in quality improvement. It is intended both for those companies that seriously aspire to win the Baldrige (the few) and for those that simply aspire to improve quality (the many).

The book is organized into three major areas: The first section explores the economic pressures that led to the development of the Malcolm Baldrige National Quality Award, as well as hard evidence of the value of pursuing quality. In section two, each of the seven Baldrige categories is demystified by looking at a Baldrige application case study. In the third section, winners are profiled along with their contributions to the quality movement.

It would be difficult to overestimate the ultimate impact of the new Baldrige way of thinking. Properly applied, the science of quality management is a CEO's dream come true. The systematic pursuit of quality has the ability to cut development and production costs, eliminate waste, streamline processes, enhance worker morale, improve customer relations, and increase market share and profits. What is more, there doesn't seem to be any sort of business—or any aspect of business—that can't benefit from an integrated system of quality management. From heavy manufacturing companies to high-tech electronics firms, from retail and service industries to hospitals and even city governments, organizations that have made the commitment to quality have reported stunning results.

No cash comes with the Baldrige Award—not directly anyway. Companies that have won the Award have made marketing hay of it, but those companies that have vied and lost have also come away big winners, with more muscular, streamlined organizations, higher profits, happier workers, and improved products and services.

There is no hidden quality agenda. The only valid reason to pursue the Baldrige Award is out of a desire to become a continuously improving quality company.

As Will Rogers once remarked: "Everyone says, 'something must be done,' but this time it looks like it might be us!"

The blueprint is here. It's time to roll up our sleeves.

Marion Mills Steeples

In the spirit of continuous improvement, suggestions and additions to this book are most welcome. Please send to:

Marion Mills Steeples
c/o ASQC Quality Press
611 East Wisconsin Avenue
P.O. Box 3005
Milwaukee, Wisconsin 53201-3005

ACKNOWLEDGMENTS

Above all else, quality is a people-driven phenomenon. This book draws on the recent, rich accounts of our country's quality breakthroughs that first created and now drive the Malcolm Baldrige National Quality Award. To name all those who have embraced this new way of thinking and have helped spread the quality message would be impossible.

Likewise, the Malcolm Baldrige National Quality Award (MBNQA) owes its success to the contributions of literally thousands of people who have accepted the quality challenge. Certainly, the Award would not have been possible without the early practitioners in the quality movement, the Award advocates who persevered to make it a reality, and all of those who have since been involved enabling the Award process work. Instrumental in the Award's rapid progress were a handful of visionary corporate leaders who reorganized their enterprises in hope of making things better. Moreover, we owe a collective debt to all the people at Baldrige-winning companies for showing us that world-class quality is an achievable standard for business in the United States. I wish to especially acknowledge Curt Reimann and the superb staff at the MBNQA Program of the National Institute of Standards and Technology (NIST). With their skill and guidance, the Award process has flourished.

Special thanks are due to a number of people who helped at various stages with the manuscript's preparation. My gratitude goes to Elaine Gowan for her dedication in compiling the early drafts; to Vicky Powell for her ingenuity in graphics development; to John Powell for his valued insights; to Peter Cunningham, Gary Kochenberger, Wendy Foster-Leigh, Paul Manoogian, Jeff Roedel, Candace Stowell, and Pat Townsend for their comments, suggestions, and support; and to Carson Reed for his encouragement and editorial assistance.

CONTENTS

THE CORPORATE GUIDE TO THE MALCOLM BALDRIGE NATIONAL QUALITY AWARD

PROVEN STRATEGIES FOR BUILDING QUALITY INTO YOUR ORGANIZATION

PART 1

THE QUALITY CHALLENGE: The Quest for Excellence

CHAPTER 1

GLOBAL ECONOMIC
REALITIES

It is for America and America alone to determine whether a system of free economic enterprise—an economic order compatible with freedom and progress—shall or shall not prevail in this century.

Henry R. Luce, 1898–1967

A SENSE OF URGENCY

Survival is the impetus for quality, as foreign competition challenges the U.S. economy. For two decades our nation's growth has been exceeded by our competitors', and many Americans now recognize that improved quality of goods and services enhances productivity, lowers costs, and increases profitability.

The U.S. economy dominated the post–World War II era, and demand for our consumer products grew rapidly during the 1950s and 1960s. For a while, American products set the standards for quality. But American business was preoccupied with efficiency over effectiveness, with price over value, with economies of scale. A seemingly insatiable appetite for consumer goods led to a mind-set that emphasized productivity at the expense of quality. For two decades, "planned obsolescence" was taught in the nation's business schools and practiced in the nation's factories.

As the quality of goods made in the United States declined, consumers lost confidence in American products and began to vote with their dollars. As consumer sophistication grew, superior quality became a critical factor in buying decisions. In 1978, fewer than four in ten U.S. consumers said quality was as important as price in their purchases. Ten years later that percentage had doubled. Customers don't have time to waste on product failure. To compete in the 1990s, American companies must deliver essentially perfect products. That has been the competition's goal, and the marketplace records their gains.

Since 1975, the United States has imported more than it exported. This trend in the balance of trade continued through the last half of the 1970s and into the 1980s. Export of U.S. goods increased from $254 billion in 1987 to $322 billion in 1988; however, imports continued to rise from $406 billion to almost $423 billion. Through the 1980s, the United States imported $920 billion more goods and services than it exported. The trend continues. In 1990, $394 billion was exported, while $495 billion was imported.

Evidence of the crisis abounds: Detroit auto factories supplied 71.3 percent of the U.S. market in 1980. By 1991, that market share skidded to 62.5 percent. In the early 1980s, two of the world's largest banks were American. By 1991, Citicorp, America's biggest bank, ranked eleventh. Eight of the ten top banks were Japanese. There are practically no U.S. companies in the consumer electronics industry. While 94 percent of the computers sold in the United States in the 1980s were American made, that figure dropped to 66 percent by 1991. The U.S. share of the global semiconductor market shrunk from 57.2 percent to 36.5 percent.

Overview of Quality Management

While concepts of quality can be traced to the craft guilds of the Middle Ages, the scientific approach to improved quality began with railroad management, with the movement toward "scientific management," and with the advent of modern statistical methods in the early part of this century. Two creators of modern statistics, Sir Ronald A. Fisher and Walter A. Shewhart, laid the groundwork in the 1920s. Pioneering work in statistical quality control (SQC) was done by Shewhart at Bell Telephone Laboratories. Later other industrial theorists, including the now-renowned quality experts W. Edwards Deming and Joseph M. Juran, refined and broadened the usefulness of those techniques.

In the early 1940s, the U.S. Department of War converted quality theory into a practical means for fighting World War II. Classified under the name Z-1 in the United States and Standards 600 in England, statistical methods and quality control played an important role in helping the Allies build needed military might to win the war.

After WWII, with its industries in ruin, Japan experienced a quality crisis worse than the current U.S. situation. Ironically, it was the U.S. occupation of Japan that prescribed the use of statistical methods to help the defeated nation rebuild its industries. To reconstruct its economy, the Japanese set out in earnest to improve quality. During the 1950s, they enlisted the help of American advisors, notably Drs. Deming and Juran. Japanese senior managers began to master total quality control and they began to integrate a broader management philosophy of quality values throughout all business activities. The Union of Japanese Scientists and Engineers (JUSE), founded in 1946, was there to coordinate and guide the effort. JUSE also established massive worker-education programs and launched the Deming Prize in 1951, to further stimulate quality improvement.

Japanese quality caught up with that of the West in the 1970s, as sharply improved Japanese products flooded the marketplace. By the late 1970s, Japanese electronics and autos had gained major U.S. market shares. These high-quality yet affordable products drew attention. Incredulous executives from such American companies as Xerox and Motorola toured Japanese plants and discovered defect levels 500 to 1,000 times better than those in comparable U.S. facilities.

Our competitors know well that the primary effect of concentrating on improved quality is customer impact. Brand names like Nikon, Sony, Seiko, and Honda have achieved the status of the German cameras and Swiss watches of an earlier era. Buyers flock to high-quality products and overseas manufacturers build market share and further reduce unit costs. Today's consumers are sold on Japanese cars and cameras, and other foreign products—German machine tools, Italian shoes—and escalating import prices haven't diminished their demand.

With a 20-year head start, Japanese businesses have a strong lead in the race for improved quality; they continue to increase that lead by systematic application of Total Quality Management principles.

Nevertheless, American business has recently made dramatic quality improvements. More than 87 percent of the largest U.S. industrial corporations have expanded their quality initiatives since 1987, according to an executive survey conducted by Organizational Dynamics, a Massachusetts consulting firm. Naturally enough, the greatest improvements have been seen in those American industries most threatened by foreign competition. In 1989, computer manufacturer Hewlett-Packard achieved its ten-year goal to improve quality tenfold. U.S. automakers boosted quality. Prior to 1969, U.S. auto warranties were typically three months or 4,000 miles; in 1991, Chrysler covered selected models for seven years or 70,000 miles. When Stanley Works, the 140-year-old toolmaker in New Britain, Connecticut, was hit in the early 1980s with market-share erosion caused by Asian imports, the company fought back with quality circles and worker training. Scrap rates dropped from 15 percent to 3 percent over a six-year period. Since 1980, Stanley's profits have more than doubled.

Quality has the potential to turn around our national trade deficit. As the quality of U.S. goods increases, so do sales to foreign countries, including Japan. In the tough market of auto parts, Monroe Auto Equipment, a Tenneco division, put on an all-out quality effort. Productivity in its 36 plants increased 26 percent from 1986 to 1990; annual sales are near $900 million—an increase of 70 percent. A recent shipment of 60,000 shock absorbers to Toyota was rated Zero Defects.

However, the rules keep changing—standards keep rising. Despite incremental quality gains made by U.S. businesses, foreign competitors continue to expand market share, and the trade deficit continues to grow.

The strategic importance of quality to the United States has not gone unnoticed. U.S. Secretary of Commerce Robert Mosbacher has cautioned that lack of high-quality production at competitive cost is America's Achilles' heel. President George Bush declared high-quality U.S. goods and services the priority most vital to American prosperity and national security. The quality crisis is no longer restricted to a handful of industries targeted by the Japanese. As expectations rise, world demand for quality is emerging as the single most critical factor in the success of any business, from corporations to the corner store.

THE CASE FOR CHANGE

U.S. businesses that do not produce high-quality products and services will not survive the 1990s. Consumers are too sophisticated. Today's shopper is cognizant that foreign products and services are equal to, and in many cases better than, those made in America.

In the recent past, the primary concern of many businesses has been financial vitality in the short term. Corporate image was at the mercy of business cycles and the pressure was on operations to produce volume. Short-term thinking precluded long-term results as we mortgaged the future for the present.

Causes for the current problems date back to events that occurred more than one hundred years ago. Development of the Taylor scientific management approach in the United States at the turn of the century inadvertently set the stage for the quality crisis that hit in the 1960s and 1970s.

Fredrick W. Taylor invented time and motion studies to help improve industrial productivity. A central tenet of Taylorism was separation of functions. As a result, quality was separated from planning, production, and distribution. This separation required systematic inspection to control and assure the quality of goods and services. The popular spread of Taylor's theories through American industry made productivity rise, but it also created the Byzantine management structures that pervade many of America's companies.

Ironically, Taylorism was meant to improve the efficiency of American industry but made continuous improvement of quality and effectiveness next to impossible. Responsibilities for quality became vague. As functional units increased in number and internal political power, quality declined. Quality Assurance professionals, using ever more sophisticated techniques, still struggled with defects as a consequence of the separation of their function from the other units of the company. The result is that products and services in the United States require more labor hours than those made in Japan. The more complex the operation, the worse the ratio between labor costs and the waste of rework.

Inspection to Integration

It appears U.S. industry has finally begun to recognize the tremendous cost of relegating quality to a separate or specialized function. The loss of customers, the loss of market share, the loss of competitive edge began the drive away from ineffective traditional methods of attempting to inspect quality into products. Awareness is growing that, to be competitive in the global marketplace, management must use an integrated approach for increasing customer satisfaction through improving quality. Only by integrating quality in all processes, all systems, and all practices can quality be optimized. By systematically preventing problems, products and services

FIGURE 1.1
Evolution of the Quality Movement

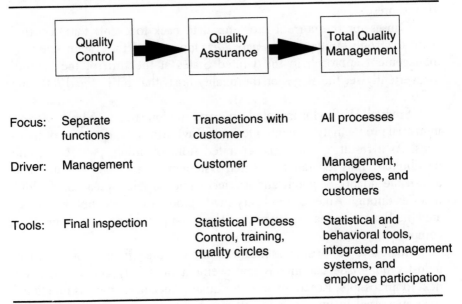

	Quality Control	Quality Assurance	Total Quality Management
Focus:	Separate functions	Transactions with customer	All processes
Driver:	Management	Customer	Management, employees, and customers
Tools:	Final inspection	Statistical Process Control, training, quality circles	Statistical and behavioral tools, integrated management systems, and employee participation

can be delivered to customers at lower costs and at higher levels of satisfaction.

Over the course of 50 years, from America to Japan and back again, these management methods of imbedding quality into the entire corporation have evolved to become known as Total Quality Management (TQM).

CHAPTER 2

QUALITY MADE IN THE USA

We have to encourage American executives to get out of their boardrooms and onto the factory floor to learn how their products are made and how they can be made better.

Malcolm Baldrige, Secretary of Commerce, 1981–1987

INITIAL AWARD SUPPORT

The origin of what is now the Malcolm Baldrige National Quality Award can be traced to a series of events that began in the early 1980s. Various groups of industry and government leaders began looking in earnest at the seriousness of America's declining position in the global marketplace. One group of concerned executives formed the National Advisory Council for Quality (NACQ) in 1982. NACQ searched for ways to increase the U.S. competitive edge. Another group, the American Productivity Center—now the American Productivity and Quality Center (APQC)—in 1983, sponsored productivity and quality conferences whose outcome was a recommendation to establish a national quality award similar to Japan's Deming Prize. After the September 1983 White House Conference on Productivity, an April 1984 report called for annually awarding a national productivity achievement medal.

As international competitive pressure grew in the mid-1980s, so too did the interest in a national productivity and quality award. Jackson Grayson, APQC's chairman, felt strongly enough about the issue that he proposed that the president of the United States present such an award to signify its importance. Frank Collins, rear admiral and executive of quality assurance for the Defense Logistics Agency, chaired a private-sector group, the National Organization for the United States Quality Award. As the push for an award matured, so did the general consensus that it should focus on comprehensive quality management. By the fall of 1985, the Collins-led group had developed draft criteria and funding strategies.

Legislative Efforts

Congressman Don Fuqua (D-Florida), then chair of the House Committee on Science and Technology, was approached in January 1985 by John Hudiburg, chairman and CEO of Florida Power & Light, to develop legislation for the award. Early in 1986, the House Subcommittee on Science, Research, and Technology began investigating the pursuit of quality by U.S. businesses. In August 1986, Fuqua introduced a bill to establish a national quality award. While it did not win passage that year, support for the initiative grew.

In January 1987, the legislation was reintroduced. It passed in the House of Representatives on June 8, 1987. Then on July 25, 1987, Secretary of Commerce Malcolm Baldrige was killed in a rodeo accident. As "Mac" Baldrige had been a supporter of the award as a way to improve our country's competitive position, the award was renamed in his honor. This action accelerated the bill's passage by the Senate. On August 20, 1987, President Reagan signed the bill, thus creating Public Law 100–107 and confirming that quality had indeed become a matter of national strategic importance.

Ronald Reagan stated at the inauguration of the Malcolm Baldrige National Quality Award, January 25, 1988:

> *The economic liberty and strong competition that are indispensable to economic progress were principles "Mac" Baldrige stressed, whether as a successful businessman or as a dynamic and effective Secretary of Commerce. They are the engines of growth, jobs, and prosperity in any society, along with the good management and attention to quality and customer needs that the Award will promote.*

The purpose of the National Quality Award program is to help the United States improve quality and productivity by:

- Stimulating companies to attain excellence for the pride of achievement.
- Recognizing outstanding companies to provide examples to others.
- Establishing guidelines that business, governmental, and other organizations can use to evaluate and improve their own quality efforts.
- Providing information from winning companies on how to manage for superior quality.

A biographical sketch of Mac Baldrige and the Malcolm Baldrige National Quality Improvement Act of 1987 appear on the following pages.

Malcolm Baldrige was nominated as Secretary of Commerce by President Ronald Reagan on December 11, 1980, and confirmed by the United States Senate on January 22, 1981.

During his tenure, Baldrige played a major role in developing and carrying out administration trade policy. He took the lead in resolving difficulties in technology transfers with China and India. Baldrige held the first cabinet-level talks with the Soviet Union in seven years, which paved the way for increased access by U.S. firms to the Soviet market. He was highly regarded by the world's preeminent leaders.

Leading the administration's effort to pass the Export Trading Company Act of 1982, Baldrige was named by the president to chair a cabinet-level trade strike force to search out unfair trading practices and recommend ways to end those practices. He was the leader in the reform of the nation's antitrust laws.

Baldrige's award-winning managerial excellence contributed to long-term improvement in the economy and the efficiency and effectiveness of government. Within the Commerce Department, Baldrige reduced the budget by more than 30 percent and administrative personnel by 25 percent.

Baldrige worked during his boyhood as a ranch hand and earned several awards as a professional team roper on the rodeo circuit. He was Professional Rodeo Man of the Year in 1980 and was installed in the National Cowboy Hall of Fame in Oklahoma City in 1984.

Malcolm Baldrige died July 25, 1987, in a rodeo accident in California. His service as Secretary of Commerce was one of the longest in history. He was possibly the most colorful Secretary of Commerce and one of the most beloved.

Source: National Institute of Standards and Technology

H.R. 812

One Hundredth Congress of the United States of America

AT THE FIRST SESSION

*Begun and held at the City of Washington on Tuesday, the sixth day of January,
one thousand nine hundred and eighty-seven*

An Act

To amend the Stevenson-Wydlyer Technology Innovation Act of 1980 to establish the
Malcolm Baldrige National Quality Award, with the objective of encouraging American
business and other organizations to practice effective quality control in the provision of
their goods and services.

*Be it enacted by the Senate and House of Representatives of the United States
of America in Congress assembled,*

SECTION 1. SHORT TITLE.

This Act may be cited as the "Malcolm Baldrige National Quality Improvement Act of 1987".

SEC. 2. FINDINGS AND PURPOSES.

(a) FINDINGS.–The Congress finds and declares that–

(1) the leadership of the United States in product and process quality
has been challenged strongly (and sometimes successfully) by foreign
competition, and our Nation's productivity growth has improved less than
our competitors over the last two decades;

(2) American business and industry are beginning to understand
that poor quality costs companies as much as 20 percent of sales revenues
nationally, and that improved quality of goods and services goes hand in
hand with improved productivity, lower costs, and increased profitability;

(3) strategic planning for quality and quality improvement programs, through a commitment to excellence in manufacturing and services, are becoming more and more essential to the well-being of our
Nation's economy and our ability to compete effectively in the global
marketplace;

(4) improved management understanding of the factory floor, worker
involvement in quality, and greater emphasis on statistical process
control can lead to dramatic improvements in the cost and quality of
manufactured products;

(5) the concept of quality improvement is directly applicable to small
companies as well as large, to service industries as well as manufacturing,
and to the public sector as well as private enterprise;

(6) in order to be successful, quality improvement programs must be
management-led and customer-oriented and this may require fundamental changes in the way companies and agencies do business;

(7) several major industrial nations have successfully coupled rigorous private sector quality audits with national awards giving special
recognition to those enterprises the audits identify as the very best; and

(8) a national quality award program of this kind in the United
States would help improve quality and productivity by–

H.R. 812—2

    (A) helping to stimulate American companies to improve quality and productivity for the pride of recognition while obtaining a competitive edge through increased profits,

    (B) recognizing the achievements of those companies which improve the quality of their goods and services and providing an example to others,

    (C) establishing guidelines and criteria that can be used by business, industrial, governmental, and other organizations in evaluating their own quality improvement efforts, and

    (D) providing specific guidance for other American organizations that wish to learn how to manage for high quality by making available detailed information on how winning organizations were able to change their cultures and achieve eminence.

(b) PURPOSE – It is the purpose of this Act to provide for the establishment and conduct of a national quality improvement program under which (1) awards are given to selected companies and other organizations in the United States that practice effective quality management and as a result make significant improvements in the quality of their goods and services, and (2) information is disseminated about the successful strategies and programs.

SEC. 3 ESTABLISHMENT OF THE MALCOLM BALDRIGE NATIONAL QUALITY AWARD PROGRAM.

    (a) IN GENERAL – The Stevenson-Wydler Technology Innovation Act of 1980 (15 U.S.C. 3701 et seq.) is amended by designating sections 16, 17, and 18 as sections 17, 18, and 19, respectively, and by inserting after section 15 the following new section:

"SEC. 16. MALCOLM BALDRIGE NATIONAL QUALITY AWARD.

    "(a) ESTABLISHMENT. – There is hereby established the Malcolm Baldrige National Quality Award, which shall be evidenced by a medal bearing the inscriptions 'Malcolm Baldrige National Quality Award' and 'The Quest for Excellence'. The medal shall be of such design and materials and bear such additional inscriptions as the Secretary may prescribe.

    "(b) MAKING AND PRESENTATION OF AWARD. – (1) The President (on the basis of recommendations received from the Secretary), or the Secretary, shall periodically make the award to companies and other organizations which in the judgment of the President or the Secretary have substantially benefited the economic or social wellbeing of the United States through improvements in the quality of their goods or services resulting from the effective practice of quality management, and which as a consequence are deserving of special recognition.

    "(2) The presentation of the award shall be made by the President or the Secretary with such ceremonies as the President or the Secretary may deem proper.

    "(3) An organization to which an award is made under this section, and which agrees to help other American organizations improve their quality management, may publicize its receipt of such award and use the award in its advertising, but it shall be ineligible to receive another such award in the same category for a period of 5 years.

H.R. 812—3

"(c) Categories in Which Award May be Given. – (1) Subject to paragraph (2), separate awards shall be made to qualifying organizations in each of the following categories –

"(A) Small businesses.

"(B) Companies or their subsidiaries.

"(C) Companies which primarily provide services.

"(2) The Secretary may at any time expand, subdivide, or otherwise modify the list of categories within which awards may be made as initially in effect under paragraph (1), and may establish separate awards for other organizations including units of government, upon a determination that the objectives of this section would be better served thereby; except that any such expansion, subdivision, modification, or establishment shall not be effective unless and until the Secretary has submitted a detailed description thereof to the Congress and a period of 30 days has elapsed since that submission.

"(3) Not more than two awards may be made within any subcategory in any year (and no award shall be made within any category or subcategory if there are no qualifying enterprises in that category or subcategory).

"(d) CRITERIA FOR QUALIFICATION. – (1) An organization may qualify for an award under this section only if it –

"(A) applies to the Director of the National Bureau of Standards in writing, for the award,

"(B) permits a rigorous evaluation of the way in which its business and other operations have contributed to improvements in the quality of goods and services, and

"(C) meets such requirements and specifications as the Secretary, after receiving recommendations from the Board of Overseers established under paragraph (2)(B) and the Director of the National Bureau of Standards, determines to be appropriate to achieve the objectives of this section.

In applying the provisions of subparagraph (C) with respect to any organization, the Director of the National Bureau of Standards shall rely upon an intensive evaluation by a competent board of examiners which shall review the evidence submitted by the organization and, through a site visit, verify the accuracy of the quality improvements claimed. The examination should encompass all aspects of the organization's current practice of quality management, as well as the organization's provision for quality management in its future goals. The award shall be given only to organizations which have made outstanding improvements in the quality of their goods or services (or both) and which demonstrate effective quality management through the training and involvement of all levels of personnel in quality improvement.

"(2)(A) The Director of the National Bureau of Standards shall, under appropriate contractual arrangements, carry out the Director's responsibilities under subparagraphs (A) and (B) of paragraph (1) through one or more broad-based nonprofit entities which are leaders in the field of quality management and which have a history of service to the society.

"(B) The Secretary shall appoint a board of overseers for the award, consisting of at least five persons selected for their preeminence in the field of quality management. This board shall meet annually to review the work of the contractor or contractors and make such suggestions for the improvement of the award process as they deem necessary. The board shall report the results of the award activities to the Director of the National Bureau of Standards each year, along with its recommendations for improvement of the process.

H.R. 812—4

"(e) INFORMATION AND TECHNOLOGY TRANSFER PROGRAM. – The Director of the National Bureau of Standards shall ensure that all program participants receive the complete results of their audits as well as detailed explanations of all suggestions for improvement. The Director shall also provide information about the awards and the successful quality improvement strategies and programs of the award-winning participants to all participants and other appropriate groups.

"(f)   FUNDING.– The Secretary is authorized to seek and accept gifts from public and private sources to carry out the program under this section. If additional sums are needed to cover the full cost of the program, the Secretary shall impose fees upon the organizations applying for the award in amounts sufficient to provide such additional sums.

"(g)   REPORT. –   The Secretary shall prepare and submit to the President and the Congress, within 3 years after the date of the enactment of this section, a report on the progress, findings, and conclusions of activities conducted pursuant to this section along with recommendations for possible modifications thereof.".

   (b)   CONFORMING AMENDMENT. – Section 9(d) of such Act (15 U.S.C. 3708(d) is amended by striking" or 16" and inserting in lieu thereof "16, or 17".

Speaker of the House of Representatives.

Vice President of the United States and President of the Senate.

APPROVED

AUG 2 0 1987

AWARD PROGRAM ORGANIZATION

The National Quality Award legislation placed responsibility for the Malcolm Baldrige Award in the Department of Commerce. Figure 2.1 depicts the Award program organization.

National Institute of Standards and Technology
An agency of the department—the National Bureau of Standards (now the National Institute of Standards and Technology, or NIST)—was charged to create and manage the Award program. Long involved in setting technical quality standards and measurements for U.S. industry, NIST was the logical choice for administering the National Quality Award.

Board of Overseers
The Secretary of Commerce appoints a Board of Overseers of at least five persons, selected for their renown in the quality management field. The overseers review the work of the contractor (the American Society for Quality Control), make improvement recommendations, and advise the

FIGURE 2.1
Malcolm Baldrige National Quality Award Organization

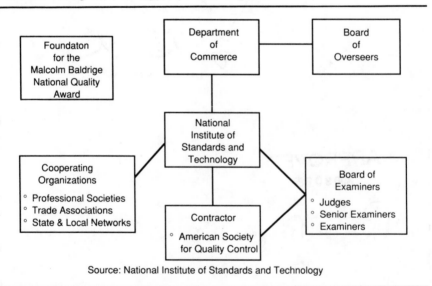

Source: National Institute of Standards and Technology

Secretary of Commerce and the Director of NIST. Overseers monitor the overall effectiveness of the Award and serve as the program's national conscience.

Board of Examiners

All Baldrige Award applications are reviewed by members of the Board of Examiners, which is comprised of over 200 quality experts. The Board of Examiners is a stratified group consisting of judges, senior examiners, and examiners. Annually, board members are selected through a competitive application process based on their experience, expertise, and peer recognition in the field of quality improvement. NIST appoints the judges. Senior Examiners are selected by the judges and approved by NIST. An examiner selection committee determines the Examiners. The board is a geographically diverse group drawn from service and manufacturing companies, government, academia, and trade and professional groups. Examiners do not represent any company or organization.

Each year, all Examiners are required to participate in a three-day training course based on the Award, its processes, scoring system, and criteria. This is a time to "recalibrate" the Examiner team and reduce scoring variability among the Examiners. Case studies are used to simulate the Award processes.

The growth in the scope of the Award is reflected in the expansion of the Board of Examiners, as Figure 2.2 illustrates.

Contractor

NIST contracts with private sector quality professionals for much of the day-to-day operation of the Award process. In the first three years of the program there were two contractors: the American Society for Quality

FIGURE 2.2
Malcolm Baldrige National Quality Award Board of Examiners

	1988	1989	1990	1991	1992
Judges	9	9	9	9	9
Senior Examiners	21	27	40	40	43
Examiners	70	98	128	178	214
Total	100	134	177	227	266

Source: National Institute of Standards and Technology

Control (ASQC) and the American Productivity and Quality Center (APQC). Together they formed a consortium to work with NIST and provide for the nuts-and-bolts operation of the Award. This included assistance in criteria development, training programs, the application review process, publicity, the Award ceremony, and the annual Quest for Excellence conference featuring Award winners. Since 1991, ASQC, a nonprofit association of professionals in the quality field, has been the sole contractor administering the Award.

Malcolm Baldrige National Quality Award Foundation

The legislation that created the Award envisioned a strong public-private partnership of government and industry banding together to improve the country's competitive position. No government funds were appropriated for the Award program. The private sector has shown its support by raising money, volunteering, and sharing quality information. The Foundation for the Malcolm Baldrige National Quality Award was organized in 1988 to establish the endowment that, along with applicant fees, supports the Award program. Through the leadership of the Board of Trustees, the foundation raised $10.4 million. Senior executives from supporting companies serve as trustees. The foundation is kept completely separate from the Award program, which is housed at NIST. This ensures the integrity of the Award selection process.

Cooperating Organizations

Cooperating organizations include a growing number of professional societies, trade associations, as well as state and local networks. These groups disseminate information on the Baldrige Award findings to foster quality improvement. This process contributes substantially to the National Quality Award's (NQA) information transfer activities.

BALDRIGE BLUEPRINT FOR QUALITY

The purpose of the Baldrige Award is to recognize U.S. companies that excel in quality management. The Award promotes:

- Awareness of quality as a vital competitive element.
- Understanding of quality excellence requirements.
- Sharing of successful quality strategies and their implementation benefits.

FIGURE 2.3
Malcolm Baldrige National Quality Award Winners

	1988	1989	1990	1991	Total
Manufacturing Companies	2	2	2	2	8
Service Companies	0	0	1	0	1
Small Businesses	1	0	1	1	3
Total	3	2	4	3	12
Maximum Possible	6	6	6	6	24

Source: National Institute of Standards and Technology

There are three Malcolm Baldrige National Quality Award (MBNQA) applicant categories: manufacturing companies, service companies, and small businesses.

Each year there can be a maximum of two Awards presented in each category. The rigorous competitive examination process selects only the best of the best. If the Award's challenging standards are not met, no Award is given. In the NQA's first four years, only 12 of the 24 possible Awards have been presented. This is illustrated by Figure 2.3, which shows Award winners by category.

Quality Excellence Requirements
The Baldrige Award has become the U.S. standard of excellence for total quality management. Baldrige winners deliver goods and services that are competitive with the best in the world. They attain this status by successfully applying TQM principles to every aspect of their business. The following essentials for total quality are embodied in the Baldrige criteria:

- Customers define quality.
- Senior corporate leadership must create clear quality values and build them into company operations.
- Excellent quality evolves from well-designed and well-executed systems and processes.
- Continuous improvement must be integrated into the management of all systems and processes.
- Companies must develop goals and strategic and operational plans to achieve quality leadership.
- Shortened response time for all operations and processes must be part of quality improvement efforts.

- Operations and decisions of the company must be based on facts.
- All employees must be appropriately trained, developed, and involved in quality improvement activities.
- Design quality and error prevention must be key elements of quality systems.
- Companies must communicate quality requirements to suppliers and work to elevate their performance.

These quality excellence requirements are embedded in the three-level examination framework that is designed for reliable evaluation and diagnosis. In the Baldrige criteria there are the seven examination categories, which contain examination items, and areas to address. Figure 2.4 illustrates the Award's three levels.

Examination Categories

The major components of a total quality management system are contained in the Award's seven examination categories:

1.0 Leadership

2.0 Information and Analysis

3.0 Strategic Quality Planning

4.0 Human Resource Development and Utilization

5.0 Management of Process Quality

6.0 Quality and Operational Results

7.0 Customer Focus and Satisfaction

The total value of all examination categories is 1,000 points. The NQA's category point allocations are depicted in Figure 2.5.

Examination Items

Examination items are the main elements of the examination categories. Each category contains at least two items. In the seven categories, there are approximately 30 examination items. Each item deals with a key quality component. Applicant responses are written to these item requirements.

FIGURE 2.4
Malcolm Baldrige National Quality Award Criteria

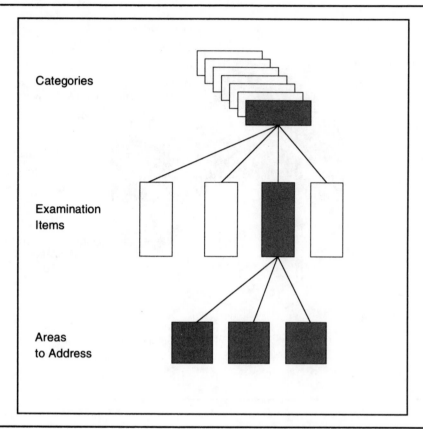

Areas to Address

Areas to address describe the intent of the examination items. Each examination item has between two and six areas to address (the average is about three). There are approximately 90 areas to address. They provide more specific information on the requirements in each examination item.

FIGURE 2.5
Malcolm Baldrige National Quality Award Point Allocation

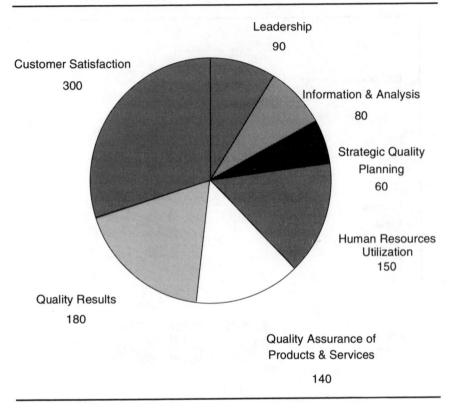

The complete current NQA examination categories, items, and areas to address are in the Application Guidelines.*

---

*To obtain an original copy of the MBNQA Application Guidelines and other materials pertinent to the Award contact:

Malcolm Baldrige National Quality Award
National Institute of Standards and Technology
Route 270 and Quince Orchard Road
Administration Building, Room A 537
Gaithersburg, MD 20899
Telephone: 301-948-3716

or simply use the perforated card contained in this book and a copy of the current MBNQA Application Guidelines will be sent directly to you.

The Baldrige Award's examination structure provides the blueprint for a quality system that can be applied to all businesses, large or small, manufacturing or service. While the Baldrige Award was created to acknowledge quality improvement among private, for-profit industries, the application framework is equally adaptable to other types of organizations such as government, schools, health care, etc. This adaptability is the reason the Award examination is referred to as a quality standard and the explanation for thousands of organizations not actually applying for the Award using the NQA Guidelines.

Development of the Baldrige Criteria

Dr. Curt Reimann, formerly a research scientist at NIST, has served as the Baldrige Award Administrator since the program began. He spearheaded the development of a highly credible, rigorous award system. Fundamental to this system are the criteria—the standards that are foundation of the Award. Reimann, working with U.S. quality leaders, attacked this formidable task by assessing the criteria used in existing awards, such as the NASA Excellence Award and the Deming Prize, and by reviewing the criteria proposed by the National Organization for the United States Quality Award. The results of these labors were the seven examination categories and the complete Baldrige Award system. Dedicated effort delivered the first MBNQA application guidelines in February 1988, ready for the first Award cycle.

The seven categories that are the nucleus of the Baldrige Award look deep into an organization, to its attitudes and implementation of total quality management. While continuous improvement is built into the Award program plan, the seven categories are its fundamental components: Leadership is the driver of the quality bus; Information and Analysis are the the fuel; Strategic Quality Planning is the map; Human Resources are the engine; Quality Assurance is the route; Quality Results are the landmarks; and Customer Satisfaction is the destination. The relationships of the seven Categories are illustrated in Figure 2.6.

Dynamic Process

In keeping with its mission, the NQA program is also involved in a continuous improvement process. As new information is gleaned from the Award program, it is incorporated so that the next year's processes and

FIGURE 2.6
Overview of Baldrige Framework

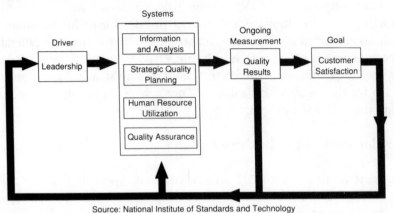

Source: National Institute of Standards and Technology

Source: National Institute of Standards and Technology

materials will be even more useful. Review of all features of the Award program is conducted annually to ensure the system meets current needs and reflects wide consensus. Comments are collected from the Board of Examiners, the Board of Overseers, Baldrige Award applicants, and other companies using the Baldrige process. Guideline instructions, Award criteria, examiner training, site visit process, feedback reports, and applicant eligibility are all subjected to continuous improvement. The basic value system and examination approach have been consistent since the inception of the Award. The seven categories and their 1,000 point value are constant. This assures continuity of the NQA guidelines core structure for those companies preparing for the Award.

The first round of annual improvement sessions was held in December 1988. Improvements for the 1989 Award cycle included:

- Streamlining the application and evaluation process.
- Narrowing the scope of categories to minimize overlap.
- Emphasizing quantitative methods and use of benchmark and comparative data.

For 1990, the changes featured:

- Tightening the criteria by reducing the number of examination items.

- Rephrasing examination items to make them more applicable to all industries.
- Enhancing instructions to clarify examination items.

Primary upgrades in 1991 were:

- Adjusting examination items to give greater weight to results.
- Improving overall examination integration through more item notes and use of direct references.
- Improving the accessibility of Baldrige Award information for use in training and self-assessment.

Essential changes for 1992 were:

- Dividing the Award criteria and Award application forms and instructions into two documents.
- Emphasizing productivity, cycle-time management, and business planning linkage.
- Expanding integration and results.

Figure 2.7 shows the streamlining of the Award criteria's three-level examination framework since the NQA began.

To compare the changes, the 1988 to 1992 Baldrige categories and examination items are located in Appendix A.

FIGURE 2.7
Malcolm Baldrige National Quality Award Continuous Improvement

MBNQA *Framework*	1988	1989	1990	1991	1992
Categories	7	7	7	7	7
Examination Items	62	44	33	32	28
Areas to Address	278	192	133	99	29

Source: National Institute of Standards and Technology

CHAPTER 3

REASONS TO PURSUE BALDRIGE

The true beauty of the competition is that there are no losers. Everyone wins—those who compete and those who do not. Competitors—whether they receive an award or not—gain from the measures they take to meet the award guidelines.

Robert Mosbacher, Secretary of Commerce

The goals of the Baldrige Award program as stipulated by the original legislation are to recognize quality achievement in individual companies, to share successful quality strategies, and to promote quality awareness among the nation's businesses. With the realization that awareness and information sharing are part of the Baldrige Award spectrum comes an understanding that the Baldrige program is much more than a contest. To institute a national quality system, which is the objective of the legislation, there needs to be a recognition tool for rewarding excellence, communication devices for information transfer, and a means for companies to be aware of quality as a competitive device.

SELF-ASSESSMENT TOOL

To achieve its goals, the Malcolm Baldrige National Quality Award Program provides companies with multifaceted opportunities for improvement, including self-assessment, information sharing, and the definition and acceleration total quality systems. To date, by far the largest and most significant use of the Baldrige Award process involves self-assessment. The vast majority of Baldrige users are organizations that do not apply for the Award. Rather, they use the Baldrige criteria as a mechanism to conduct analyses of overall efforts and the efforts of individual functions or plants and, in many cases, suppliers and business partners.

It is crucial that an organization have a sense of where it stands relative to its challengers in the whole quality race, and of how it measures up to the best practicing companies. Organizations are using Baldrige as a self-help method to upgrade their own capabilities and performance. The application guidelines provide an objective, externally directed blueprint. The criteria set high standards and are useful in comparing units with different organizations and practices.

For example, prior to Xerox Business Products and Systems winning the NQA in 1989, the company used the Baldrige criteria as a diagnostic tool. Xerox's Baldrige self-assessment was merciless. It allowed the company to pinpoint areas in its quality system that were strengths and those that were areas for improvement. This self-appraisal was a powerful way to bring the people in the company together using solid, verifiable information. At the completion of its evaluation of the seven categories, Xerox had identified 513 "warts" (in Baldrige terms, areas for improvement). These "warts" were later categorized and prioritized into the company's five-year planning process, with the senior management team taking ownership and account-ability to assure attainment.

Federal Express, a 1990 Baldrige Award winner, is among a number of companies that originally went through a Baldrige self-assessment with only the goal of self-improvement in mind. But by the time the company completed the process, senior management reasoned that they might at least rate a site visit, and they opted to apply.

Most organizations benefit substantially from conducting a Baldrige self-analysis. Looking at both positive and negative factors yields valuable insights. Companies often discover a number of competencies that have previously been overlooked. In identifying the areas for improvement, the NQA framework crystallizes ideas about what is lacking and how to get better. Lessons learned from the pluses and minuses can be of tangible benefit to moving ahead in quality: Strong areas can be used to propel forward momentum while weak areas are addressed and improved.

Self-assessment using the Baldrige examination categories encourages team commitment. Understanding the practical requirements of making quality improvements promotes better communications. The process also encourages senior management's involvement and commitment.

For those seeking to know where their organization stands relative to the NQA process, a logical first step is to conduct an assessment according to the examination criteria. By responding to the 7 categories, examination items, and areas to address, a company can begin to see how far along it is in its quality journey.

The findings from a review of Baldrige applicant evaluations from

1988 through 1990 provide valuable comparisons for groups conducting self-assessments. Analysis of the data reveals that in many companies only a partial quality system is in place and there is a lack of quality strategy, quality measures, and awareness of best practices. Customer systems tend to be reactive not proactive. In general, it has been found that companies have the greatest problems in clearly defining quality.

The strongest NQA applicants are those with clear, aggressive quality goals, those which have established benchmarks based on industry and world leaders. Quality companies are response time-drivers. Quality companies use every feasible type of customer "listening post." All employee training and education, management and non-management, are comprehensive, evaluated, and reinforced. Quality improvement systems are in place in all operations and integrated across all functions.

The Baldrige Effect

In its relatively short four-year history, the Baldrige Award has emerged as a focal point for our country's quality renewal. The fact that organizations in growing numbers are requesting Baldrige guidelines, conducting self-assessments, and submitting applications testifies to value of the Award.

In 1988, the first year of the Award, 66 companies applied. Though it was anticipated that in the Award's second year, applications would sharply increase, the number of applicants actually dropped to 40. Nevertheless, during this two-year period there was a dramatic increase in the number of application guidelines distributed. In 1988, 12,000 guidelines were requested. By 1989, that number had jumped fivefold to 65,000.

This phenomenon can be labeled the "Baldrige Effect." Literally thousands of businesses took a hard look at the rigorous criteria and opted to delay their application. It also seems clear that thousands of U.S. organizations requesting application guidelines have more interest in the Award's improvement potential than its competitive aspects. Shown in Figures 3.1 and 3.2 is the extraordinary growth in application requests compared to actual applications submitted.

The Baldrige Effect continues. In 1990, there were 97 total applicants—a decided growth over the previous year's 40. At the same time the number of requests for Application Guidelines exploded to over 180,000— a 277 percent increase! In 1991, 106 hopeful companies applied for the Baldrige Award. Requests for application guidelines continue to climb and now outnumber applicants by about 2,000 to 1.

FIGURE 3.1
Malcolm Baldrige National Quality Award Application Guidelines Requested,
1988–1991

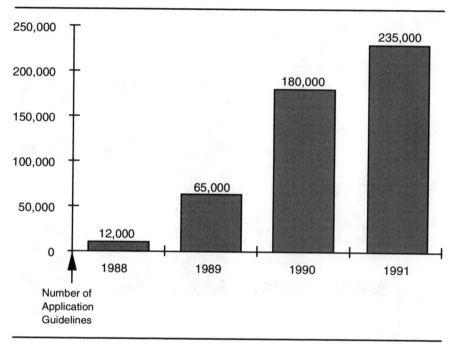

As shown in Figure 3.3, in the Award's first five years, manufacturing companies accounted for 46 percent of all applicants, service for 17 percent, and small businesses for 37 percent. The trends within each of the three categories reveal steady applicant progression in both service companies and small businesses. While still high overall, manufacturing has declined proportionately. Manufacturing's generally higher numbers can be attributed to greater competitive pressures and more substantial quality systems (much of quality practice began in manufacturing). According to a report done by the Department of Commerce, applications in all sectors are predicted to grow over the next five years based on the Awards' history and the thousands of companies currently tooling up. With an expanding number of organizations gaining an understanding of the importance of the NQA, there will continue to be a marked advancement in the ability of the United States to compete in a marketplace that demands quality products and services.

FIGURE 3.2
Malcolm Baldrige National Quality Award Applicants, 1988–1992

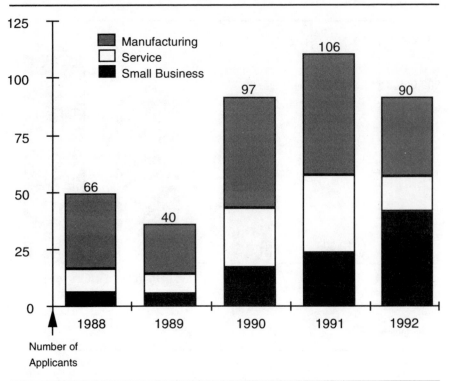

FIGURE 3.3
Malcolm Baldrige National Quality Award Applicants

	1988	1989	1990	1991	1992	Total
Manufacturing Companies	45 (68%)	23 (58%)	45 (46%)	38 (36%)	31 (34%)	182 (46%)
Service Companies	9 (14%)	6 (15%)	18 (19%)	21 (20%)	15 (17%)	69 (17%)
Small Businesses	12 (18%)	11 (27%)	34 (35%)	47 (44%)	44 (49%)	148 (37%)
Total	66	40	97	106	90	399

Source: National Institute of Standards and Technology

INFORMATION-SHARING NETWORKS

Information sharing is another major goal of the Baldrige Award program. The aim of this activity is to stimulate the creation of networks of companies, trade and professional organizations, universities, and individuals for the purpose of exchanging information about Total Quality Management (TQM), generally and the Baldrige process, specifically.

There are a number of ways to access the cumulative wisdom of quality companies. Through conferences, seminars, and workshops across the country, TQM intelligence is being exchanged at an unprecedented rate. These quality sharing sessions offer an outstanding opportunity for groups and individuals to learn more about the Baldrige Award and to network with those companies that have been intimately involved in the Baldrige process. In 1990, more than 3,000 presentations were given about the NQA. Speakers included Award winners, NIST Quality Award Program representatives, and members of the board of examiners. In 1991, that number more than doubled.

The legislation that created the Award requires that Baldrige recipients share their quality strategies as a means of fostering quality management improvement throughout the country. However, no one ever imagined that the Baldrige winners would "open the kimono" as far as has been the case. The transfer of information from Award recipients to others has been phenomenal. It has greatly helped raise the nation's awareness of TQM and has fostered an uncharacteristically high degree of cooperation among companies in the pursuit of excellence.

Information transfer includes communication within companies, between companies and suppliers, and among companies seeking to share accounts of quality. The Baldrige process provides a focus on what to prioritize and offers a framework for comparing strategies, methods, progress, and benchmarks. The criteria contribute a common quality vocabulary that makes discussion between different companies possible.

This information interchange focuses people on their commonalities rather than their differences. The NQA program has created a forum for service companies and manufacturing companies to communicate more than they ever have in the past. In this process, some of the best manufacturing companies confess that in the last analysis they, too, are service companies and need a service orientation to survive. Service companies have discovered that their view of the customer has frequently left their quality system vague. Meeting with manufacturing quality assurance professionals has led many service companies to design more analytical quality processes and concrete quality systems.

Annually, NIST sponsors the Quest for Excellence conference, which features companies that have won the Award sharing their strategies on each of the examination categories. Company representatives describe how their quality efforts met the challenging criteria and give specific improvement results. The first year of the Quest for Excellence Conference (QE I), the heads of the three winning companies—Bob Galvin of Motorola, John Marous of Westinghouse, and Arden Sims of Globe Metallurgical—described their leadership role in winning the Award. At the second conference, dubbed QE II, David Kearns of Xerox and Roger Milliken of Milliken & Company were center stage. At QE III, it was John Grettenberger of Cadillac, Larry Osterwise of IBM Rochester, Fred Smith of Federal Express, and John Wallace of Wallace Company. QE IV featured Winston Chen of Solectron, Ronald Schmidt of Zytec, and Raymond Marlow of Marlow Industries.

War Stories

First-year winners Motorola and Globe have more than met their obligation of providing information about their quality improvement programs. Motorola has participated in hundreds of conferences, served on panels at professional trade seminars, and hosted monthly on-site Baldrige Briefing sessions. Globe has sent a representative across this country as well as abroad to Moscow and Singapore.

In the process of fulfilling the Baldrige Award requirement that winners share their quality strategies, these companies and their employees have become popular heros—venerated veterans of the quality war. Envoys of the winning companies are much sought-after speakers at conventions and meetings, with eager listeners hoping to learn the secrets of their success. There is something eminently appealing about hearing someone who has been there tell what it actually takes to make TQM a reality. While this information transfer presents resource and logistics problems, the winners seem undaunted. Their spirit seems to emanate from a sense of patriotism and pride along with the awareness that their hour in the Baldrige spotlight creates a tremendous marketing advantage.

Education and Training

The NQA process is being used as an adjunct in education and training, particularly at the management levels. The Baldrige criteria represent a distillation of the major issues managers need to understand to effectively operate a business. The advantages of using the criteria for instruction are twofold: First, to delineate TQM's component parts and second, to introduce the concept of a systematic means to achieve excellence. This use of the Baldrige Award is not accidental. It was the intention of its creators that the Award process be an eye-opening catalyst for change. Nothing a company can do will add more to its knowledge and reveal more about its operations than education and analysis using the Baldrige guidelines.

Many companies have set up internal Baldrige-type examiner training courses. In this way, the organization can conduct its own Baldrige evaluation. Frequently this is done in conjunction with the company's internal quality award that is based on the NQA criteria. This in-house competition often serves as a rehearsal for applying for the Baldrige Award. Several companies pursue this route, among them Westinghouse, AT&T, and DuPont.

TOTAL QUALITY ACCELERATION

A third major area of use for the Baldrige Award is as a sound way to accelerate a company's progress in total quality management. Xerox officials, for instance, believe that using the Baldrige criteria advanced the company's quality progress by three or four years. Acceleration occurs through effective, efficient integration of TQM components into all the company's systems and processes.

A key value of the Baldrige method is its ability to imbed quality throughout the organization. This benefit not only occurs in companies just beginning their journey toward total quality, it also helps "unstick" companies where further deployment of quality is needed to gain better results. For example, as their expectations ratchet up, customers expect more from the total experience with a company. If the products or services bought are of high quality, but the accompanying billings are inaccurate, customers will tend to look to the competition for their next purchase. By effectively integrating quality, all elements of a company—the total enterprise—can be strong and competitive. Leading companies are doing just that.

In 1990, Rockwell International Corporation's Digital Communications Division (DCD) applied for the Baldrige Award. While not a finalist, the company found that the NQA regimen gave it the means to analyze and refine the organization's diverse programs, as well as redefine and integrate improved quality in its existing systems. DCD used the Baldrige feedback report to determine further upgrades to its Total Customer Satisfaction initiative.

Even on the most basic levels, the Award criteria is a comprehensive checklist of all the issues that need to be assessed, and their interrelationships. Because the Baldrige guidelines address the full range of quality issues, it is valuable in setting up new systems, as well as in renewing established ones. It would be difficult to find a more complete, integrated picture of total quality management.

Mentor Graphics Corporation, based in Beaverton, Oregon, stands out as an industry leader in electronic design automation (EDA) software. In 1989, the company competed for the National Quality Award to sharpen its quality focus. Gerard Langeler, Mentor's president, stated, "Applying for the Baldrige forced us to write down what we were doing. We got to a few places where we drew blanks. There were a lot of things we weren't measuring." The Baldrige criteria has been integrated into the company's product development process. Mentor's intent is to win the Award by 1994. Langeler adds, "Winning the Baldrige Award is the goal, but the journey is more important."

The Award criteria embodies the most important diagnostic progress indicators needed for planning and managing total quality. The Baldrige application process requires that a company describe *in detail* all aspects of its quality management methods, processes, and results. The evaluation process looks for the interconnections—the alignment of business functions. This is the most difficult thing to do. The goal is to have a cohesive, systematic approach.

Businesses are using the NQA Guidelines as part of their strategic planning process. For example, the strategy of the world's largest connector maker, AMP, Inc. of Harrisburg, Pennsylvania, is to keep its prices fixed and maintain its 15 percent compound annual growth through better quality. AMP is utilizing Baldrige to help guide its total quality system to meet those targets. The company first applied for the Award in 1988 and competed again in 1991.

While traditional approaches have frequently relegated quality to an obscure unit in an organization, Baldrige requires a thorough alignment of all quality management activities. The stringent Baldrige criteria provide standards for organizations to check their overall progress toward becoming world-class competitors.

In 1989, Wallace Company conducted a Baldrige self-assessment to see how its TQM efforts measured up. Out of the possible 1,000 points, Wallace scored itself 210. This tough analysis was essential in targeting improvement areas. Senior leadership then condensed the time frame for the company to compete for the Baldrige Award from two years to one and one-half years. Based on its ultimate success of winning the Award in 1990, Wallace recommends that companies considering applying for the Award take the plunge. "If you apply, you really become a winner," says president Sonny Wallace. "You will get feedback that is better than anything you can buy. It points out your strengths and weaknesses, and you will know more about your company as a result of having done it than any other way I know."

The Baldrige process is an excellent means for comparison to best practicing companies. This benchmarking activity provides a system to establish improvement goals through analysis of the competition, incorporation of findings into functional and operating plans, and then continual reassessment to reach a leadership position.

The Baldrige Award does not prescribe quality approaches or techniques. Nor does it establish quality or performance measures. Naturally, these will vary from company to company. What Baldrige does is to present the concepts that are essential to being world-class, such as customer-driven quality, continuous improvement in all operations and activities, benchmarking against industry and world leaders, and having all employees trained and involved in quality initiatives. It is the responsibility of each company to use the Baldrige framework as a blueprint and focus on the key elements vital to building a well-constructed quality process for itself.

In 1982, as a response to intense global competition, Solectron Corporation, a San Jose electronics manufacturer, launched its quality program. Winston Chen, Solectron's president, believes Baldrige to be a strong focal point for improving U.S. competitiveness. In 1989, this 1,600-employee company applied for the Baldrige Award along with industry giants such as Xerox. Solectron did not reach the final round of the on-site visit evaluation. Chen's determination was steady. Solectron applied again in 1990. While not a winner, the company used Baldrige process to advance its quality crusade and accrued many benefits. Finally in 1991, in its third attempt at the Baldrige, Solectron emerged victorious. "The Malcolm Baldrige National Quality Award criteria establishes an excellent roadmap for a company to continuously improve its quality," an elated Chen proclaimed. "Baldrige absolutely works!" As a result of Solectron's Baldrige application and improvements made from feedback reports, sales increased 284 percent and profits were up 283 percent in the past three years.

Basically, the NQA gives any company the means to assess where it is in relation to key elements needed to be regarded as world-class, and the blueprint to build a quality system suited to its own unique needs.

CHAPTER 4

QUALITY WORKS! THE PROOF

The whole process we're engaged in is a total process. It's not departmentalized, and one needs to recognize that and get everybody thinking about the total process, which starts with the conceptual idea and ends when you book your accounts receivable on the balance sheet of your company.

Roger Milliken, Chairman and CEO, Milliken and Company

Question: Why are an increasing number of U.S. firms adopting total quality management (TQM)?

Answer: It works!

It is as straightforward as that. Hard data confirm what many have long observed: In the relentlessly competitive global marketplace, quality leads to success.

In addition to ample testimonials of Baldrige winning companies, a 1991 United States General Accounting Office (GAO) study of the 1988 and 1989 top-scoring Baldrige applicants, "Management Practices, U.S. Companies Improve Performance Through Quality Efforts," attests to the rewards of pursuing the quality quest.* Overall corporate performance of these quality-focused companies improved in four key measurable areas: employee relations, operating procedures, customer satisfaction, and financial performance. In virtually every case market share grew, profitability improved, productivity rose, customer satisfaction advanced, and employee satisfaction increased.

The General Accounting Office undertook this study in response to a request from Congressman Donald Ritter (R-Pennsylvania) and 29 other members of Congress. The task was to examine the impact of TQM practices on companies' performance.

---

*The GAO Report, "Management Practices, U.S. Companies Improve Performance Through Quality Efforts" (GAO/NSIAD-91-190) can be obtained by contacting the U.S. General Accounting Office, P.O. Box 6015, Gaithersburg, MD 20877, phone 202-275-6241.

The project, headed by Allan I. Mendelowitz, Director of GAO's International Trade, Energy, and Finance Issues Division, developed its methodology by interviewing experts from business, professional and trade associations, universities, and government agencies, and by reviewing both quality management literature and previous GAO quality studies.

After GAO research determined that "the most widely accepted formal definition" of total quality management exists in the criteria for the Baldrige Award, the office decided to rely on the NQA results for its work.

Twenty of the 22 Baldrige contenders in 1988 and 1989 that received site visits participated in the project (see Figure 4.1). The seven listed in bold type are Baldrige winners: Globe Metallurgical Inc., Motorola Inc., and Westinghouse Electric Corporation's Commercial Nuclear Division for 1988, and Milliken & Company and Xerox Corporation's Business Products and Systems for 1989. Two companies that received site visits in 1989 did not emerge victorious that year, but applied again in 1990 and won: General Motors Corporation's Cadillac Motor Car Company, and International Business Machines Corporation, Rochester.

A significant conclusion drawn from the research is that TQM is applicable to both large and small companies as well as to both service and manufacturing businesses. Also of significance is the finding that companies studied were able to achieve substantial improvement in performance, on average, within two and one-half years of initiating a quality improvement process.

At the time the GAO Report was released, Mr. Mendelowitz announced the results had been so impressive that the GAO intended to establish a TQM process of its own.

Presented here is a summary of the four measurement indicators described in the GAO Report covering the 1988 and 1989 Baldrige site visited companies. In addition, the 1988, 1989, and 1990 Baldrige winners provide specific examples of the benefits of total quality management.

EMPLOYEE RELATIONS ENHANCED

To gauge the impact of TQM processes on employee relations, the GAO examined performance in the following areas: employee satisfaction, attendance, turnover, safety and health, and number of employee suggestions for quality and productivity improvements. Of the 52 observations obtained

FIGURE 4.1
Malcolm Baldrige National Quality Award 1988 and 1989 Site Visited Companies

- Corning Inc., Telecommunications Products Division
  Corning, NY
- Digital Equipment Corporation
  Maynard, MA
- Eastman Kodak Company, Eastman Chemicals Division
  Kingsport, TN
- Ford Motor Company, North American Auto Division
  Dearborn, MI
- General Motors Corp., Allison Transmission Division
  Indianapolis, IN
- **General Motors Corp., Cadillac Motor Car Company**
  Detroit, MI
- **Globe Metallurgical Inc.**
  Beverly, OH
- Goodyear Tire and Rubber Company
  Akron, OH
- GTE Corporation, Telephone Operations
  Irving, TX
- Hoechst Celanese Corp., Chemical Group
  Dallas, TX
- **International Business Machines Corp.**
  Rochester, MN
- International Business Machines Corp.
  Endicott, NY
- L.L. Bean Inc.
  Freeport, ME
- **Milliken & Company**
  Spartanburg, SC
- **Motorola Inc.**
  Schaumburg, IL
- Paul Revere Insurance Group
  Worcester, MA
- Seagate Technology, Small Disk Division
  Oklahoma City, OK
- Timken Company, Bearing Division
  Canton, OH
- USAA Insurance Company, Property and Casualty Division
  San Antonio, TX
- **Westinghouse Electric Corp., Commercial Nuclear Fuel Division**
  Pittsburgh, PA
- Westinghouse Electric Corp., Westinghouse Furniture Systems
  Grand Rapids, MI
- **Xerox Corporation, Business Products and Systems**
  Fairport, NY

Source: U.S. General Accounting Office

FIGURE 4.2
Employee-Relations Indicators

Performance indicator	Number of responding companies	Direction of indicator		
		Positive (favorable)	Negative (unfavorable)	No change
Employee satisfaction	9	8	1	0
Attendance	11	8	0	3
Turnover	11	7	3	1
Safety/health	14	11	3	0
Suggestions received	7	5	2	0
Total	**18***	**39**	**9**	**4**

*Indicates the total number of companies providing data and not the total number of responses for all performance indicators.

Source: U.S. Government Accounting Office

from the participating companies, 39 were positive. (See Figure 4.2.) A comparison of the employee-related indicators is shown in Figure 4.3.

Summary of GAO Findings of Baldrige Award Site Visited Companies, 1988 and 1989

- An average annual improvement of 1.4 percent in overall employee job satisfaction was shown in eight of nine participating companies that conducted employee surveys.
- Above average industry attendance rates were found in 9 of 11 reporting companies.
- Lower (better) employee turnover than industry averages was reported in 7 of the 11 participating companies. In a typical company, the decline was from a 10 percent annual turnover to 9.4 percent— an average 6 percent improvement in employee retention.
- Safety and health rates were better than industry averages in 12 of 14 companies. Lost work days due to occupational injury and illness showed an average annual improvement rate of 1.8 percent.
- Increase in the total number of quality improvement suggestions submitted was present in five of seven companies (the decline of suggestions at the other two companies was attributed to heightened use of improvement teams).

FIGURE 4.3
Employee-Related Indicators

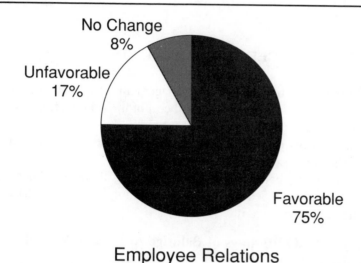

Employee Relations

Results of Baldrige Award Winners 1988, 1989, and 1990

- Milliken's suggestion system, Opportunity for Improvement (OFI), yielded 262,000 OFIs during 1989, or 19 per associate, with a completion rate of 87 percent. By 1990, the number of OFIs had jumped to 472,884, or 39.3 per associate, with an 85 percent completion rate.
- At the Commercial Nuclear Fuel Division at Westinghouse, employee suggestions increased from 425 in 1985 to 2,000 in 1988.
- Cadillac's employee turnover rate has been cut in half, and at 0.3 percent it is one of the industry's lowest. The company has also had a 33 percent improvement of injury and illness rates.
- In 1990 comparisons of IBM Rochester to industry averages, the company's safety record was 57 percent better, its absenteeism rate was 48 percent less, and its turnover rate was 88 percent less. The Rochester site's participation in the annual corporate-wide employee survey was 94 percent, which was the highest of any IBM division. Participation in the company's suggestion system increased 35 percent from 1987 to 1989.

- At Federal Express, from 1985 to 1990 more than 91 percent of surveyed employees reported they were proud to work for the company.

OPERATING PROCEDURES IMPROVED

To gauge the effect of total quality management on operations, the companies studied measured the quality and cost of their products and services. Operating indicators include reliability, timeliness of delivery, order-processing time, errors or defects, production lead time, inventory turnover, quality costs, and cost savings.

Data from the companies yielded 65 observations, of which 59 indicated improvement. (See Figure 4.4.) Operating Indicators' relationships are illustrated in Figure 4.5.

Summary of GAO Findings of Baldrige Award Site Visited Companies, 1988 and 1989

- The average annual improvement in reliability was 11.3 percent for the 12 reporting companies. Product and services reliability means

FIGURE 4.4
Operating Indicators

Performance indicator	Number of responding companies	Direction of indicator		
		Positive (favorable)	Negative (unfavorable)	No change
Reliability	12	12	0	0
Timeliness of delivery	9	8	1	0
Order-processing time	6	6	0	0
Errors or defects	8	7	0	1
Product lead time	7	6	0	1
Inventory turnover	9	6	1	2
Costs of quality	5	5	0	0
Cost savings	9	9	0	0
Total	20*	59	2	4

*Indicates the total number of companies providing data and not the total number of responses for all performance indicators.

Source: U.S. Government Accounting Office

FIGURE 4.5
Operating Indicators

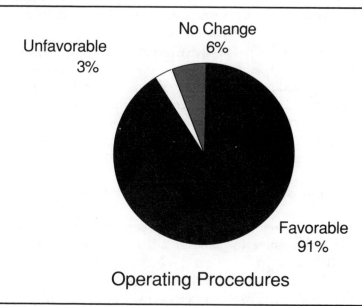

Operating Procedures

the absence of errors or breakdown while in use and is measured by recalls, claims, or other means.

• Timeliness of delivery improved in eight of the nine reporting companies. On-time delivery improved 4.7 percent on an average annual basis.

• A reduction (improvement) in order-processing time occurred in all six reporting companies. Overall average annual order-processing time improved 12 percent.

• A reduction in errors or defects was reported in seven of the eight reporting companies. It should be noted that the defect rate at the remaining company was unchanged from its manufacture of nearly 100 percent error-free products. Overall reduction in errors was 10.3 percent on an annual basis.

• Shortened product lead times (cycle times) were found in six of the seven reporting companies. Product lead time is the time from design to delivery of the new products or services. Overall product lead time was reduced (improved) 5.8 percent.

• Increased inventory turnover—one good measure of a company's operating efficiency—was reported in six of nine reporting companies. Inventory turnover is the cost of goods sold divided by average yearly inventory. Overall, the companies' average annual inventory turnover increased 7.2 percent.

- Quality costs improved in all five reporting companies on an average annual basis of 9 percent. Costs of quality include the costs of quality failures (rework, scrap, and lost profits) as well as the costs of quality detection and prevention (inspection, training, and audits).

- Cost saving from quality improvement suggestions increased for all nine reporting companies. The range in average annual cost savings was $1.3 million to $116 million per year.

Results of Baldrige Award Winners 1988, 1989, and 1990

- Milliken improved from having 75 percent on-time deliveries in 1984 to becoming the industry's best, with 99 percent on-time deliveries, in 1988.

- Since 1981, Milliken has had a 60 percent reduction in the cost of non-conformance. Milliken's productivity has increased 42 percent since the start of its Pursuit of Excellence push for Total Quality Management in 1983.

- Since 1989, Motorola's quality improvements have reduced by $250 million annually the cost incurred through internal and external failures. In Motorola's cellular telephone operation there was a 30 to 1 reduction in factory cycle time and a 90 percent reduction in defects per unit. In its semiconductor product sector there was a 71 percent reduction in product selection errors and a 53 percent decline in shipping errors.

- At the Commercial Nuclear Fuel Division (CNFD) of Westinghouse, first-time through yields for fuel rods increased to 87 percent in 1987, up from less than 50 percent in 1984. On-time delivery was 100 percent over a three-year period.

- At Xerox, defects per 100 machines dropped 78 percent between 1984 and 1989; unscheduled maintenance decreased by 40 percent; service response time went down 27 percent. Xerox's cost of quality was cut by $116 million through aggressive production-schedule tightening, scrap reduction, and other improvements.

- Since 1983, IBM Rochester has reduced product development time by more than half, manufacturing cycle time has been cut 60 percent, and product reliability has increased threefold. Implementing continuous-flow manufacturing from 1986 to 1990 reduced cycle time, increased manufacturing capacity by five times, produced a 42 percent savings per system, and cut assembly-line time in half. From 1986 to 1989, productivity improved 30 percent. Since 1984, engineering change costs have been reduced 45 percent.

- Cadillac has reduced time required for major styling changes from 175 weeks to between 50 and 85 weeks. Customer order response time (the time from order to delivery) has improved 47 percent since 1987. Since 1986, quality reliability and durability of products has improved 65 percent or better.

- At Wallace, inventory turn has dramatically improved, becoming the industry's highest at 4.3 turns. On-time deliveries were 92 percent in 1990, up from 75 percent in 1987.

CUSTOMER SATISFACTION INCREASED

Companies have moved their quality efforts from addressing only technical specifications to focusing on meeting customers' needs and expectations. The companies studied measured customer satisfaction through consumer perception surveys of products and services.

In analyzing 30 observations from 17 of the participating companies, the GAO learned that 21 improved, 3 became worse, and 6 showed no change. (See Figure 4.6.) Comparison of the Customer Satisfaction Indicators is depicted in Figure 4.7.

Summary of GAO Findings of Baldrige Award Site Visited Companies, 1988 and 1989

- Customer satisfaction increased in 12 of 14 companies on an annual average basis of 2.5 percent. At the two companies that showed no change, customer satisfaction levels were already high at between 89 and 100 percent.

- Complaints declined at five of the six reporting companies at an average annual rate of 11.6 percent. Further, the increase at the sixth company is credited to a more reliable system that provided more accurate complaint identification.

FIGURE 4.6
Customer Satisfaction Indicators

Performance indicator	Number of responding companies	Direction of indicator		
		Positive (favorable)	Negative (unfavorable)	No change
Overall customer satisfaction	14	12	0	2
Customer complaints	6	5	1	0
Customer retention	10	4	2	4
Total	**17***	**21**	**3**	**6**

*Indicates the total number of companies providing data and not the total number of responses for all performance indicators.

Source: U.S. Government Accounting Office

FIGURE 4.7
Customer Satisfaction Indicators

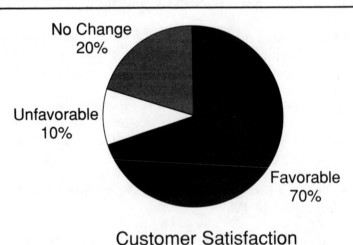

No Change 20%

Unfavorable 10%

Favorable 70%

Customer Satisfaction

- Improved customer retention was reported in 4 of the 10 reporting companies. Four companies' customer retention was stable at between 90 and 100 percent. There was a slight decline of between 0.2 and 1.2 percent in two companies.

Results of Baldrige Award Winners 1988, 1989, and 1990

- Since 1987, the percent of Cadillac owners who replaced their cars with another Cadillac improved 24 percent. The company has the most loyal customer base in the car business and is the top-rated domestic automaker according to the J. D. Powers and Associates Customer Satisfaction Index.
- Warranty coverage at Cadillac expanded from one year or 12,000 miles in 1988 to a minimum of four years or 50,000 miles in 1990. At the same time, warranty-related costs dropped 29 percent as a result of better quality. Customer satisfaction with service has increased 17 percent since 1989.
- Globe's customer complaints went from 44 in 1985 to four in 1987, a drop of 91 percent.
- From 1983 to 1988, Milliken received 41 major quality awards from its customers.
- At Federal Express, since 1987 overall customer satisfaction for domestic service has averaged better than 95 percent; for international service the average is 94 percent. In 1990, 93 percent of Fed Ex customers were completely satisfied with the ease of doing business with the company; 97 percent were completely satisfied with the company's couriers. Federal Express scored well with customers in an independent survey, where 53 percent of air-express industry customers rated Fed Ex perfect, compared to the nearest competitor at 39 percent.
- In 1990, Wallace customers rated the company 4.4 out of a possible 5, while the company's closest competitor scored 3.8.
- Xerox was the first in the copier industry to offer customers a three-year product warranty.

FINANCIAL PERFORMANCE STRENGTHENED

Improved quality also leads to improved profitability. The four measures of bottom-line results used were: market share, sales per employee, return on assets, and return on sales. Of the 40 profit-related observations obtained from the 15 reporting companies, 34 showed an increase and 6 showed a decline. (See Figure 4.8.) Indicators for Financial Performance are compared in Figure 4.9.

Summary of GAO Findings of Baldrige Award Site Visited Companies, 1988 and 1989

- At 9 of 11 reporting companies, market share increased at an average annual rate of 13.7 percent. An initial decline shown by two companies because of heightened foreign competition has been reversed.
- All 12 reporting companies showed an increase of sales per employee resulting in an average annual increase of 8.6 percent.
- Return on assets increased in seven of nine reporting companies. Two companies undergoing strong competition experienced a slight decline (0.1–0.6 percent). There was an average annual increase of 1.3 percent.
- Return on sales increased on an average annual basis of 0.4 percent in six of eight reporting companies. Two companies experienced a decline of one to two percent as a result of fierce competition.

Results of Baldrige Award Winners 1988, 1989, and 1990

- IBM Rochester was one of only six leading competitors that in 1988 and 1989 grew faster than the industry. In both years the company

FIGURE 4.8
Financial Performance Indicators

| | | Direction of indicator | | |
Performance indicator	Number of responding companies	Positive (favorable)	Negative (unfavorable)	No change
Market share	11	9	2	0
Sales per employee	12	12	0	0
Return on assets	9	7	2	0
Return on sales	8	6	2	0
Total	**15***	**34**	**6**	**0**

*Indicates the total number of companies providing data and not the total number of responses for all performance indicators.

Source: U.S. Government Accounting Office

FIGURE 4.9
Financial Performance Indicators

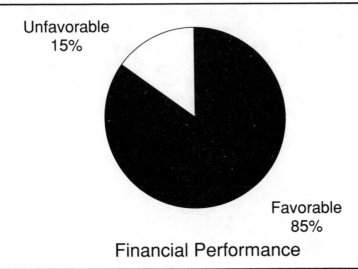

Unfavorable
15%

Favorable
85%

Financial Performance

yielded a one half percent increase in market share for its intermediate computers. In 1989, IBM Rochester's revenue growth was
twice the industry rate. During the 1980s, spending for defect-
detection equipment declined 75 percent. Write-offs, which includes
scrap and rework, have been reduced by 55 percent since 1984.

- Cadillac reversed its market share decline and is holding steady in
the tough luxury car business.

- Federal Express's market share was 43 percent in 1989, compared
to its nearest competitor at 26 percent.

- Greater customer responsiveness has expanded Wallace Company's
customer base and increased business with existing customers, as
shown in sales volume growth of 69 percent since 1986. Profits
increased 7.4 times through 1989. Market share has gone from 10.4
percent in 1987 to 18 percent in 1990.

- Globe has increased market share among high-end foundry users
from 5 percent in 1985 to better than 50 percent in 1988.

- In 1991, Xerox's market share was 16 percent, up from 8.6 percent
in the early 1980s.

The Quest

The quest for quality, and more specifically for the Baldrige Award, is an epic journey in which the hero (a company) is irrevocably transformed by the exigencies of the quest. The grail that lies at the end is not profit per se: It is the contentment and well-being of all constituencies, from employees to customers to suppliers and stockholders. The GAO Report bears out one basic conclusion: Whatever the difficulty and expense of pursuing quality, the road ahead is immeasurably more treacherous and difficult, for those who choose *not* to pursue it.

CHAPTER 5

BALDRIGE PROCESS
IN ACTION

The Baldrige Award is a participative, non-prescription program rather than a forced march to quality. Applications are evaluated by peer review. The examiners are chosen, primarily from the private sector, on the basis of their personal experience in quality management. Moreover, the Baldrige criteria provide a definition of total quality while helping a company generate evidence of progress.

From that perspective, the real goal isn't winning the Baldrige but achieving national harmony in the pursuit of excellence. Even if a company does not enter the competition, the criteria may be the key to survival in today's increasingly competitive global markets.

Curt W. Reimann, Director,
Malcolm Baldrige National Quality Award Program

ELIGIBILITY AND APPLICATION PROCESS

To be eligible for the Baldrige Award, a business must be for-profit and be located in the United States or its territories. The three eligibility categories are manufacturing, service, and small business.

The legislation that created the Award anticipated the creation of new categories. To do so requires a proposal from the Secretary of Commerce and approval by Congress. It is expected that new Award categories will be added in response to growing momentum to include other organizations, but at the time of this writing, local, state, and national government agencies; not-for-profit organizations; trade associations; and professional societies are not eligible.

An overview of eligibility restrictions for three current categories are as follows:

- A company or subsidiary must have more than 50 percent of its operations in the United States.
- If a subsidiary is applying, at least 50 percent of its base must be free of direct financial and organizational line control of the parent company.
- Individual units or partial aggregations of "chain" organizations are not eligible.
- Subsidiaries that perform business support functions are not eligible.
- A parent company and a subsidiary may not both apply in the same year, and only one subsidiary may apply in the same category in a given year.
- A Baldrige Award–winning company and all subsidiaries must wait five years to apply for another Award.

Detailed eligibility information is located in the Award Criteria.

Potential applicants are required to submit an eligibility form to determine if they meet the requirements. NIST works with interested organizations to ascertain which units of the company are eligible to submit an application.

Developed for the 1991 Baldrige examiner training, the Alpha Telco case study includes responses to all seven Baldrige categories, as well as other Award requirements, such as eligibility and application forms. An example of a completed eligibility form for the Baldrige case study that is used in Part 2 of this book appears in Figure 5.1.

FIGURE 5.1
Eligibility Form for Case Study

1991 ELIGIBILITY DETERMINATION FORM – *Page 1 of 2*

Malcolm Baldrige National Quality Award

1 **Applicant**

Company Name   Alpha Telco

Address   288 Signal Drive

City of Commerce, Central

Did the applicant officially or legally exist before April 3, 1990? (Check one.) _X_ Yes ___ No (briefly explain)

2 **Highest-Ranking Official**

Name   Donald E. Williams

Title   Chief Executive Officer

Address 288 Signal Drive

City of Commerce, Central

Telephone No. (663) 204-7171

3 **Is the applicant a for-profit business?**

(Check one.)   _X_ Yes ___ No

4 **Size of Applicant**

Total number of Employees _____ 22,268

Percent employees in the U.S. and/or territories _100_

Percent physical assets in U.S. and/or territories _100_

5 **Subsidiary Designation** (Check one.)

a. Is applicant a subsidiary, business unit, division, or like organization? ___ Yes (continue) _X_ No (go to Item 6)

b. Parent Company

Address _____

Highest Official _____

Title _____

Number of world-wide employees of parent company_____

c. Does applicant comprise over 25% of the world-wide employees of the parent company? (Check one.)

___ Yes ___ No

d. Do other units within the parent company provide similar products or services? (Check one.)

___ Yes (briefly explain) ___ No

e. Briefly describe the major business support functions provided to the applicant by the parent company or unit of the parent company, if applicable.

This form may be copied and attached to, or bound with, other application materials.

Source: National Institute of Standards and Technology

FIGURE 5.1
Eligibility Form for Case Study (Continued)

1991 ELIGIBILITY DETERMINATION FORM – *Page 2 of 2*

Malcolm Baldrige National Quality Award

5 **Subsidiary Designation** (Continued)

f. Is the applicant's parent company or another subsidiary of the parent company intending to apply in 1991? (Check one.)

___Yes (briefly explain)   ___No   ___ Don't know

_____

_____

g. Name the document supporting the subsidiary designation.

_____

Include a copy of the document with this application. See instructions on page 28 for limit on materials to be submitted.

6 **Percent Customer Base**

Is over 50% of the sales of the applicant to customers outside of the applicant's organization, its parent company, or other companies with financial or organizational control of the applicant or parent company? (Check one.)

X Yes   ___No(briefly explain)

_____

_____

7 **Fee**

Enclosed is $50 to cover the eligibility determination. Make check or money order payable to:
         The Malcolm Baldrige National Quality Award

8 **Official Inquiry Point**

Name   Ms. Brenda Webb

Title   Chief Quality Officer

Mailing Address 288 Signal Drive

             City of Commerce, Central

Overnight
Mailing Address Same

_____

Telephone No. (663) 204-7878

Telefax No.   (663) 204-8111

9 **Signature, Authorizing Official**

                                    Date Jan. 15, 1991

X   *Brenda Webb*

Name   Brenda Webb

Title   Chief Quality Officer

Address   288 Signal Drive

             City of Commerce, Central

Telephone No. (663) 204-7878

10 Eligibility Determination

confirmed 1/24/91
                 For Official Use Only

Note: *An approved Eligibility Determination Form must be submitted as part of the Application Package.*

Source: National Institute of Standards and Technology

Applications

Companies confirmed as eligible then proceed with the application process, which includes the application form, the site listing and descriptors forms, an overview of the company's business, and responses to the Baldrige examination items.

The heart of this documentation is the applicant's response to the criteria's seven categories. Applicants in the manufacturing and service categories may use a maximum of 75 single-sided pages, including graphs, figures, tables, and appendices. For the small business category the maximum is 50 single-sided pages.

Applicant fees cover the award review process, which includes application distribution, evaluation and feedback documents, as well as examiner honoraria.

Detailed instructions for completing the application are described in the MBNQA Application Forms and Instructions booklet. A completed application form for the Alpha Telco case study is shown in Figure 5.2. Figure 5.3 shows the Alpha Telco site listing and descriptors forms.

FIGURE 5.2
Application Form for Case Study

1991 APPLICATION FORM — *Page 1 of 2*

Malcolm Baldrige National Quality Award

1 Applicant

Company Name   Alpha Telco

Address   288 Signal Drive

City of Commerce, Central

2 Highest-Ranking Official

Name   Donald E. Williams

Title   Chief Executive Officer

Address   288 Signal Drive

City of Commerce, Central

Telephone No.   (663) 204-7171

3 Size of Applicant

Total Number of Employees   22,268

Total Number of Sites   5 business offices

Sales Preceding Fiscal Year *(circle one)*

0-$1M	$10M-$100M	$500M-$1B
$1M-$10M	$100M-$500M	(Over $1B)

4 Subsidiary Designation *(check one)*

☒ No **(Go to Item 5)**   ☐ Yes (continue)

Parent Company

Address

Highest Official

Title

Does Applicant comprise over 50% of parent company?
(check one)

☐ No   ☐ Yes

5 Award Category *(check one)*

☐ Manufacturing   ☒ Service   ☐ Small Business

6 Industrial Classification

List up to three most descriptive two-digit SIC Codes.
(See Page 42.)

48

7 Description of Products or Services Sold

Local and toll telecommunications

service and network-access service

*This form may be copied and attached to,
or bound with, other application materials.*

Source: National Institute of Standards and Technology

FIGURE 5.2
Application Form for Case Study (Continued)

1991 APPLICATION FORM — *Page 2 of 2*

Malcolm Baldrige National Quality Award

8 **Supplier and Dealer Networks**

Number of Suppliers   613

Numbers of External Sales Organizations:

Dealers _____   Distributors_____

Franchises _____   Other (Type/Number)_____

9 **Application Components**

Eligibility Determination Form with confirmation ____X____
(check)

Number of Site List' g and Descriptors Forms
Submitted ____1____
(number)

Application Report only____X____
(check)

Application Report and _____ Supplemental Sections
(number)

10 **Official Inquiry Point**

Name   Ms. Brenda Webb

Title   Chief Quality Officer

Mailing Address 288 Signal Drive

_____ City of Commerce, Central
Overnight
Mailing Address Same

_____

Telephone No.   (663) 204-7878

Telefax No.   (663) 204-8711

11 **Fee** *(see instructions)*

Enclosed is $ 3000 _____ to cover one
Application Report and ___0____ Supplemental Sections

Make check or money order payable to:
The Malcolm Baldrige National Quality Award

12 **Statement**

We understand that this application will be reviewed by members of the Board of Examiners. Should our company be selected for one or more site visits, we agree to host the site visit(s) and to facilitate an open and unbiased examination. We understand that the company must pay reasonable costs associated with any site visit(s).

13 **Signature, Authorizing Official**

Date March 22, 1991

X   *Brenda Webb*

Name   Ms. Brenda Webb

Title   Chief Quality Officer

Address 288 Signal Drive

_____ City of Commerce, Central

Telephone No.   (663) 204-7878

FIGURE 5.3
Site Listing and Descriptions Form for Case Study

1991 SITE LISTING AND DESCRIPTORS FORM

A. Address of Site	B. Relative Size Percent of Applicant's		C. Linkage to Written Report		D. Description of Products or Services
	Employees	Sales	Application Report	Supplemental Section	
288 Signal Drive City of Commerce Central	32	27	X		Toll and telecommunications services and network access services
528 Adams Tollway Nugget Rocky Mountain	26	19	X		Same
3142 Sandpiper Lane Seashore Coastal	19	21	X		Same
215 Harbin Hollow Tennval Smoky Mountain	13	17	X		Same
11111 Shady Lane Kingwood Woodland	10	14	X		Same

Provide all the information for each site except where multiple sites produce similar products or services. For such multiple site cases, see page 34.

This form may be copied and attached to, or bound with, other application materials.

Source: National Institute of Standards and Technology

THREE-DIMENSIONAL SCORING SYSTEM

The MBNQA evaluation process is a structured, analytical method for scrutinizing a company's quality management systems. In evaluating Baldrige Award applications, a three-dimensional scoring system is used to look at the *approach* a company is taking to quality, the *deployment* of that approach through all operations, and the *results* being achieved both within the company and with its customers. Applicants need to provide objective, quantifiable responses to comprehensively describe their total quality approach, deployment, and results. Some of the key diagnostics under each of the three evaluation dimensions are shown in Figure 5.4. The following discussion looks at three-dimensional scoring from the standpoint of how it is used by examiners during the evaluation process.

Approach

The specific tools and techniques a company uses to improve its quality fall under the heading of "approach."

Prevention Based.   In the quality war, the preferred strategy is prevention. Examiners look for a company to anticipate potential problems as opposed to traditional inspection and detection patterns. Is the company determining quality methods through action rather than reaction?

FIGURE 5.4
Malcolm Baldrige National Quality Award Scoring System

Approach	Deployment	Results
• Prevention Based	• Products, Services	• Derived from Approach
• Evaluation–Improvement Cycles	• Transactions with Customers and Supplies	• Quality Levels
• Tools and Techniques	• Business Functions, Processes, Facilities, and Employees	• Rate of Improvement
• Integrated	• Public Interactions/Responsibilities	• Sustained
		• Benchmarked

Source: National Institute of Standards and Technology

Evaluation-Improvement Cycles.   Examiners probe the degree to which the company has developed effective self-evaluation, feedback, and adaptation cycles to sustain continuous improvement. The successful applicant learns something from the process and feeds that back into the system to stimulate fundamental changes.

Tools and Techniques.   The message here is choose your weapons well. Examiners evaluate if the company's tools and techniques are appropriate for the task and if the tools are effectively used.

Integrated.   In the quality battle, the ideal tactic is integration. Examiners focus on the degree to which quality improvement tools and processes are in place within every unit of the organization and the ability of those processes to work in harmony with each other.

Deployment

"Deployment" refers to the extent that the company's approaches are implemented throughout all relevant areas in the organization.

Products and Services.   Deployment does not just apply to the characteristics of the product in the case of a manufacturer. Examiners are interested in deployment over the whole range of service issues relevant to the customers' total purchase experience.

Transactions with Customers and Suppliers.   Examiners look at the degree to which the company's quality approaches are applied to all transactions and interactions with customers and suppliers. It is important to view quality as customer-driven, not internally driven. Examiners also consider whether a company's quality deployment specifically addresses not only internal but also external conditions such as the marketplace, the competition, the regulating environment, and others.

Business Functions, Processes, Facilities, and Employees.   Investigated is whether the company's quality approach is not only articulated, but is actually functional throughout the total enterprise—in all operations, all employees, all activities, business, and services areas.

Public Interactions/Responsibilities.   A quality company is a responsive corporate citizen. Examiners evaluate whether interaction between a company and the public is integrated into a company's total quality system. Are a company's community responsibilities also subject to continuous improvement?

Results

"Results" refers to the outcomes in accomplishing the purposes addressed in the examination items.

Derived from Approach. The applicant should provide evidence of cause and effect by accounting for results in terms of specific quality-improvement actions. Examiners determine if the company's quality approach and deployment are linked to the ultimate quality improvements.

Quality Levels. Examiners analyze quality-improvement trends and scrutinize for effective demonstrations of overall quality levels.

Rate of Improvement. A world-class company is using every avenue possible to sharpen and accelerate its quality process. Does the applicant?

Sustained. Examiners probe to determine if quality improvement gains are durable. Does the company maintain its quality results over several years?

Benchmarked. Examiners look for a concerted effort by the company to make specific comparisons with industry and world leaders. Then they assess how the company measures up against the benchmarks.

One or more of the three dimensions—approach, deployment, or results—are to be addressed in every examination item. Figure 5.5 shows the specific dimension each item addresses.

The Baldrige scoring guidelines (Figure 5.6) are an invaluable tool in the evaluation process. The "green sheet," as it is known by examiners (because of the color of the card stock), provides a ready reference for scoring applications. By using its matrix system to diagnose the applicant's responses, rigorous scholarship can be applied throughout the entire application.

A score of 50% (500 on the 1,000-point Baldrige scale) indicates a

FIGURE 5.5
Malcolm Baldrige National Quality Award Information Requested

Category/Items	Approach	Deployment	Results
1.0 Leadership 　　Items:	1.1, 1.2, and 1.3		
2.0 Information and Analysis 　　Items:	2.1, 2.2, and 2.3		
3.0 Strategic Quality Planning 　　Items:	3.1 and 3.2		
4.0 Human Resource 　　Development and 　　Utilization 　　Items:	4.1, 4.2, 4.3, 4.4, and 4.5		
5.0 Management of Process 　　Quality 　　Items:	5.1, 5.2, 5.3, 5.4, and 5.5		
6.0 Quality and Operational 　　Results 　　Items:			6.1, 6.2, 6.3, and 6.4
7.0 Customer Focus and 　　Satisfaction 　　Items:	7.1, 7.2, 7.3, and 7.6		7.4 and 7.5

Source: National Institute of Standards and Technology

company has a sound, systematic process of quality management, which is the basis for moving forward to world-class levels. Companies do not score much above 50% or 60% (500–600 points) unless they demonstrate continuous improvement cycles and wide deployment and are producing substantial results.

The 1991 distribution of written scores (Figure 5.7) reveals that the majority of applicants score between 251 and 600 of the 1,000 points possible. There is not a set score to become a site-visit candidate. The judges determine site-visit candidates based on all factors presented. However, companies that have received site visits have typically scored more than 600 points.

Scoring Summary

A world-class company is effective in the three quality management dimensions. It approaches quality through a sound, systematic basis that is

FIGURE 5.6
Malcolm Baldrige National Quality Award Scoring Guidelines

Score	Approach	Deployment	Results
0%	Anecdotal, no system evident	Anecdotal	Anecdotal
10–40%	Beginnings of systematic prevention basis	Some to many areas of business	Some positive trends in the areas deployed
50%	Sound, systematic prevention that includes evaluation/ information cycles Some evidence of integration	Most major areas of business Some support areas	Positive trends in most major areas Some evidence that results are caused by approach
60–90%	Sound, systematic prevention basis with evidence of refinement through evaluation/ improvement cycles Good integration	Major areas of business From some to many support areas	Good to excellent in major areas Positive trends from some to many support areas Evidence that results are caused by approach
100%	Sound, systematic prevention basis refined through evaluation/ improvement cycles Excellent integration	Major areas and support areas All operations	Excellent (world-class) results in major areas Good to excellent in support areas Sustained results Results clearly caused by approach

Source: National Institute of Standards and Technology

refined through improvement cycles. There is excellent integration. Deployment is present in all the operation's major business and support areas. Results are world-class in major areas and range from a minimum of "good" to "excellent" in support areas. Sustained results are clearly caused by the company's approach.

In a world-class company, the Baldrige Examination Categories—Leadership, Information and Analysis, Strategic Quality Planning, Human Resource Utilization, Quality Assurance of Products and Services, Quality Results, and Customer Satisfaction—move toward a common focus.

Lower-scoring companies tend to have passive leadership, reactive customer systems, limited measures and benchmarks, partial quality sys-

FIGURE 5.7
1990 Distribution of Written Scores

Range	% Applicants in Range
0–125	2.8
126–250	13.2
251–400	35.8
401–600	34.0
601–750	14.2
751–875	0
876–1000	0

Source: National Institute of Standards and Technology

tems, and lack of evaluation and change cycles. In contrast, those with higher scores possess aggressive quality goals, benchmarks, and response-time drivers; proactive customer systems; and quantitative orientation. They have made major investments in human resources.

RECOGNIZING THE BEST OF THE BEST

There are four stages in the application review process: the first-stage review, the consensus review, the site visit review, and the judges' final review (see Figure 5.8). At all stages the Baldrige criteria are adhered to conscientiously.

The Award schedule requires eligibility determination forms to be submitted in the first quarter of the year. The first-stage review process takes place from April through June. Stage two is conducted between June and August. Site visits are carried out during September. The judges completed their final review after the site visits, with the Award ceremony in the fall. While dates may vary, the Award schedule follows essentially the same pattern each year.

First Stage Review

In the first-stage review, an application report is independently evaluated by at least four members of the Board of Examiners. This initial review serves to sort out applicants that are at a start-up stage and those that are more advanced. The Panel of Judges analyzes the examiners' findings and determines which applications shall proceed to the next stage, the consensus review.

FIGURE 5.8
Malcolm Baldrige National Quality Award Evaluation Process

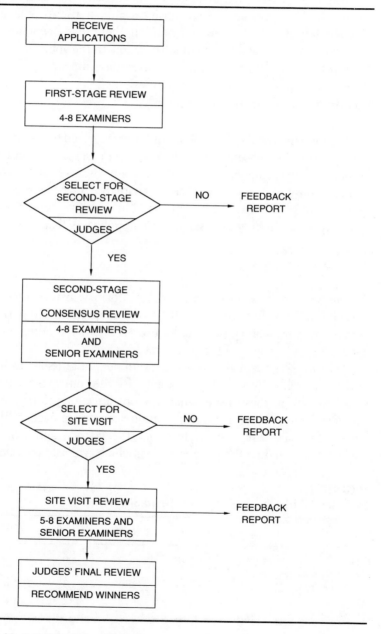

Source: National Institute of Standards and Technology

All examiner assignments to review applications are made to avoid conflicts of interest. Examiners are bound by a formal code of ethics and are required to disclose all their business affiliations. An examiner is not assigned to review a company in which there has been any affiliation. Examiners are provided only with information on the applicants they review. They receive no data regarding any other applicant.

Second Stage: Consensus Review

Four or more members of the Board of Examiners, led by a senior examiner, proceed with the consensus review. The senior examiner notes differences in the examiners' individual scores, the team discusses discrepancies, and, through consensus, reduces scoring variability. A consensus score is developed along with a set of comments. The resulting report is considered by the Judges' Panel, which selects those applicants that receive site visits.

Site Visit Review

The purpose of this review is to verify information presented in the application and clarify both the content of the application report and issues raised during evaluators' reviews. Figure 5.9 shows the number of site visits conducted by category during the first four years.

During the evaluation process, examiners note issues to be explored during a possible site visit. In preparation for the actual visit, each examiner team reviews all these issues and develops an issue-priority schedule. At least five examiners and a senior examiner comprise each of the site visit teams. The site visit team determines the agenda and works with the applicant to schedule the various events, which typically include interviews

FIGURE 5.9
Malcolm Baldrige National Quality Award Site Visits

	1988	1989	1990	1991	Total
Manufacturing companies	10	8	6	9	33
Service companies	2	2	3	5	12
Small businesses	1	0	3	5	9
Total	13	10	12	19	54

Source: National Institute of Standards and Technology

with the company's officials, tours of the facilities, and a review of pertinent records and data. Site visited companies conduct introductory and concluding presentations. The examiner team arrives at the company site on Sunday and at the completion of the visit finishes the report normally on Friday. This senior examiner report of the team's findings goes to the panel of judges.

The best way an applicant can prepare for the site visit review is to compile documentation as the application is being written. It is advised that applicants save all the data, printouts, and reports used in the application preparation (with a large company this can be a considerable amount of data). For any company planning to compete for the Baldrige Award, systematically segmenting the information into the seven Baldrige categories and then into each of the examination items and areas to address will pay off in the end. This makes it relatively easy to retrieve information during the actual visit. The Baldrige examiners attempt to validate what the applicant has already stated in the condensed words of the application. The documentation is needed to provide proof.

The site visit team does not contact customers or suppliers. The examiner team works with the application itself, the people in the company, and the documentation to verify and clarify information.

Judges' Final Review

In the fourth and final stage of the evaluation process, the judges review all applicant scores, assess site visit reports, and interview the senior examiners leading the site visit teams. The nine member judging panel raises questions and clarifies issues. Applicants (at this stage, only site visited companies are in contention) are reviewed by category (manufacturing, service, and small business). The focus is on evaluating each contender's strengths and areas for improvement and determining if a company is an appropriate national model.

The judges make their recommendations to the National Institute of Standards and Technology (NIST). As agents of the Secretary of Commerce, NIST submits the judges' recommendations to the Secretary for the Award decisions. Up to two companies in each category can win; however, if none are deemed worthy, no winners are declared.

Feedback Report

All applicants receive feedback reports at the end of the Baldrige Award cycle. Whether an applicant has gone through the first-stage review, made the round for the consensus review, received a site visit, or actually won the Award, feedback is provided. Feedback reports contain salient information companies can use to upgrade their quality efforts. The report is a valuable summary, by examination category and item, of the company's strengths and areas for improvement. Information is also given regarding the applicant review process and a distribution of applicant scores. While the company's specific score is not included (nor are the names of any applicants), the distribution of all applicants' scores is provided, and the company is informed as to the general range of its scores. Figure 5.10 contains the range of scores and general comments for each range. Each of the companies that proceeds through the final review will have received upwards of 500 person hours of evaluation from the Board of Examiners.

The Baldrige Award is the most difficult honor to win, but also the most prestigious honor conferred on a business in America today. Those who win make the pilgrimage to Washington, D.C., where they are recognized for their substantial achievements by no less than the President of

FIGURE 5.10
Interpretation of Applicant Feedback Score

Range	General Comments
0–125	No evidence of effort in any category. Virtually no attention to quality.
126–250	Only slight evidence of effort in any category. Quality issues of low priority.
251–400	Some evidence of effort in a few categories, but not outstanding in any. Poor integration of efforts. Largely based on reaction to problems, with little preventive efforts.
401–600	Evidence of effective efforts in many categories, and outstanding in some. A good prevention-based process. Many areas lack maturity. Further deployment and results needed to demonstrate continuity.
602–750	Evidence of effective efforts in most categories, and outstanding in several. Deployment and results show strength, but some efforts may lack maturity. Clear areas for further attention.
751–875	Effective efforts in all categories, and outstanding in many. Good integration and good-to-excellent in all areas. Full deployment. Many industry leaders.
876–1,000	Outstanding effort and results in all categories. Effective integration and sustained results. National and world leaders.

Source: National Institute of Standards and Technology

the United States. And while this acclaim would seem to signal the successful end of a long journey, those who would aspire to a Baldrige Award would do well to heed the consensus of that elite group of past winners: To win the Award is less an end than a beginning.

PART 2

MASTERING THE CATEGORIES
Understanding and Responding to the Seven Examination Elements

Each of the next seven chapters takes a closer look at one of the seven examination categories that make up a Baldrige application: Leadership, Information and Analysis, Strategic Quality Planning, Human Resource Utilization, Quality Assurance of Products and Services, Quality Results, and Customer Satisfaction. The examination items and all of the areas to address are illustrated via a hypothetical case study and examiner evaluation.

The Alpha Telco case study was developed for the 1991 Examiner Training Course. (Alpha Telco is a fictitious company. There is no connection between the case study and any company, either named Alpha Telco or otherwise.) The case study is an example of the content and format of an actual application for the Baldrige Award.

The examiner evaluation illustrates how an application is reviewed during the first two stages of the Award evaluation process. In stage one, the Alpha Telco application was scored by eight examiners who wrote responses to each of the examination items. In stage two, a senior examiner led the consensus process to determine the team's evaluation. The scoring itself is approximate and represents the examination team's consensus score. The key value of this evaluation and scoring process is in the comments, which discuss the applicant's strengths and areas for improvement.

Each chapter in Part 2 contains the following:

- An overview of one of the Baldrige examination categories and items.
- The case study response to the areas to address.
- The evaluation of the applicant's strengths, areas for improvement, and site visit issues.
- The examiner consensus scoring.

The case study application total score is located at the end of Chapter 12.

All the chapters in Part 2 are set up to make it easy to cross-reference the case study and the evaluation. There is even the opportunity for you to practice evaluating the case study and compare your evaluation to that of the examiners.

For each of the seven examination categories, an "Instant Index" precedes the case study. This index breaks down the chapter into sections: Case Study, Examiner Evaluation, and Consensus Scoring. This organization allows the reader to cross-reference by item. For example, after reading Case Study Item 1.3 Management for Quality, you can refer to Examiner Evaluation 1.3 Management for Quality to learn how the case was evaluated, and next to the Consensus Scoring to see how that evaluation is reflected in the scoring.

Try evaluating the case study on your own. It could prove to be enlightening. First read the Case Study Examination Item. Then list the applicant's strengths, areas for improvement, and site visit issues. A sample scoring sheet appears on page 73. You can adapt this worksheet for examination items in each category. Finally, compare your responses to the examiner evaluation. While this is not a replication on the actual evaluation process, it will give you experience in using what you know to analyze a Baldrige case study. This is an effective exercise to learn more about the disciplined, systematic Baldrige process.

Sample Scoring Worksheet

Leadership

CATEGORY 1

1.1

STRENGTHS:

AREAS FOR IMPROVEMENT:

SITE VISIT ISSUES:

CHAPTER 6

LEADERSHIP: CATEGORY 1.0

We launched Leadership Through Quality, and the results are now pouring in. Make no mistake about it, the quality process is driving this corporation today. Who says we can't have zero defects on incoming parts and outgoing finished machines? And who says that we can't have 100 percent customer satisfaction? Well not me, and not any Xerox person with our new set of expectations.

David T. Kearns, Chairman and CEO (1982–1991), Xerox Corporation

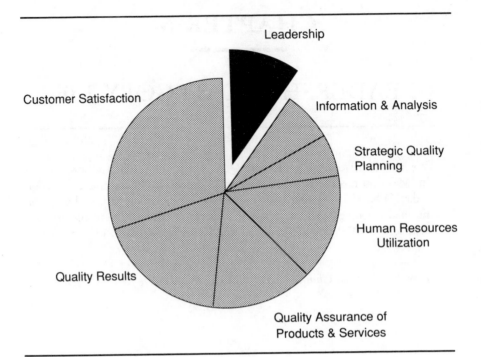

Examination Category/Items	Maximum Points
1.0 LEADERSHIP	100
1.1 Senior Executive Leadership	40
1.2 Quality Values	15
1.3 Management for Quality	25
1.4 Public Responsibility	20

EXAMINATION CATEGORY OVERVIEW

1.0 LEADERSHIP (100 points)

Leadership has proven to be key in the continuous quality improvement process. Quality "programs" assigned to workers while management continues to focus on short-term productivity and profits are a formula for disaster. Early on, American companies infatuated with quality "techniques" such as quality circles learned the painful lesson that without quality leadership, there can be no sustained quality improvement.

> *The Leadership category examines how senior executives create and sustain clear and visible quality values along with a management system to guide all activities of the company toward quality excellence. Also examined are the senior executives' and the company's quality leadership in the external community and how the company integrates its public responsibilities with its quality values and practices.*

- Examiners look at the senior executives' leadership in creating quality values, in building those values into the way the company does business, and how the executives and the company project those values outside the company.
- Evaluations are based upon the appropriateness, effectiveness, and extent of the executives' commitment to quality, and of the company's community involvement in relation to the size and type of business.
- Whether or not the company has a quality department or officer, or a regulatory affairs office or officer, are not considered in the evaluation.

Items

1.1 Senior Executive Leadership (40 points)

> *Describe the senior executives' leadership, personal involvement, and visibility in developing and maintaining an environment for quality excellence.*

1.2 Quality Values (15 points)

> *Describe the company's quality values, how they are projected in a consistent manner, and how adoption of the values throughout the company is determined and reinforced.*

1.3 Management for Quality (25 points)

Describe how the quality values are integrated into day-to-day leadership, management, and supervision of all company units.

1.4 Public Responsibility (20 points)

Describe how the company extends its quality leadership to the external community and includes its responsibilities to the public for health, safety, environmental protection, and ethical business practice in its quality policies and improvement activities.

INSTANT INDEX

CASE STUDY

Overview

Alpha Telco provides advanced communication services, mainly local and certain toll telecommunications service and network-access service, in five states: Central, Coastal, Rocky Mountain, Smoky Mountain, and Woodland. The company provides two basic types of telecommunications services within Local Access and Transport Areas (LATAs), specific geographical areas that are generally centered on a city or other identifiable community of interest. The first of these services is the transporting of telecommunications traffic between telephones and other equipment on customers' premises located *within* the same LATA (intraLATA service); this can include toll service as well as local service. The second service is providing exchange access, which links a customer's telephone or other equipment to the network of transmission facilities of interexchange carriers (IXCs) that provide telecommunications service primarily *between* LATAs (interLATA service) and, in some states, within LATAs. Other communications services offered by the company include data transmission, transmission of radio and television programs, and private-line voice and teletypewriter services.

1990 AlphaTel revenues amounted to $2.7 billion. The company earned $347 million and has a very strong financial performance record: return on capital (ROC) was 15.1 percent and return on equity (ROE) was 19 percent; both figures were in the 95th percentile for all local telephone companies in the United States.

On December 31, 1990, the company had approximately 5,084,000 customer lines providing service to about 90 percent of the population and 70 percent of the areas of the five-state region. (The remainder of the region is served by other telephone companies.) Sixty-five percent of these lines serve residential customers, 32 percent business, 1.5 percent public telephone, and 1.5 percent special access. About 33 percent of the company's customer lines are located in the City of Commerce and its surrounding metropolitan area. Another 24 percent are in exchanges serving 19 other community areas of 50,000 or more population. As of December 31, 1990, 96.4 percent of all customers were served by the company's 462 electronic central offices.

Interexchange carriers provided about 23 percent of AlphaTel's 1990 revenue. One IXC customer accounted for 75 percent of that amount; the top three IXCs accounted for 94 percent.

AlphaTel's business and residence customers demand uncompromising reliability, immediate availability, timeliness of installation and repair, and knowledgeable, courteous customer representatives and operators. They also expect convenient business hours and accessible business offices. AlphaTel's interexchange carrier customers consider accuracy of service orders and bills to be major requirements.

The telecommunications industry is capital intensive, requiring major investments in infrastructure. AlphaTel has been making and expects to continue to make large construction expenditures to meet the demand for communications service and to improve such services. The total investment in the telecommunications plant increased from $5.8 billion as of December 31, 1985, to about $7 billion as of December 31, 1990. In that same time frame, the company's annual construction expenditures have been $496 million (1986), $670 million (1987), $652 million (1988), $591 million (1989), and $578 million (1990); they are expected to be about $603 million in 1991. Because AlphaTel is prohibited from manufacturing any telecommunications equipment, it depends totally on outside equipment manufacturers for products and supplies.

The telecommunications industry is also labor intensive. As of December 31, 1990, the company had 22,268 employees, of whom about 15,800 are represented by the International Brotherhood of Electrical Workers (82 percent) and the Communications Workers of America (18 percent), both of which are affiliated with the AFL–CIO. During 1992, three-year union contracts agreed upon in 1989 will expire. The company expects that bargaining for new contracts with one or both of the unions will begin in April 1992.

Profit-sharing plans for nonmanagement employees were instituted in 1987 for the first time at the company. Over 90 percent of AlphaTel's work force had never worked anywhere else before joining the company.

The telecommunications services industry is increasingly competitive, driven by significant customer sensitivity to feature availability, price, reliability, and convenience. Differentiation is largely based on price and service (convenience, accuracy, and responsiveness). This means that dissatisfied customers seek alternative vendors. While AlphaTel's markets were not competitive prior to 1984, recently the company has seen competition in most major service lines and markets. The only market where significant competition has not occurred is basic local exchange service. However, the company expects that wireless services will directly compete for the local exchange market by the end of the decade. In 1989, intraLATA toll competition was allowed in AlphaTel's two largest states.

1.0 LEADERSHIP

1.1 Senior Executive Leadership

a.   The quality initiative at Alpha Telco (AlphaTel) received its impetus in 1985, when the Executive Quality Council (EQC), which comprises the chief executive officer (CEO) and his six direct reports, agreed that changes in the marketplace and competitive pressures required the company to modify both its focus and its strategy. The initiative is led by CEO Don Williams, who has announced that he expects all management within the company to become familiar with and endorse the Malcolm Baldrige National Quality Award criteria. To that end, Mr. Williams and his reports have each assumed ownership of one of seven Baldrige Categories (Category 5 has two owners, and Category 6 is, in a sense, owned by all the senior executives). The Category owner is responsible for developing plans and objectives for the company that reflect the Items and Areas to Address within his or her Category.

Recognizing that their examples influence employee behavior and attitudes, Mr. Williams expects the senior executives to be visible in reaffirming the company's quality goals at every opportunity. To that end:

- Mr. Williams, the Category 1 owner, makes the opening comments at every session of the company's Quality Awareness course (see also Item 4.3), attends at least one quality improvement team (QIT) workshop each month (see also Item 4.2), and writes a column in *AlphaBetics*, the company's bimonthly quality newsletter.
- Brenda Webb, the company's chief quality officer (CQO) and Category 4 owner, works with the directory of AlphaTel's Quality Institute to develop its curriculum, semiannually evaluates the quality progress of each of the organizations headed by the other members of the EQC, and delivers the opening comments at all recognition functions.
- Together, Mr. Williams and Ms. Webb evaluate the goals and plans of the other members of the EQC. In particular, they ensure that

the goals set represent a balance of incremental and breakthrough gains. The other members of the EQC, all of whom are executive vice presidents (EVPs), help the senior managers in their respective departments set departmental and organizational goals (see also Item 4.2).

- The executive vice presidents also participate in various other quality-related activities. Each is a member of his or her department's Quality Management Team (QMT), which comprises selected supervisors and managers. These teams evaluate each department's progress toward goals at monthly meetings and also recommend candidate teams and individuals for the company's various quality awards (see also Item 4.4).

In addition, AlphaTel's senior executives maintain a high day-to-day profile in the company. The company's new headquarters building, for example, does not have an "executive row." Rather, each EVP has an office in the heart of the activity of his or her department. This ensures that each EVP has daily contact with department personnel. (This also means that executives do not have window offices, which are instead given to support staff.) With this degree of accessibility, top management is able to communicate with employees in several ways:

- Mr. Williams meets biweekly for informal lunches with 10 or 12 managers who report directly to general managers and managing directors. He also presides over monthly orientation breakfasts with all new employees.
- John Conlee, AlphaTel's chief operating officer (COO), hosts weekly small-group lunches, meeting in the course of each year with all exempt employees at or under the level of general manager or managing director. He also has monthly breakfast meetings with groups of nonexempt employees by department. These extend to breakfast meetings in individual field locations.

In addition to these activities, senior executives monitor the company's "quality pulse" in several other ways. Each EQC member:

- Calls or visits at least two key customers each month. To make the visits more effective, the majority of each visit is spent "on the floor," in customer service centers or data centers where the EVPs can see firsthand how the customers are using AlphaTel's services.
- Participates in monthly Corporate Customer Call Days, when one

of the senior executives takes complaint calls from customers and then takes steps to see that the problems are solved.

- Works on a customer-contact job for one day per quarter. EQC members participate as installers, operators, or customer-service representatives in either the business office or the repair bureau.

b. To ensure that the members of the EQC were equipped to manage quality effectively, they all participated in a one-week quality process training course and then spent another week training their direct reports. This process cascaded down through the organization, with the help of a facilitator and a quality training specialist. Although the process took over two years to filter down to all 22,000 employees, the EQC demonstrated its commitment to the initiative by being patient with it.

Because the quality performance of AlphaTel is directly related to the leadership abilities of the senior executives, all of them share in the responsibility for that performance. For example, salary increases and bonuses are tied not only to the overall financial performance of the company, but also to each department's progress toward quality goals (Table 1.1). This progress is evaluated semiannually by the EVP and the CQO, and the CQO reports the findings to the CEO. Similarly, each EVP rates his or her organization's VPs and managers in terms of quality performance as either exemplary, competent, or inadequate. Personnel rated inadequate are ineligible for promotion, and only those rated exemplary are considered for promotion to VP or SVP. In developing these ratings, the EVPs rely not only on their own assessments, but also on the results of the annual Employee Opinion Survey (EOS), which provides a section for employees' ratings of management staff (see also Item 4.4).

c. Mr. Williams is currently the chairman of the Quality Institute of the National Communications Forum (NCF). In this capacity, he has

TABLE 1.1
Management Incentive Award Structure

Year	Quality	Financial	Strategic
1987	20	50	30
1988	25	45	30
1989	35	40	25
1990	40	40	20

brought several world-renowned business leaders to make presentations at the NCF. Other EQC members participate in regional and state quality organizations, and each one delivers a quality-related speech at least once a quarter to either a civic group or a trade organization. All are involved as members or officers of several organizations, including the National Conference of Standard Laboratories, National Association of Quality Control, and American National Standards Institute.

1.2 Quality Values

a. AlphaTel has a very simple—but far-reaching—quality policy: The customer comes first. Every AlphaTel employee is given the freedom to work in whatever manner supports this policy. Supporting the quality policy are AlphaTel's four Quality Absolutes:

- Quality is defined as conformance to standards, not as goodness.
- Quality is achieved through prevention, not inspection.
- Quality performance means Zero Defects, not "that's close enough."
- Quality is measured by the price of nonconformance, not by indexes.

b. The customer focus embodied in the company's quality policy is the first message all new employees receive upon joining AlphaTel. In fact, the first hour of every monthly orientation session is devoted to this message, so that employees understand from the outset that the company's purpose is to serve its customers. The message is reinforced daily in nearly every venue. The statement appears at the top of every internal memorandum, on all internal publications, and in every classroom and conference room. AlphaTel's customers are made aware of it as well: The statement appears on all invoices and phone bills, as well as on every page of the company's yellow pages.

Mr. Williams's column in *AlphaBetics* is a useful vehicle not only for reinforcing the company's basic quality philosophy, but also for disseminating the CEO's personal observations of how the system is working (or not working). He uses this space to tell about corporate quality achievements, introduce new ideas that other companies have used with success, provoke discussion with an occasional "contrarian" piece, and highlight best practices within the company. Most of these columns are expanded in subsequent issues of the newsletter.

c. To verify that each AlphaTel employee takes the quality policy to heart, one part of the annual employee appraisal and evaluation asks the employee to cite one or more personal actions that demonstrated a customer focus. For the purposes of this citation, customers can be either internal or external. Thus, one installer was able to note that she permitted an end-user customer to use her car phone to let his employer know he was going to be late. A reprographics employee, recognizing the urgency of a department manager's copying request, personally drove to the stationery supplier to pick up a certain color and weight of stock, rather than wait for delivery.

AlphaTel performs a biennial employee survey to assess employees' awareness of the company's quality values and their belief that AlphaTel's operations reflect these values. The annual performance evaluations of employees also include discussions of the company's quality values, with particular emphasis on employees' areas of responsibility. Employee acceptance is reinforced in two major ways:

- Survey results are used to identify areas where employees' understanding and/or beliefs indicate problems. This information is used to schedule ad hoc refresher courses or revise existing courses accordingly. Where appropriate, the CQO and her staff clarify or elaborate on policies in *AlphaBetics*.
- Departments that do not show high levels of employee acceptance are provided assistance in their efforts to increase employees' awareness of AlphaTel's values. This assistance may include special training sessions, extra posters and guidebooks, and more visibility on the part of the EVP.

1.3 Management for Quality

a. As mentioned in Item 1.1, each department has a Quality Management Team that evaluates progress toward quality goals. This team is made up of selected supervisors and managers, but selection to this team does not imply that the team member has exemplary status. In fact, AlphaTel has found that including an individual rated inadequate is often helpful in improving that person's rating, because the close involvement of teamwork with other committed employees is an empowering and invigorating experience.

Although AlphaTel is moving away from a strictly hierarchical organization, the EQC feels that some kind of vertical structure is useful in planning. In essence, vertical levels are determined by "time frame of concern":

- First-line supervisors are most concerned with their departments' near-term (less than a year) performance and goals, particularly in the context of the day-to-day operations of the departments.
- Middle managers are responsible for medium-term (one- to three-year) plans; this is the level at which the company's stretch objectives are set.
- Upper management is most concerned with long-term (5–10-year) prospects.

By including all levels in the department's QMT, AlphaTel effectively makes each person aware of how his or her time frame of concern affects the performance of others.

b. In addition to the "umbrella" QMT, each department at AlphaTel has interdepartmental teams linking units that have internal customer-supplier relationships. These teams are charged with creating agreements based on the customer's needs and the supplier's capabilities. Department managers, while not necessarily team leaders, are nevertheless responsible for ensuring that their departments remain true to both the spirit and the letter of those agreements.

c. In addition to the CQO–EVP progress reviews (see also Item 1.1) and individual performance reviews (see also Item 4.1), the progress of each department's quality plans is reviewed quarterly in the department-level QMT meetings. In particular, the department is expected to show positive progress toward its quality goals, or to explain negative trends and develop plans to address adverse indications. Departments and subdepartment groups not performing to expectations are asked to reconsider the ambitiousness of those plans in the light of the current environment. If the department managers agree that they tried to do too much too soon, they are within their rights to downgrade their goals. AphaTel has found that few managers do so; far more are willing to accept new resources to help them meet their goals, and no one is shy about requesting budget supplements to do so.

d. One of the many resident teams at AlphaTel is a QIT dedicated to analyzing the company's management processes. This QIT is charged with reviewing the company's quality results vis-à-vis its goals, and making recommendations whenever it appears that management processes are ineffectual in certain areas. The QIT is composed of designates from each EVP, so that each department is represented. To ensure that this QIT is credible and that its recommendations are considered, it is chaired by a member of the company's board of directors, and all reports are sent directly to the chairman of the board.

When the relevant process team or process owner receives the recommendations, which are directional and not prescriptive, the team or owner is then responsible for modifying the existing process or developing an alternative one. The methodology for doing so is described fully in Category 5.0.

The inculcation of quality values into day-to-day management is evaluated in the annual performance reviews, wherein each supervisor, manager, and VP is required to summarize his or her team activities for the year. The company does not expect everyone to be a team leader, but active team participation is a significant determinant of promotions, salary increases, and bonuses. Supervisors, managers, and VPs are also evaluated by their subordinates in the Employee Opinion Survey (see also Items 1.1 and 4.4).

1.4 Public Responsibility

a. AlphaTel has a strong and effective quality program and is eager to share many of its "secrets" with interested companies and organizations. To that end, individual employees who are asked to speak at civic functions are given every liberty to do so, provided they include the company's quality message in their address. The company has also underwritten a public television series on quality "gurus" and is a major sponsor of the American Society of Quality Control.

AlphaTel has also endowed a Statistical Process Control professorship at Rocky Mountain State University (RMSU), including funds and resources for all teaching materials. Within broad guidelines set by the endowment—candidates must have industry experience, for example, and appointments are limited to two years (to ensure a continual influx of fresh ideas and approaches—RMSU is free to select its own candidates for this position).

One of the most ambitious company efforts, however, is the development of a state quality award in Central, AlphaTel's largest operating territory, to be modeled along the lines of the Malcolm Baldrige National Quality Award. Mr. Williams and Ms. Webb are working closely with state officials, executives from other companies, and management consultants to create the optimal application form and process for state-based corporations. The plan is to have the guidelines in place for a 1992 award. Ms. Webb has been asked to serve as the first director of the board of examiners.

   b.   When the divestiture of the Bell System became a reality in 1984, AlphaTel discovered that most of its technical resources actually resided at AT&T Bell Laboratories. To keep its own staff at high proficiency, therefore, AlphaTel participates in a technical-exchange program (TEP) with both Bell Laboratories and BellCore, the research consortium of the Regional Bell Operating Companies (RBOCs). The company also encourages all of its personnel to participate in professional societies and underwrites one to three memberships per employee per year. Employees who are appointed to standards or quality-related committees of their societies are given the time and resources—including all travel expenses related to committee meetings—to pursue society activities. Those who are asked to deliver invited or keynote lectures at society meetings, or who are asked to chair technical sessions, are also given the time and expenses to fulfill their obligations.

   c.   The general public often regards telecommunications as an environmentally "clean" business. AlphaTel recognizes, however, that manufacturing processes that create silicon chips, microprocessors, and the like use chlorofluorocarbons (CFCs) and other potentially hazardous solvents. Therefore, the company works with its vendors and suppliers to minimize the consequences of this work. It is an active researcher into alternatives to CFCs and polychlorinated biphenyls (PBCs) and has told all suppliers that disposal of hazardous materials shall be in accordance with strict regulations as a condition of purchasing; in all cases, AlphaTel's regulations are tighter than federal and state mandates. All AlphaTel QITs that work with suppliers are required to understand and enforce these regulations.

   In all matters related to environmental protection and waste management, AlphaTel is a partner with the Environmental Resources Defence Council (ERDC) in establishing goals and standards and in monitoring compliance. Specifically:

   • AlphaTel and ERDC have agreed that AlphaTel and its suppliers shall cut pollution 50 percent from 1990 levels by year-end 1993.

Suppliers who do not wish to comply with this standard are dropped. Others are given technical assistance by ERDC in reaching the standard, which also specifies a progress-toward-goal schedule.

- AlphaTel and its suppliers have established a recycling consortium, which is open to all companies in AlphaTel's service area, to handle all paper, glass, cans, and the three polymers—polyethylene, high-density polyethylene, and polypropylene—that constitute 90 percent of disposed plastic. The company estimates that its waste-disposal costs—the company disposes of 100,000 pounds of paper alone every month—will be reduced by 60 percent when the recycling effort is fully deployed, and it expects to reach this level by year-end 1991. AlphaTel has also entered into an agreement with Procter & Gamble to purchase products developed from that company's efforts to recycle disposable diapers.

- ERDC will audit AlphaTel and its suppliers quarterly to verify compliance with the established standards. ERDC has ultimate responsibility for monitoring pollution, and AlphaTel regards that group's decisions as final.

EVALUATION

1.0 LEADERSHIP

1.1 Senior Executive Leadership

Strengths

- The chief executive officer (CEO) and his six direct reports, which include the chief quality officer (CQO), form the Executive Quality Council (EQC). The council was formed in 1985, indicating both sustained visibility of quality as a priority and sustained senior management involvement.

- The senior executives' approaches to leadership, personal involvement, and visibility include a variety of regular quality-related activities:

  1. The CEO makes opening comments at every session of the company's quality awareness course, attends one quality improve-

ment team (QIT) workshop per month, and writes a column for the company newsletter.

2. The CQO is involved with the director of the company's Quality Institute in the development of the quality curriculum.

3. Each member of the EQC is also a member of a departmental Quality Management Team (QMT) which, on a monthly basis, evaluates the department's progress toward quality goals and recommends teams and individuals for recognition and rewards.

4. Each EQC member has direct contact with customers through calls or visits taking complaint calls and participating in customer contact jobs such as installation, etc.

- The approaches taken to maintaining senior executive involvement and focus on quality are:

1. Each member of the EQC has ownership of one of the National Quality Award categories.

2. Senior executives' salaries are tied to each department's progress toward quality goals.

3. All managers are rated on quality performance, and those rated inadequate are not eligible for promotion.

- All members of the EQC have received one week of training, after which they then spent another week training their direct reports.

- The CEO is chairman of the Quality Institute of the National Communications Forum. Other executives give at least one speech per quarter and are involved in organizations such as ANSI.

Areas for Improvement

- The level of knowledge and expertise of the senior executives about quality is not clear. There is no indication given in this Item that the members of the EQC have further developed or refined their quality management skills beyond the initial one week of training or are involved in any ongoing activities to improve their knowledge. One week of training in five years in not likely to be sufficient. (Note: There is indication in Item 4.3 that they have had SPC training.)

- While a number of meetings between the senior executives and customers or employees are mentioned, it is not clear what the profile of quality is at these meetings relative to other business considerations.

- There is little indicated participation of senior management in recognition or rewards.
- There appears to be no involvement of senior executives with suppliers.
- The degree of senior executives' communication of quality outside the company seems limited.
- While there are some incentives in place for reinforcing the importance of quality, there does not appear to be any systematic process for building the quality values into leadership throughout the company.
- There is little indication of a strategy or rationale underlying the senior management's activities. In particular, it is not clear that their leadership activities are responsive to the leadership needs of the organization as determined from data such as that generated by the Employee Opinion Survey. In addition, it is unclear how the various activities are coordinated to be most effective. Thus, there does not appear to be a well–thought-out leadership process.

Site Visit Issues

- Determine the degree of focus on quality in the various meetings with customers and employees that are mentioned. Examine the minutes or other documentation from some of the meetings with employees.
- Determine the kinds of speeches that are made by the EQC members in regional and state organizations.
- Examine the senior executives' schedules to verify the extent of their involvement in quality-related activities.

1.2 Quality Values

Strengths

- The quality policy is that the customer comes first. This demonstrates one clear organizational value. The quality policy is supported by four "Quality Absolutes."

- There are several approaches used for communicating the company's "customer comes first" quality policy:
  1. The quality policy is communicated immediately to new employees during the first hour of the new employee orientation sessions.
  2. The quality policy is printed on all company stationery and internal publications and on every page of the company's yellow pages.
  3. The quality policy is posted on all classroom and conference room walls.
  4. The CEO reinforces the policy in his column in the company newsletter.
- The annual performance evaluation process reinforces the quality policy by requiring that employees cite an example of a customer-focused action they have taken and by including discussions of the company's quality values.
- The biennial Employee Opinion Survey is also used to assess the adoption of customer focus as a primary value. There appears to be some mechanism for acting on the survey's results. Actions taken when general weaknesses are identified include refresher courses, revising the training curriculum, and clarification by the CEO in his newsletter column. Actions taken when a department shows weakness include special training and increased visibility by the department's senior executive.

Areas for Improvement

- The quality policy appears inadequate. There is no mention of fundamental TQM values such as quality, importance of self-improvement, teamwork, management-by-fact, cooperation, etc. In addition, the link between the quality policy and the four quality absolutes is not clear. Further, there is no indication of the extent to which terms like "conformance to standards" are operationalized so that they are understood by all employees.
- Communication activities are minimal. There appears to be no mature, systematic process for communicating the quality values throughout the company or integrating them with plans or day-to-day operations. In addition, communication of the policy seems to rely almost exclusively on written forms.

- There appears to be no aggregation of the performance evaluation data about customer-focused actions for assessment of the deployment of the quality values.
- Exactly how the Employee Opinion Survey is used to measure the deployment of the values is not clear.

Site Visit Issues

- Examine the Employee Opinion Survey to determine its effectiveness in assessing the communication and adoption of the quality values. Also examine the Survey results to determine the effectiveness of the company's approaches to communicating the values.
- Ask some employees at all levels of the company about the quality values and how they affect their work.

1.3 Management for Quality

Strengths

- The primary approach for involving all levels of management in leadership for quality appears to be the departmental Quality Management Teams.
- The key approach to promoting cooperation is the formation of interdepartmental teams linking units that have internal customer/supplier relationships.
- Each department's Quality Management Team reviews progress toward quality plans and goals quarterly. Other reviews of departmental quality plans are made jointly by the chief quality officer and each of the executive vice presidents.
- The management process Quality Improvement Team is the primary approach described for improving the quality management process. This team has cross-functional membership composed of delegates selected by each of the executive vice presidents.
- The integration of quality into day-to-day management is also encouraged by the rating of each manager according to his or her quality leadership level. In addition, during the annual performance reviews supervisors, managers, and executives are required to summarize their team activities, and these activities are a significant determinant of promotions. Supervisors and managers are also evaluated by their subordinates in the Employee Opinion Survey.

Areas for Improvement

- The exact roles and functioning of the Quality Management Teams are never specifically described.
- The effectiveness of the annual performance evaluation process is not clear. In particular, how the accuracy and quality of the quality leadership ratings and team participation ratings is ensured is not discussed.
- There is no indication of aggregation of data about quality leadership, team participation, or other involvement in quality from the performance evaluation process. This is needed to assess trends in involvement and leadership and determine the effectiveness of management approaches taken.
- The extent of the deployment of interdepartmental teams is not indicated. It is also not clear how this approach ensures management cooperation, since the application suggests that even indirect involvement of management in these teams may be very limited.
- The planning process and review of plans seems to be informal. It is unclear how the reviews are done and what the outputs of the review process are. In addition, it is not clear how the QMT reviews relate to reviews by the CQO and the members of the EQC.
- Exactly how the evaluation of supervisors and managers by their subordinates in the annual Employee Opinion Survey is used is not clear.
- The only approaches taken for involving all levels of management are the QMTs and the annual employee performance review assessments of quality leadership and team participation.

Site Visit Issues

- Determine exactly what the role of the QMTs is and how they function, how often they meet, etc. Item 1.1 says that the QMTs meet monthly, but Item 1.3 says that they review progress to plans quarterly. Determine what happens at the meetings.
- Determine the extent to which the QMTs are successful in deploying quality involvement and leadership to *all* levels of management and supervisors.
- Examine the annual employee evaluation system and determine how it supports quality management.

- Examine a case in which a department that was not performing was "asked to reconsider the ambitiousness" of its plans.

1.4 Public Responsibility

Strengths

- AlphaTel has promoted quality awareness externally by endowing an SPC Professorship at Rocky Mountain State University and underwriting a public television series on quality "gurus." With direct participation by the CEO and CQO, AlphaTel is helping to develop a state quality award in Central.
- AlphaTel employees speak at a variety of civic functions. AlphaTel supports employee participation in external groups by giving time off for participation, paying for memberships, paying for some travel, etc.
- AlphaTel works with and encourages its vendors in the area of environmental protection. AlphaTel is a partner with the Environmental Resources Defense Council (ERDC) and has established goals for vendors of cutting pollution by 50 percent from 1990 levels. The ERDC will audit compliance by suppliers.
- AlphaTel has established a recycling consortium with its vendors.

Areas for Improvement

- The extent of outside promotion of quality awareness and the effectiveness of encouraging employee leadership and involvement are not demonstrated. No data are given indicating the number of speeches given by employees to groups outside the company, the number of employees that have memberships in various quality-related organizations, etc.
- In spite of the role of communications in public safety (emergency numbers, 911, etc.), there is no mention of any public safety activities.
- The extent of public responsibility and external quality leadership which is described seems minimal for an organization of this size.

Site Visit Issues

- The pollution reduction program with suppliers is new. Goals of a 50% reduction by 1993 from 1990 levels have been set. Determine the extent to which this program is deployed or the deployment is thoroughly planned.

- Review data on employee participation in quality activities outside the company.
- Review the company's newspaper and magazine clip files for evidences of quality promotion and leadership outside of the company.

SCORING

SCORING CONSENSUS SUMMARY WORKSHEET	Total Points Possible A	Percent Score 0–100% B	Score (A × B) C
1.0 LEADERSHIP 100 Possible Points			
1.1 Senior Executive Leadership	40	63%	25.2
1.2 Quality Values	15	44%	6.6
1.3 Management for Quality	25	53%	13.3
1.4 Public Responsibility	20	54%	10.8
Category Total	100		55.9
	SUM A		SUM C

**Category 1.0
LEADERSHIP**

Percent Score

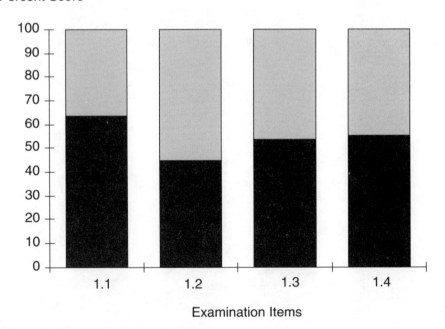

Examination Items

CHAPTER 7

INFORMATION AND ANALYSIS: CATEGORY 2.0

Our service standard is total customer satisfaction, 100 percent on-time deliveries, 100 percent accurate information about each and every shipment. But we measure our service failures in absolute terms using daily reports from the SQI (Service Quality Index). . . . We use these mathematical indices to reduce absolute failures every day. The point is this, the ability to mathematically measure the quality of our service is fundamental to improving it.

Frederick W. Smith, Chairman, President, and CEO, Federal Express Corporation

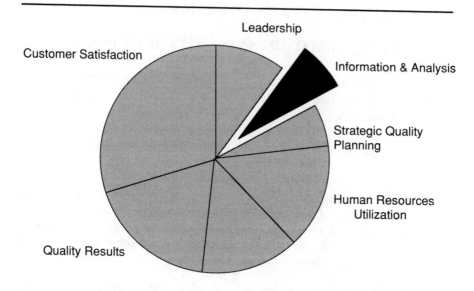

Examination Category/Items	Maximum Points
2.0 INFORMATION AND ANALYSIS	70
2.1 Scope and Management of Quality Data and Information	20
2.2 Competitive Comparisons and Benchmarks	30
2.3 Analysis of Quality Data and Information	20

EXAMINATION CATEGORY OVERVIEW

2.0 INFORMATION AND ANALYSIS (70 points)

Continuous quality improvement is a science that relies completely on a steady flow of accurate information about the processes that generate a company's products and services.

To be effective, management must base its decisions on information from every constituency: workers, agents, vendors and, of course, customers.

> *The Information and Analysis category examines the scope, validity, use, and management of data and information that underlie the company's overall quality management system. Also examined is the adequacy of the data, information, and analysis to support a responsive, prevention-based approach to quality and customer satisfaction built upon "management by fact."*

- Evaluations focus on the scope, validity, and use of data to improve quality. Are all constituencies represented with a reporting system? Are the data in a useful form? Are they accurate? Do the company's solutions/responses logically reflect the data?

- Evaluations do not depend upon how activities are organized or whether or not the company has an information department or officer or uses particular technologies to analyze data or to make data available throughout the company.

Items

2.1 Scope and Management of Quality Data and Information (20 points)

Describe the company's base of data and information used for planning, day-to-day management, and evaluation of quality, and how data and information reliability, timeliness, and access are assured.

2.2 Competitive Comparisons and Benchmarks (30 points)

Describe the company's approach to selecting quality-related competitive comparisons and world-class benchmarks to support quality planning, evaluation, and improvement.

2.3 Analysis of Quality Data and Information (20 Points)

Describe how data and information are analyzed to support the company's overall quality objectives.

INSTANT INDEX

CASE STUDY

2.0 INFORMATION AND ANALYSIS

2.1 Scope and Management of Quality Data and Information

a.   In selecting items to include in its quality-related data base, AlphaTel asks if the item affects customers and if inclusion of the item would be useful in helping the company achieve its quality goals. In the first instance, AlphaTel categorizes each item on the basis of when and how pervasively the customer effect would be felt. For example, cable bought from a supplier might not affect a customer for several months, depending on when that cable is used in an installation. When that cable is used, however, it will affect many customers, so cable purchase-related items would be given a high-level data base priority. Similarly, expense reimbursements affect relatively few company employees (mainly the sales staff), but the effects are almost immediate. These data, too, would receive high-level data base priority.

In determining whether an item would help AlphaTel achieve its quality goals, the company recognizes that many of those goals are predicated on how other companies are performing in the relevant areas. Not only does the company wish to maintain its lead in the many areas in which it is considered a paragon, but it also desires to approach and exceed those companies regarded as world-class in other practices and achievements.

To accomplish its major objectives in compiling quality-related data, AlphaTel uses numerous measurement systems to evaluate both quality level and improvement, and does so for internal and external processes. These are summarized in Table 2.1.

In addition to the data sources listed in Table 2.1, AlphaTel has a separate system that deals specifically with Process Management data (see also Category 5.0). This system, called PROMISE (Process Management Interactive Selection and Evaluation), stores relevant data from the PASS, PANL, and PIM modules of the company's Process Management system, and does so for product- and service-oriented processes as well as internal processes.

b.   The majority of the quality data at AlphaTel resides in an on-line information system called AlphaNumerics (also called the Numbers), which is accessible throughout the company in each department's quality library and from any networked workstations. The leader of each data-gathering QIT is responsible for ensuring that his or her team's activities and results are input to the system at least weekly; the input-coding system makes it possible for the leader (or whoever is designated by the team) to recognize when an item repeats or contradicts an existing entry. The staff of the CQO reviews all new input monthly to monitor the activities and participation of employees.

Whenever a new QIT is formed, for whatever purpose, team members are expected to review the data base for pertinent information. The Numbers detail the problem statement, output summary, solutions chosen, and results. In addition, a team member is named as a primary contact in case the new QIT needs complete documentation of project activities (since much of this documentation is necessarily in printed form, rather than on-

TABLE 2.1
AlphaTel Sources of Quality Data

Source	Description	Competitive Benchmarks (Item 2.2)	Quality Planning (Item 3.1)	Employee Perceptions (Item 4.5)	Results Benchmarks (Item 6.1)	Customer Needs (Item 7.1)
External Sources						
Metromail, Atlas, Donnelly	Census data; demographic profiles		✓			
Federal Communications Commission	National customer satisfaction norms	✓	✓		✓	✓
Total Research Corporation	Surveys of AlphaTel markets, including customer perceptions of company and competitors	✓	✓		✓	✓
Dun & Bradstreet	Market data and background reports of companies in service areas		✓	✓		✓
Market Assessments, Inc.	Surveys of commercial customers	✓	✓		✓	✓
MMH Service 100™	Industry HR Trends and data	✓		✓		
Global Research Corporation	Market share and perception data		✓			
Internal Sources						
Employee Opinion Survey	Survey of all employees			✓		
FAMIS	Financial reporting system		✓			
AlphaNumerics (Numbers)	Quality measurement system		✓	✓	✓	
CNA and Tel-Us	Interviews, focus groups, statement inserts, direct mail	✓	✓		✓	✓
SAFE	Accident and illness reports		✓	✓		
AlphaBits	Access to dispersed sources		✓		✓	
Vendor Auditing Tracking System	Internal perceptions of vendor products and services	✓	✓		✓	

line). Projects are grouped in the Numbers under 32 business categories that correspond to Baldrige application items, making it easier to locate specific kinds of team projects.

    c.   Every source listed in Table 2.1 is periodically reviewed for accuracy and relevance by the staff of the CQO. If they determine that little useful data has been derived from a particular source—the frequency with which that source is called up is one measure of its usefulness—then the company seeks new sources of comparable data. If it is determined that a complete line of data is of little use to the company's QIT, then that item is no longer sought.

    Similarly, a data base QIT conducts periodic benchmarking of comparable systems in other organizations and also within AlphaTel. When a best practice is identified either internally or externally, the QIT evaluates its usefulness for AlphaTel and recommends its adoption and deployment. This QIT also solicits users of the various data sources for comments as to the accessibility and timeliness of the data.

2.2 Competitive Comparisons and Benchmarks

    a.   As is true for all local phone companies, AlphaTel is concerned with improving both defect rate and cycle time. To evaluate defect rate, the company assesses transmission quality, call set-up time, and service availability. Substandard performance in any of these areas is regarded as a defect. To evaluate cycle time, the company tracks provisioning intervals and trouble duration and repair time. All regional and long-distance phone companies must consider these factors, so comparisons with the RBOCs, independent telephone companies, interexchange carriers, and foreign entities (British Telecom and Nippon Telephone & Telegraph) are generally performed along these lines.

    Internal comparisons are similarly made among the five states and various operating areas within AlphaTel and are disseminated through internal communications on a monthly basis.

    b.   Competitive and benchmark data are acquired as follows:

- Transmission quality, call set-up time, and service availability are evaluated using a proprietary technology descended from studies first conducted in the mid-1960s by AT&T Bell Laboratories. The technology, which is part of AlphaTel's Performance Management

System, is used to convert subjective customer responses to objective technical measures. The studies are conducted by AlphaTel network personnel, and they enable the company to compare its technical performance with that of other telephone companies and interexchange carriers (see also Item 6.1).

• Service quality is evaluated by third-party opinion-analysis firms such as the Yankee Group and Benchmark Technologies. Limited service data are also available from the state public utility commissions (PUCs) and the FCC. AlphaTel uses these data to assess its progress toward goals and to determine if those goals need to be more aggressive.

• The state PUCs and the FCC are the primary sources of competitive data on customer satisfaction. These data, combined with data from AlphaTel's Customer Needs Assessment (CNA) and Tel-Us surveys (see Item 7.6) and surveys from Total Research Corporation, detail the company's standing in the perceptions of its current and prospective customers.

• Employee data are derived primarily from the MMH Service 100™ and AlphaTel's own Employee Opinion Survey. The local chambers of commerce also provide limited data on such matters as salaries and the cost of living. All sources are consulted in the company's constant reevaluation of its salary and benefits programs.

• Internal operations are benchmarked by third-party consulting firms that specialize in analysis of business processes.

c.   In determining new sources of benchmark data, AlphaTel continually seeks out best practices and world-class companies. The practices are often those cited in published compendia, and the companies are often those which have won or received site visits for the Baldrige Award or have won major state or foreign prizes, such as the Canadian Award for Business Excellence, the Deming Prize, and the Minnesota Quality Award. In reviewing this information, AlphaTel seeks benchmark criteria it has not used before and quality measures it does not currently track. Even though the company measures more than 100 areas of performance, this is fewer than the 250+ that Xerox measures. Accordingly, the company benchmarks Xerox's benchmarking process as an analysis and improvement tool.

In 1991, AlphaTel will begin a major initiative to accelerate its benchmarking efforts in three directions. First, AlphaTel is participating with three other U.S. companies to conduct a study of customer service practices and results for 20 overseas telephone companies. Second, AlphaTel is extending the scope of its telecommunications analysis to include several small, efficient U.S.–based independent telcos and four more foreign telcos. Third, AlphaTel will conduct benchmarking studies for all of its support units, including legal, human resources, purchasing and materials management, motor vehicles, buildings and real estate, accounting, and public relations/public affairs. For this study, AlphaTel will benchmark its performance against U.S. telephone companies and leading service providers.

2.3 Analysis of Quality Data and Information

a.   AlphaTel uses standard statistical tools to assess the meaning of all the items in the quality data base. For example, trend charts reveal internal performance along several measures as a function of time, and Pareto analysis reveals the causes of substandard performance. Combined with benchmark data, these analyses show how the company compares with competitors and other service-oriented companies. The company also uses cross-correlation techniques to assess the relationships between apparently disparate data trends (see, for example, Item 7.1).

Revelations from these analyses are included in the assessing QIT's final report, copies of which are sent to the CQO and the QMT leaders and VPs or managers of the affected departments. Each departmental recipient is then expected to respond in some manner, and that response is also sent to the CQO. The response may be a call for further data, study, or analysis, or for the formation of a QIT to develop improvements. At the very least, the department is expected to revisit its plans and priorities in the light of the newly revealed shortcomings.

b.   Some departments within AlphaTel have established process owners (POs), individuals or groups of individuals who have responsibility and accountability for the overall performance of specific services (see 5.3.D.). The POs have the authority to determine which data are necessary and how those data should be collected in an efficient and timely manner. The success of this concept in those departments may lead to implementation of process ownership.

AlphaTel's Process Management methodology (Category 5.0) contains steps to ensure that data analysis reveals opportunities for modifying or enhancing data-collection activities. In order to properly evaluate and control their processes, process teams require data that are relevant and accessible. Thus, the company developed AlphaBits, a system that captures data from geographically dispersed systems and enables users to link the data and generate information that was previously inaccessible. Information that is accessible through AlphaBits includes customer information, service and usage patterns, market forecasts, service costs, tariffs, and prices. Process teams can use these data, if pertinent, in their process analysis activities.

EVALUATION

2.0 INFORMATION AND ANALYSIS

2.1 Scope and Management of Quality and Information

Strengths

- AlphaTel's criterion for selecting data is whether or not it helps the company to achieve its goal of satisfied customers. The scope of data collected appears to include customer data, some employee-related data, and some benchmark data.
- There are several on-line data base systems which are networked and widely accessible. The PROMISE system stores data from the PASS, PANL, and PIM modules of the Process Management System (the continuous improvement process), and the AlphaNumerics system stores quality-related data.
- The PROMISE system's software helps to ensure its data's integrity by signaling when repeat or contradictory data are entered.
- All data sources listed in Table 2.1 are reviewed periodically for accuracy and relevance by the staff of the CQO.
- A data base QIT exists and conducts periodic benchmarks of comparable systems. This QIT also solicits comments from data base users.

Areas for Improvement

- Other than the general criterion that data must help AlphaTel achieve its goal of satisfying its customers, no process or specific criteria for selecting the data is described.

- The scope of the data seems limited. No data are mentioned concerning training, safety, health, suppliers, complaints, etc.
- While the categories of data collected are mentioned in general terms, it is not clear specifically what data are collected. In particular, it is not clear what data are in the PROMISE and the Alpha-Numerics data bases.
- There is essentially no approach described for ensuring quality, reliability, consistency, etc. of the data. In addition, the roles of the QITs in data collection are not clear, and it is not apparent how the accuracy and reliability of their activities are ensured.
- How often periodic reviews of data sources and benchmarks are done is not indicated.
- The data and collection improvement process appears informal and not well deployed.
- How the cycle time from data gathering to access is improved is not addressed.

Site Visit Issues

- Determine exactly what data are in the PROMISE and Alpha-Numerics data bases.
- Determine exactly what the roles of the QITs in data collection are and how the accuracy and reliability of their activities are ensured.
- Find out how often data are input. The application mentions that data input must be at least weekly, but it does not mention whether or not important measures are input daily or more frequently.
- Determine how often periodic reviews are done by the staff of the CQO, and whether or not these are the only reviews that are done.

2.2 Competitive Comparisons and Benchmarks

Strengths

- AlphaTel maintains data for comparison to the Regional Bell Operating Companies, British Telecom, and Nippon Telephone & Telegraph. The main areas of comparison are defect rate (transmission quality, call set-up time, and availability) and cycle time (provisioning intervals, trouble duration, and repair time.)

- AlphaTel has a well-defined process for benchmarking, which is described in Item 3.1.
- Benchmark data include service-quality data from opinion-analysis firms and from the state PUCs and the FCC. AlphaTel also performs customer surveys and an Employee Opinion Survey.
- AlphaTel's approach to new services of benchmark data is to continually seek out world-class companies, including winners of the Baldrige and other quality awards.
- AlphaTel's approach to improving its benchmark process is to benchmark Xerox's benchmarking process. AlphaTel has plans to increase its benchmarking activities in 1991.

Areas for Improvement

- The almost exclusive focus of the benchmark data appears to be comparison of narrowly focused telecommunications variables to other telephone companies. Also, there is no relationship described between the company's plans, goals, or priorities and the benchmarks selected.
- The scope of benchmark data appears to be severely limited. There are few process benchmarks mentioned; no customer-contact process benchmarks; and few employee, internal operations, supplier, or support-area benchmarks.
- It is not clear how mature or thoroughly deployed AlphaTel's benchmarking process is. In particular, it is unclear how long AlphaTel has used the benchmarking process described in Item 3.1, how many processes have been benchmarked, how what is to be benchmarked is determined, and how data from the benchmarks are used in planning and in the quality-improvement process.

Site Visit Issues

- A list of companies benchmarked is given in Item 3.1. It includes Proctor & Gamble, GE, and American Express for service; Motorola, Xerox, Federal Express, and CSX for process improvement; and Florida Power & Light and Ford for policy deployment. Data from these benchmarks, however, are not mentioned in this item. Determine the extent to which these companies have actually been benchmarked and how data from the benchmarks have been used.

- Item 3.1 claims 110 benchmarks. Verify this and determine exactly what the benchmarks are.
- Determine how long AlphaTel has used the benchmarking process described in Item 3.1 and how many processes have been benchmarked.
- Determine the extent to which the plans for extending the scope of benchmarking are well developed and in the process of being implemented.
- Review the benchmark data in the areas of service, quality, customer satisfaction, and employees.
- Determine how benchmark data are organized and stored. Are they part of one of the data base systems? Also determine the extent to which the benchmark data are available for use in the quality improvement process (e.g. by the QITs).

2.3 Analysis of Quality Data and Information

Strengths

- AlphaTel's approach to analysis is to use the standard statistical tools and quality tools such as the Pareto Diagram in the analysis of its quality-related data. AlphaTel also mentions cross-correlation analysis.
- Collection and analysis of data are part of the Process Management process described in Items 5.1 and 5.2, which is the QIT improvement process.

Areas for Improvement

- Use of analysis is very limited. In addition, analysis appears informal and not extensively deployed.
- How analysis supports major processes (planning, customer-expectations analysis, etc.) and continuous improvement is not addressed.
- No process for improving analyses is described.

Site Visit Issues

- Examine the analyses sections that are a part of the Process Management process to assess their scope. Determine the extent to which effective analysis is actually done by the QITs.

- Determine what types of analysis support major processes such as planning.

SCORING

SCORING CONSENSUS SUMMARY WORKSHEET	*Total Points Possible* A	*Percent Score 0–100%* B	*Score (A × B)* C
2.0 INFORMATION AND ANALYSIS 70 Possible Points			
2.1 Scope and Management of Quality Data and Information	20	48%	9.6
2.2 Competitive Comparisons and Benchmarks	30	52%	15.6
2.3 Analysis of Quality Data and Information	20	33%	6.6
Category Total	70		31.8
	SUM A		SUM C

Category 2.0
INFORMATION AND ANALYSIS

Percent Score

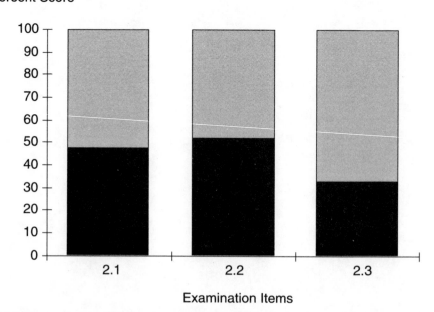

Examination Items

CHAPTER 8

STRATEGIC QUALITY PLANNING: CATEGORY 3.0

Today the Cadillac business plan is the quality plan, and every employee has input into the business.

John O. Grettenberger, General Manager, Cadillac Motor Car Company

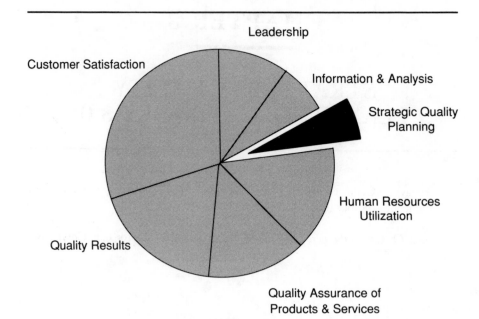

Examination Category/Items	Maximum Points
3.0 STRATEGIC QUALITY PLANNING	60
3.1 Strategic Quality Planning	35
3.2 Quality Goals and Plans	25

EXAMINATION CATEGORY OVERVIEW

3.0 STRATEGIC QUALITY PLANNING (60 points)

By definition, continuous quality improvement is a long-term competitive strategy. Although companies often enjoy immediate benefits (including increased profitability) from beginning a quality-improvement process, the focus is clearly on the long-term. Integrating a quality culture into a company is a lengthy and sometimes frustrating process. Articulating a clear vision for the future is the key to keeping everyone on track.

> *The Strategic Quality Planning category examines the company's planning process for achieving or retaining quality leadership and how the company integrates quality improvement planning into overall business planning. Also examined are the company's short-term and longer-term plans to achieve and/ or sustain a quality leadership position.*

- Evaluations focus on the company's approach to planning. Do stated quality goals represent a true "stretch" for the company? Are the methods for achieving those goals clearly articulated?

- Evaluators will look for competitive and benchmark data, which are essential for planning quality leadership because they make possible clear and objective quality comparisons. The sources of such data may be both competitive and noncompetitive companies that have set the standard of excellence in the area relevant to the company. Evaluators take into consideration the limits of a company's resources as well as the peculiarities of the company's competitive environment.

- However, if a company operates in a local or regional market and there are other noncompeting companies in similar markets elsewhere, the company would be expected to reach beyond its local or regional market for competitive and benchmark data on key product, process, and service features.

- Evaluations of planning are based upon the thoroughness and effectiveness of processes, including the validity of the information and how it is used.

- Evaluations do not depend upon how planning activities are organized or whether or not the company has a planning department or officer.

Items

3.1 Strategic Quality Planning Process (35 Points)

Describe the company's strategic quality planning process for short-term (1–2 years) and longer-term (3 years or more) quality leadership and customer satisfaction.

3.2 Quality Goals and Plans (25 points)

Summarize the company's goals and strategies. Outline principal quality plans for the short term (1–2 years) and longer term (3 years or more).

INSTANT INDEX

CASE STUDY

3.0 STRATEGIC PLANNING PROCESS

3.1 Strategic Quality Planning Process

a.   AlphaTel's overall business plans are developed in the Corporate Planning Department (CPD), which coordinates all strategic and tactical plans put forward by the board of directors. Every year, the CPD develops a three-year corporate business plan (CBP) that describes the direction that the directors and senior officers of the company would like AlphaTel to take. The plan is essentially a statement of overall business and quality objectives that the CPD determines are necessary if the company is to maintain its position not only as a responsive telco, but also as an outstanding company in general. The CBP provides a strategic foundation upon which the one- to two-year and operational plans of the company's departments will be based.

The departmental operational plans, in turn, contain quality improvements resulting from the activities of the company's various QITs, as well as changes in operations based on input and training received from the Quality Institute. These short-term plans are reviewed quarterly for progress and effect by the department QMTs and the EQC, and they are updated semiannually. These reviews and updates then feed forward into the CBP process: The corporate planning department updates its own plans based on these revisions and modifications. Finally, the CBP as modified feeds forward to the board of directors for review and update.

b.   In general, AlphaTel's corporate business plan arises from considerations of state regulations, customer requirements and expectations, financial performance, identified corporate best practices, and supplier and process capabilities. The need to consider federal and state regulations is clear: As a telephone company, AlphaTel is subject to the mandate and decisions of the state PUC regarding such factors as rate structure and service levels for many of its markets and services. Other cited factors are discussed in further detail below.

Customer Expectations.   Customer contribution to the planning process generally comes in the form of focus group and survey comments. Further details are in Item 7.1.

Competitive and Benchmark Data.   As a local exchange company, AlphaTel competes with RBOCs and other telephone companies only in limited arenas. For example, it does not provide exchange or toll service outside its own service area. Nevertheless, AlphaTel management believes that effective short- and long-term strategies rely not only on goals set from within, but also on a complete analysis of the successes and shortcomings of similar organizations. Thus AlphaTel benchmarks RBOCs in an effort to integrate competitive analysis into every decision on network architecture, capabilities, and operations. The company's goal is to be at least on a par with the best-performing of the RBOCs in the areas of customer satisfaction, network quality, on-time provisioning, dedicated services, and defect rates.

To evaluate maintenance and provisioning processes in the customer service centers, customer interactive systems, and training, AlphaTel looks to such companies as Procter & Gamble, General Electric, and American Express as recognized world-class service organizations. For process improvement, the company looks to Motorola, Xerox, Federal Express, and CSX. For policy deployment, the company benchmarks Florida Power & Light (FPL) and Ford Motor Company. FPL is also the recognized standard for excellence in utility-customer relations.

Once benchmark data are available, AlphaTel seeks first to meet the industry benchmark for a given standard of performance and then to meet world-class standards. The next task is to maintain continuous improvement in all benchmark categories, of which there are currently 110. This involves identifying the top company in each category, projecting its trajectory over the term of the current CBP, and working to surpass that level.

AlphaTel's benchmarking process involves four distinct phases.

- The first phase is planning, wherein the company determines what will be benchmarked (e.g., residence installation intervals). The measurement criteria (e.g., the difference between promised due date and actual intervals) are determined next, followed by data-collection methods.

- In the analysis phase, the process determines benchmark companies' strengths and compares AlphaTel's performance in those areas to that of the benchmark companies. Specifically, the process seeks to find which companies are better in an area than AlphaTel and how they do a better job, what practices make them better and what AlphaTel can learn from them, and how AlphaTel can develop applications to adapt the lessons learned.

- The third phase is integration, wherein AlphaTel establishes measurable goals and targets and works them into the formal business plans. It is in this phase that improvement plans are converted to targets and folded into performance assessments and reviews. This stage is also where a unit's integration of benchmarking into overall planning activities is evaluated.

- The next phase is implementation, which also includes constant assessment. This assessment asks several questions:
  1. What are the actions accomplishing?
  2. How do the accomplishments compare with the benchmark companies' current and projected strengths?
  3. What parts of the plan need to be adjusted or modified?
  4. Where is the continuous improvement going to occur, and is there a recalibration process in place?

(A fifth phase of benchmarking—maturity—develops when the company has achieved leadership status in a benchmark criterion and entails continuous improvement and recalibration into the work process.)

Employee Input and Capabilities.

Employee input to AlphaTel's planning process comes principally from two venues: the recommendations of the various QITs and comments made in the annual Employee Opinion Survey (see also Item 4.4). The QIT reports are sent to departmental QMTs (see also Item 2.3), which often take the comments or recommendations therein contained under advisement at their monthly meetings. These recommendations often migrate upward to EQC meetings, at which the decision may be made to include them in planning agendas. In general, however, each district or department is given sufficient latitude to deal with QIT recommendations at that level.

AlphaTel studies both the Employee Opinion Survey and personnel evaluations to determine the need for new courses. To facilitate this, the CQO and her staff work with the quality director to investigate new courses that have been developed by the various training arms of the ASQC and the IEEE, among others. Technical staff familiar with these courses are asked their opinions about the courses' rigor and relevance to AlphaTel.

Supplier Input and Capabilities.

Supplier input to the planning process generally begins with the vendor agreement, a contract between AlphaTel and the supplier that outlines the responsibilities of both parties. This agreement is exactly that—a bilateral and mutually beneficial statement of expectations and obligations that considers each party's capabilities and flexibility. The agreement is reviewed quarterly during visits to the supplier by a department manager or vice president. During these visits, each party has the right to comment on the other's performance as regards the contract. Substantive supplier comments are forwarded to the department QMT for further consideration or action. In order to ensure that AlphaTel's supplier base is as strong as possible, the company has reduced its supplier base by half since 1986 and makes current-supplier "best practices" available to vendors who wish to restore the relationship. All current vendors are aware that the company provides this information to their competitors.

One of the major responsibilities of the departmental QMTs is that of converting customer expectations into company expectations of suppliers. To that end, AlphaTel is very active in discussing with suppliers the feasibility of translating customer requirements into new technologies or processes. In many cases, a company-supplier team works to evaluate whether solutions exist for certain customer-defined needs, or if new solutions need to be developed.

    c. During the planning process, each department commits to achieving objectives in the areas of leadership, human resource utilization, information and analysis, quality assurance of products and services, quality results, and customer satisfaction. Progress in meeting the objectives, which are regarded as minimum commitments, is tracked through departmental quality councils and reviewed by the executive quality council. Departments must also address other quality issues that arise during the year.

Quality improvement tasks are included in the budget review process. In 1990, for example, $65 million was budgeted for quality projects. The projects were allocated back to the departments, with the expectation that some projects would be a pure investment in quality while others would result in savings from improved productivity. Each department ensures that the needed resources for each quality initiative are deployed to all work units and suppliers where appropriate.

The program evaluation process can begin at any level of the organization, but the ultimate portfolio (all the projects and their respective financials) to be selected is approved by the EQC. No major changes can be implemented without the council's approval; once a portfolio has been selected for implementation, therefore, it carries the full weight of senior executive support. Their commitment includes the financial and human resource requirements to implement the approved portfolio.

    d. AlphaTel's planning process includes an annual review with appropriate modifications of the strategic plan and quality programs. It encourages continual checks and balances, including operations reviews of day-to-day field activities as well as surveys of internal department quality by external professional organizations. An example of this is the internal customer/department survey by the network operations planning department. The AlphaTel Quality Policy clearly identifies the integration of the company's quality focus into the overall plan for quality. This provides the means to judge overall quality within the organization.

3.2 Quality Goals and Plans

a.   AlphaTel's overriding goal is to be the best-run telecommunications company in the world. The company's senior management and directors believe that as AlphaTel strives for and reaches this objective, all other benefits will accrue naturally. To this end, the company is fully committed to doing business in a manner that is consistent with the framework of the Malcolm Baldrige National Quality Award. This framework, which has customer satisfaction as its foundation, constitutes a vehicle to corporate excellence and will be supported by several underpinning short- and long-term objectives. AlphaTel expects that achievement of these objectives will lead to a general acknowledgment that the company is at the forefront of customer satisfaction through technology and service.

b.   By year-end 1992, AlphaTel expects to have achieved the following goals:

- Ninety-nine percent first-time correction rate.
- Ninety-seven percent kept appointments on maintenance calls.
- Ninety-five percent of residential and small business installations completed within three days.
- Sixty percent of access lines served by digital central offices.
- Ten percent increase in number of employees satisfied with AlphaTel (as reported in the Employee Opinion Survey).
- New carrier billing system.

These objectives imply an aggressive deployment of training and capital resources, and all work units are aware that personnel will have to be made available to attend the courses at the Quality Institute. Indeed, every employee of AlphaTel is expected to attend 40 hours of quality training and 32 hours of technical training every year (see also Item 4.3). The company has set aside a training budget of $28 million, which will be administered by the Quality Institute. To ensure that employees are not called back to their jobs during the training sessions, all formal training will be done off-site beginning in February 1991, when the Institute's new classroom building will be completed. This facility will provide all training capabilities, including media rooms, ergonomically designed classrooms, study carrels, interactive terminals, and a complete technical library.

AlphaTel has committed a capital budget averaging $600 million for each of the next five years. More than half of this amount is dedicated to programs to increase the quality and reliability of the network: digital COs, SS7, OSP upgrades, and new information systems (e.g., CABS and CRIS).

All departments at AlphaTel have discretionary budgets specifically for the evaluation of new and emerging technologies. Funds can be used for anything from the purchase of reference materials to fact-finding trips.

In general, AlphaTel does not enter into any vendor agreements unless the supplier can demonstrate both the ability and the willingness to meet the company's quality requirements. Suppliers who are "on the cusp" are offered the opportunity to participate in certain of the Quality Institute's courses in statistical process control, quality measures, or human systems. AlphaTel has notified its suppliers that by 1992 they must demonstrate adherence to the Baldrige framework. Further detail, including AlphaTel's plans to help its suppliers meet the company's quality objectives, can be found in Item 5.7.

    c.   AlphaTel has the following objectives for the longer term:

- New customer billing system by 1994.
- Ninety-seven percent large business met/exceeded expectations by 1995.
- Ninety-four percent small business met/exceeded expectations by 1995.
- Ninety-four percent residential met/exceeded expectations by 1995.
- Network reliability of 99.999 percent for carrier access services by 1995.
- Eighty-five percent automated provisioning on residence inward orders by 1996.

Again, these objectives imply an aggressive deployment of personnel and resources, to which AlphaTel is committed. They will also require continued monitoring of customer expectations and satisfaction, and more extensive benchmarking efforts (see also Item 2.2).

d.   AlphaTel believes that its quality plans and programs will have a far-reaching competitive impact.

- Interexchange carriers will have no service-related incentive to by-pass AlphaTel's network. Combined with stringent cost-control measures, AlphaTel should protect the approximately 23 percent of its revenue base represented by this market.
- CO Digitization and SS7 deployment will enable AlphaTel to offer its customers new services more quickly than it could previously.
- Training enhancements will ensure that the company's primary measures of network quality and customer satisfaction (as enumerated in Items 6.1 and 7.7) will increase.
- Improvements in cost and quality position will enable the company to seek regulatory reform in the three states where it is still under traditional rate-of-return (ROR), rate-base regulation. Regulatory freedom in turn will provide AlphaTel the flexibility to change prices to meet market conditions, and to eliminate price as a competitive disadvantage. AlphaTel believes that it can distinguish itself on the basis of superior service and delivery availability in every market.

AlphaTel has every reason to believe that its quality program will help the company maintain or enhance its leading position in some areas, improve its position in the others, and bring it to a position of worldwide prominence among telecommunications and service companies.

EVALUATION

3.0 STRATEGIC QUALITY PLANNING

3.1 Strategic Quality Planning Process

Strengths

- AlphaTel's Corporate Planning Department develops a three-year corporate business plan based on strategic and tactical plans put forward by the board of directors. This plan is a statement of overall business and quality objectives. The departments develop one- and two-year tactical and operational plans from the corporate business plan.

- The plans are based on data and information from a number of sources: customer data from focus groups and surveys, regulatory data, competitive and benchmark data, employee data from QITs and the Employee Opinion Survey, supplier comments.
- A well-defined benchmarking process is described. AlphaTel benchmarks Proctor & Gamble, General Electric, and American Express for services, and Motorola, Xerox, Federal Express, and CSX for processes. FPL and Ford are benchmarked for policy deployment.
- Departments commit to goals in each of the areas of the Baldrige Criteria. Progress is tracked through the departmental quality councils and is reviewed by the executive quality council.

Areas for Improvement

- The importance and status of quality in the business plans is not clear.
- The planning process is not described. As a result, the extent to which the planning process is well defined and deployed is not clear.
- The planning process does not appear to encourage input from all important groups. The channels for participation by and information flow from customers, employees, and suppliers seem unlikely to encourage a free flow of information.
- Exactly how the data sources listed are used to support the planning process is not clear.
- The quality improvement projects for each year are approved by the executive quality council. Once approved, there is no opportunity to change them.
- A systematic process for improving planning is not described.

Site Visit Issues

- Determine the importance and status of quality in the corporate business plan.
- Determine the role of the EQC in planning.
- Examine the role of benchmarking in the planning process. Verify the 110 claimed benchmarks and determine their scope. A number of benchmarks are described in this item, but there is little additional evidence that benchmarking is well deployed in other areas of the application, including Item 2.2.

- Determine if the $65 million spent on quality improvement represents a substantial investment relative to the number of employees and gross sales.
- Deployment of the plans seems to be primarily through departmental commitments to achieve goals. Determine the maturity and effectiveness of this deployment and implementation process.

3.2 Quality Goals and Plans

Strengths

- AlphaTel has specific short-term goals for first-time correction rate, kept appointments on maintenance calls, residential and small business installations completed within three days, access lines served by digital central offices, and employee satisfaction.
- Resources committed to the short-term goals includes a substantial investment in training (40 hours of quality training and 32 hours of technical training per year for each employee), $600 million for capital improvements in each of the next five years, and departmental discretionary budgets for evaluating new technology.
- Longer-term objectives include a new customer billing system and goals for large business, small business, and residential satisfaction; network reliability; and automated provisioning on residence inward orders.
- AlphaTel predicts that its plans and goals will result in: no incentive for inter-exchange carriers to bypass AlphaTel's network, faster new-service offerings, increased measures of network quality and customer satisfaction, AlphaTel's ability to seek regulatory reform in three states.

Areas of Improvement

- The major quality goal listed is a broad vision, and thus is very general and vague. No specific major quality goals or plans for achieving the goals are described.
- While general goals are described, there is little description of plans indicating how the goals will be attained, how the plans will be implemented, and how major requirements will be met.
- There is no comparison of projections with competitors or other

telephone companies. Also, the projections are not very specific, and it is not clear how they are directly related to the goals and plans described.

Site Visit Issues

- Examine both the corporate business plan and some of the departmental plans. Also, determine how the goals have changed over the last few planning cycles.
- In order to assess deployment of the goals, ask some employees at all levels of the company what their area's primary short-term goals are, and how they relate to the overall goals of the company.

SCORING

SCORING CONSENSUS SUMMARY WORKSHEET	Total Points Possible A	Percent Score 0–100% B	Score (A × B) C
3.0 STRATEGIC QUALITY PLANNING 60 Possible Points			
3.1 Strategic Quality Planning Process	35	48%	16.8
3.2 Quality Goals and Plans	25	49%	12.2
Category Total	60		29.0
	SUM A		SUM C

Category 3.0
STRATEGIC QUALITY PLANNING

Percent Score

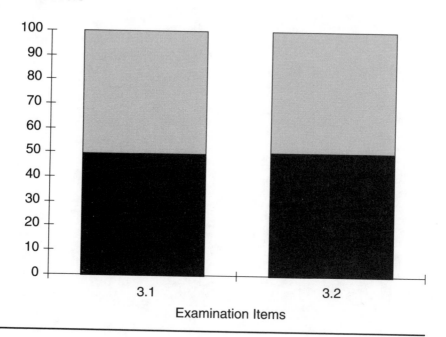

Examination Items

CHAPTER 9

HUMAN RESOURCE UTILIZATION: CATEGORY 4.0

People have an ability to do things that appear to be almost impossible. These expectations may seem to be a little bit above one's abilities, but if one reaches out to those expectations, one can very often discover how much more they can accomplish.

Robert W. Galvin, Chairman of the Executive Committee, Motorola, Inc.

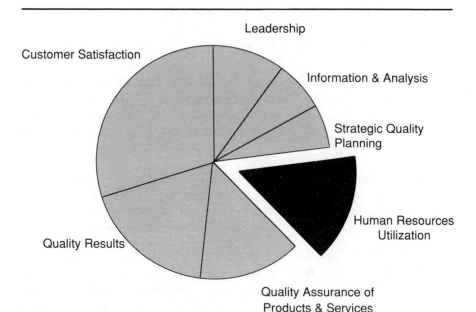

Examination Category/Items	Maximum Points
4.0 HUMAN RESOURCE UTILIZATION	150
4.1 Human Resource Management	20
4.2 Employee Involvement	40
4.3 Quality Education and Training	40
4.4 Employee Recognition and Performance Management	25
4.5 Employee Well-Being and Morale	25

EXAMINATION CATEGORY OVERVIEW

4.0 HUMAN RESOURCE UTILIZATION (150 points)

Continuous quality improvement depends on the maximization of the talents and abilities of a company's entire work force. To achieve world-class quality, it is imperative that a company empower its workers—but empowering workers without providing education and training is a sure formula for corporate suicide.

The Human Resource Utilization category examines the effectiveness of the company's efforts to develop and realize the full potential of the work force, including management, and to maintain an environment conducive to full participation, quality leadership, and personal and organizational growth.

- Evaluators focus on the company's efforts to develop and involve the entire work force in total quality. Have employees been adequately educated in quality theory and practice? Does the company have a shared "vocabulary for quality"? Are employees empowered with decision-making abilities regarding quality improvement? Are employees recognized/rewarded for their support of quality objectives? Does the company demonstrate commitment to human resource development through education, training, and a concern for employee well-being and morale?

- Evaluators take into consideration the limits of a company's resources as well as the logistical difficulty of instituting human resources programs.

- Evaluations depend upon the appropriateness and effectiveness of approaches to human resource development and do not depend upon whether or not the company has either a human resource department or officer, or training and education specialists or facilities. For example, education and training might be accomplished in a variety of ways such as through schools, contract, or through training given by customers.

Items

4.1 *Human Resource Management (20 points)*

Describe how the company's overall human resource management effort supports its quality objectives.

4.2 Employee Involvement (40 points)

Describe the means available for all employees to contribute effectively to meeting the company's quality objectives; summarize trends and current levels of involvement.

4.3 Quality Education and Training (40 points)

Describe how the company decides what quality education and training is needed by employees and how it utilizes the knowledge and skills acquired; summarize the types of quality education and training received by employees in all employee categories.

4.4 Employee Recognition and Performance Measurement (25 points)

Describe how the company's recognition and performance processes support quality objectives; summarize trends in recognition.

4.5 Employee Well-Being and Morale (25 points)

Describe how the company maintains a work environment conducive to the well-being and growth of all employees; summarize trends and levels in key indicators of well-being and morale.

INSTANT INDEX

CASE STUDY

4.0 HUMAN RESOURCE UTILIZATION

4.1 Human Resource Management

a. The human resource implications of AlphaTel's short- and longer-term quality goals and plans are briefly defined in Item 3.2. On a larger scale, the company's quality considerations and human resource management have always been inextricably linked. Because the company is customer-focused, its human resource plans are built around the need to meet customer expectations. Thus, the deployment of personnel—both short-term and longer-term—is driven by the quality focus of the corporate business plan.

This is not to say that personnel have no voice in this deployment. Indeed, AlphaTel has found that employees lend valuable advice in the deployment/redeployment process; after all, they know their own capabilities better than anyone and are eager to participate in processes that shape the future of the company.

AlphaTel has a short-term goal of sending every employee through the three-course (eight-day) Quality Basic Training program (see also Item 4.3). This will ensure that everyone in the company is conversant with basic quality principles. The company also wishes to increase employee participation in the various aspects of the quality initiative to 75 percent within the next two years.

Employees are constantly reminded that their participation in AlphaTel's quality initiative is crucial to the success of the initiative and the company. Recognizing that many people do not respond well to large groups, the company does not mandate a minimum team size; two people can make up a team if they feel they can be effective together. And team makeup need not be limited to departments or even the company. Indeed, AlphaTel fosters partnerships with both customers and suppliers.

The company is also active in creating partnerships with the Communication Workers of America (CWA) and the International Brotherhood of Electrical Workers (IBEW), which represent nearly 90 percent of all hourly employees. Employees are encouraged to participate in union activities, and the company is willing to negotiate reduced hours with people interested in pursuing union offices. This commitment to union partnerships is manifest in the 1989 contract with the CWA, which pledges employee support to continuous quality improvement while reducing quality costs through teamwork and quality tools and processes.

In the longer term, the goal of the AlphaTel quality initiative as regards its personnel is to develop quality leaders at all levels of the company. By doing so, the company expects to be in a position to enter the next century with a pervasive and unambiguous quality culture; one that can be considered a role model for the world-class company of the 21st century.

b. Increasingly, the human resources (HR) function at AlphaTel has served as a catalyst for departments to address many of the critical personnel issues that will face the company in the 1990s. During the past three years, HR has analyzed and provided the operating departments with assistance on such issues as the aging of the work force, the education level of entry-level employees, profiles of prospective customer-contact personnel for attitudes that predict human interaction capabilities, bilingual requirements in the work force, creative utilization of full-time/part-time labor pool, and revising the performance appraisal process to place a heavy emphasis on quality.

The goal of these activities is not to create foolproof hiring and career development criteria (unless such a thing were, in the opinion of the majority of HR experts, even remotely possible). Rather, the company wishes to be able to attract people who are comfortable with the company's culture and way of doing business. The company also wishes to project itself as a company that would be considered before all others by uncompromising and quality-focused professionals. To that end, AlphaTel wishes to achieve a 75 percent job offer acceptance rate for technical and professional staff, to reduce turnover of all staff to 6 percent in the first four years of employment and 3 percent thereafter, and to develop clear career paths for all types of employees.

c. AlphaTel uses the results of the Employee Opinion Survey to determine the primary causes of employee satisfaction or dissatisfaction. These data highlight areas where the company needs to strengthen or renew its emphasis, and areas where the company needs to continue successful efforts. The company also reviews attrition reports to determine most probable causes of employee turnover. Each year's results become the baseline on which improvement targets are set.

4.2 Employee Involvement

a.   In addition to the executive- and department-level quality teams, AlphaTel has inter- and intradepartmental quality management and improvement teams (QITs). Some, like the Residential Fiber Optic Study Team, have long-term goals and open agendas. Others, like the Major Customer Billing Task Force, come together for specific purposes and disband when the task has been accomplished.

Teams that involve customers and suppliers stay in place as long as AlphaTel serves those customers and purchases from those vendors. On certain long-term contracts, team turnover may occur annually or semiannually, to allow broader employee participation. Such teams are likely to be cross-functional and interdepartmental.

One example of group participation is the 540 work groups that encompass AlphaTel's 7,000 installers and maintenance technicians. Each work group manages its own workload, including vacations and overtime, and applies the principles of participative management to improve its results as a work group. The members of the group also maintain data on customer satisfaction and the costs of delivering service.

On a larger scale, union-management study teams analyze the need to assign unprofitable work performed by a bargaining-unit staff to a third party. The team assesses the existing work process and the bid from an outside vendor, and recommends improvements to the process. Thus far, seven such study teams have saved AlphaTel over $7 million; the employees, meanwhile, have been gainfully redeployed.

AlphaTel also encourages employees to make suggestions as thoughts occur to them (as opposed to waiting for meetings or evaluations). Therefore, every personal computer or workstation in the company is connected to an on-line suggestion box, which automatically routes suggestions and comments to the designated recipient. Employees are encouraged to identify themselves as the originators of suggestions so that the company may reward them accordingly, but they are not required to do so. Recipients are required to acknowledge the suggestion within 24 hours and to respond appropriately within 72 hours. Appropriate responses can range from answering the query to pledging to raise the issue at the next QIT or QMT meeting.

More conventional means of contributing include the Employee Opinion Survey, letters to the quality newsletter, department meetings, an employee hot line to the company's Quality Service Center, and direct talks with someone able to answer the question or solve the problem.

    b.   AlphaTel employees know that the quality policy of putting the customer first puts the burden of doing so directly on the employee. Employees also know, however, that they are given extraordinary liberties to do so. Thus, all installation and service personnel are taught how to respond when circumstances prevent business as usual. The company provides them with a discretionary fund to compensate customers who have been inconvenienced by installation or service problems, whether or not AlphaTel was at fault.

Employees are also instructed to act first and seek approval later whenever doing so would provide earlier satisfaction to a customer. Of course, they are required to report these circumstances as soon as possible, with the understanding that they will not be penalized. An employee's action may even become policy. One service engineer lent an obviously pregnant customer a cordless phone (the base was attached to the network interface in the basement) while her electrician corrected faulty house wiring. Now AlphaTel routinely provides emergency assistance even if the service interruption is beyond the company's control.

Empowerment is not limited to first-line customer-contact employees. For example, billing employees are encouraged to review bills before sending them out. One clerk who did so saw unusual calling-card activity interspersed with normal charges. On her own initiative, she called to verify that the charges were not the customer's—who had left her calling card and PIN at an airport phone booth—and eliminated them before sending out the bill. She also deactivated the missing card and issued a new PIN.

AlphaTel does not have any plans to give employees further responsibility and authority to act on behalf of customers. Rather, it wishes by year-end 1992 to increase the percentage of customer-contact employees who use the liberties that already exist from the present rate of 26 percent to 75 percent. This will demonstrate that employees recognize that the liberties exist. The company also expects a like proportion of all employees to develop (or at least suggest) new ways of exercising their authority.

c.   Different involvement mechanisms are best suited to different classes of employees. For example, customer-contact employees demonstrate their involvement in the company's primary focus by using their liberties to act on behalf of customers. Administrative personnel are most effective when they work as part of a team. And technical and professional staff are best measured by the rate at which they develop process, product, and service improvements.

Perhaps the truest indicator of the effectiveness of employee involvement, however, is the percentage of employees making quality suggestions that eventually are implemented (defined by AlphaTel as participation rate). AlphaTel feels that simply recording the number of suggestions per employee can be misleading, since most of the suggestions may come from relatively few employees. Therefore, the company records how many employees make implemented suggestions. The company also records how many employees are active in two or more teams.

d.   Overall trends in employee involvement, empowerment, and innovation are shown in Table 4.1. AlphaTel has made significant strides in most areas.

4.3 Quality Education and Training

a.   Quality training at AlphaTel is divided into four categories that depend on the employee category. The company's goal is to provide 72 hours of training per year to each employee, 40 hours in quality courses and 32 hours in skills courses.

- Basic quality curriculum courses are given to all employees and are offered bimonthly. The quality director ensures that each class has a mix of employees to facilitate the broadest exchange of ideas and opinions. Courses in this curriculum include Effective Team Building, Quality Awareness, Team Awareness, and Quality Improvement Tools and Techniques, among others.

- Advanced quality courses are designed for employees in leadership positions, whether in day-to-day work or in team situations. Courses include Situational Leadership, Motivating Employees, Cost of Quality, Competitive Benchmarking, Developing Customer-Supplier Relationships, Vendor Quality, Process Management, and others.

TABLE 4.1
Trends in Employee Involvement

Employee Involvement Measure	1986	1987	1988	1989	1990	1992 Goal
Departmental Quality Meetings						
Number of Meetings	6	12	18	36	72	
Employee Involvement (percent)	15	40	62	70	75	90
Technical and Professional	3	12	35	54	59	75
Administrative and Support	21	47	78	91	96	100
Customer Contact	12	25	45	52	57	75
Managerial and Above	22	66	91	100	100	100
Suggestion Box						
Number Submitted		1113	4455	17,915	24,495	
Number per Employee		0.05	0.2	0.8	1.1	12
Implementation Rate (percent)		32	38	52	65	75
Participation Rate (percent)		1	5	34	49	75
Customer-Focused Acts						
Installation and Repair Personnel	0	5	37	189	344	1000
Customer Service Personnel	0	23	111	223	445	1200
Other Personnel	0	4	25	41	32	
Quality Improvement Teams						
Number of Teams	44	89	222	370	512	
Employee Involvement (percent)	2	4	11	17	23	45
Technical and Professional	0	3	10	15	18	25
Administrative and Support	5	12	25	40	45	75
Customer Contact	0	0	4	8	12	20
Managerial and Above	6	12	16	21	33	50
Number of Completed Projects	36	97	307	556	643	

- Customer-contact courses are available to any employee who has regular dealings with suppliers and end-user customers. Operators, installers, customer service personnel, and purchasing personnel are given courses in Effective Listening and Conflict Avoidance, among others.
- Skills courses in management, communications, and computer skills

are open to all employees. Employees are encouraged to attend these courses based on the development portion of their performance appraisals.

In addition to the formal curriculum, AlphaTel has specific requirements for its new technical personnel; these employees are all assigned to work units involving the customer-service organization before they receive their final assignments. This ensures that they get a firm grounding in the requirements and expectations of customers before they proceed with technical responsibilities. Customer-contact personnel go through 10 weeks of phone training, service training, and communications courses before they receive their assignments.

Beginning in February 1991, all courses will be taught at the new classroom building, which is located in a corner of AlphaTel's office park. All instructors have received graduate-level training in the courses they teach, and most are full-time AlphaTel employees (the remainder are either professors from local colleges and universities or visiting experts from such companies as Motorola and 3M). Because registration for courses occurs shortly after each employee's performance evaluation and development session, attendance is mandatory except for certain personal conflicts; in no case, however, is an employee's supervisor permitted to expect the employee to perform job-related activities when class is in session.

In some cases, the employee and his or her supervisor may determine that AlphaTel's curriculum does not contain a course they deem essential to the employee's development. In that case, the employee may choose to take a night course at a local college or university; the company will, of course, reimburse tuition in return for a passing grade. In exceptional cases, the employee may be permitted to take a daytime course if a comparable course is not taught in the evening.

Part of every supervisor's job is to evaluate an employee's performance after attendance at one of the company's quality courses. This evaluation may be in the form of simple observation, discussions with team leaders, or review of the employee's output. Because an employee is expected to know more after finishing a course, the supervisor increases the employee's responsibilities to include specifically the concepts learned in the course. Thus, a Statistical Process Control (SPC) graduate is instructed to develop and maintain run-and-control charts, and a Leadership graduate is expected to volunteer to be a team leader.

b.   The trends in quality training are presented in Tables 4.2 and 4.3. In particular, Table 4.2 shows that cost per student has steadily in-

TABLE 4.2
AlphaTel Quality Education and Training

	1988	1989	1990
Total Company Employees	21,604	22,045	22,268
Total Training Hours	785,089	797,588	809,442
Total Costs (millions)	$20.10	$22.40	$24.70
Avg. Hrs. Trained per Employee	36.34	36.18	36.35
Cost Per Student Hour	$25.71	$28.08	$30.46

creased, a reflection of the investments that AlphaTel has made in new course development.

c.   AlphaTel assesses the effectiveness of its various courses and curricula in several ways. One is the postcourse questionnaire, sent within a month to all recent graduates. This survey asks the employee to rate the course's relevance to his or her day-to-day activities and seeks advice on those activities which were not addressed sufficiently in the course. A related survey is sent to the employee's supervisor. Employees who attended customer-contact courses are rated on the basis of before and after customer-satisfaction scores. A lack of improvement indicates either insufficient learning on the part of the employee or inadequate teaching on the part of the instructor. These data are also used to evaluate the overall effectiveness of the instructor and curriculum.

Participants evaluate each training course at its completion and again after six months. In 1990, an average of 37 percent of all employees rated quality training as very effective, and 51 percent rated it as effective at the close of the sessions. A training QIT consisting of both managers and first-line supervisors, which reports to the executive quality council, annually evaluates all training data and establishes future objectives.

4.4 Employee Recognition and Performance Measurement

a.   While AlphaTel believes that employees should be rewarded and recognized for quality work, the company also feels that a certain level of performance is simply a condition of employment. Further, the company feels that the truly deserving employee achieves lasting results using quality tools and processes. In general, results not driven by quality tools are not indicative of a change in process and will probably not be enduring.

To encourage group efforts, AlphaTel provides a larger portion of

TABLE 4.3
AlphaTel Quality Curriculum (Percentage of Population Attended)

Curriculum[1]	1986[2]	1987	1988	1989	1990	Cumulative[3]
	Quality Orientation					
All new employees	—	100	100	100	100	100
	Basic Quality Tools					
Technical and Professional	5	18	37	65	41	100
Administrative and Support	1	1	39	44	51	94
Customer Contact	1	4	40	55	43	100
Managerial and Above	9	20	45	60	42	100
	Statistical Process Control					
Technical and Professional	22	18	32	30	5	100
Administrative and Support	3	14	21	21	24	74
Customer Contact	0	6	12	18	21	55
Managerial and Above	21	36	45	10	6	100
	Advanced Quality Skills					
Technical and Professional	0	6	10	17	21	48
Administrative and Support	0	0	3	12	15	27
Customer Contact	0	3	12	11	12	35
Managerial and Above	5	13	23	41	23	95
	Customer Contact					
Technical and Professional	0	8	12	14	21	52
Administrative and Support	5	12	15	12	24	66
Customer Contact	10	16	21	27	34	100
Managerial and Above	2	12	17	22	26	74

[1]The totals represent employees who have completed the core courses in each curriculum.

[2]The annual total represents the percentage of employees of record as of January 1 of that year who attended the courses noted.

[3]The cumulative total represents the percentage of employees of record as of 1990 January 1 who attended the courses noted sometime within the five year period. It does not reflect employees hired or terminated in 1990; it may also include employees who repeated courses.

recognition vehicles to teams than to individuals. While district-, department-, and company-level achievement awards are available to individuals, cash awards—especially bonuses—are available only when groups of employees achieve specified levels of customer satisfaction. Thus installers, operators, and customer-service reps are all grouped into geographic teams.

No one in the team qualifies for a bonus unless all team members meet customer-satisfaction performance standards.

Employee recognition programs at AphaTel are specifically aimed at improving the work force's use of quality tools and techniques, and at fostering teamwork. While results are important, the methods used to achieve those results are even more so. The goal of the various recognition programs is to inculcate an AlphaTel team spirit.

Employees are welcome to suggest changes to the recognition programs through the various vehicles mentioned in Item 4.2. Otherwise, they are encouraged to set targets for themselves at their annual performance reviews and planning sessions, where they establish performance objectives based on their areas of responsibility and set recognition targets for the coming year. Naturally, no one is penalized for failing to reach his or her stated recognition objectives. Perhaps this is why more than 90 percent of such targets are met every year.

b. AlphaTel had found that the most valued forms of recognition and praise are those that are given spontaneously and informally and those that are awarded at the department or team level. The company does not track them, because they are widespread and unique. The company does track employees' own comments about these recognition initiatives, however. According to the Employee Opinion Survey, the percentage of employees who feel that their efforts are being noticed and recognized at the team or department level has increased from 26 percent in 1986 to 77 percent in 1990.

The company also tracks department- and company-level awards for contributions to quality improvement. These measures do not consider the number of awards given or the total cash presented. Rather, they track the number of employees receiving awards, as that is regarded as a more accurate barometer of employee involvement. Since 1986, the number of employees receiving department- or company-level commendations or awards has increased from 90 to 816; the number receiving cash bonuses (according to the present criteria) has increased from 535 to 6,015.

c. The Employee Opinion Survey (Table 4.4) is the primary vehicle for soliciting employee reactions to the company's recognition and performance measurement systems. The survey provides specific data on employee satisfaction with all performance and recognition measures—salaries, opportunities for contributions, bonuses, and the like. There is also a QIT

TABLE 4.4

AlphaTel Employee Opinion Survey (Percentage Ranking in Top Two of Five Categories)

	1985	1987	1989
Overall Satisfaction			
Overall satisfaction with AlphaTel	59	64	81
AlphaTel is a good place to work	60	70	80
Job Satisfaction			
Satisfaction with job	59	67	74
I like the kind of work I do	76	80	87
Quality of Service			
Quality of customer service	80	78	89
I can do what is necessary to meet my customer's requirements	60	73	79
Overall quality of work in my work group	81	89	87
AlphaTel is easy to do business with	35	49	50
Teamwork			
People I work with cooperate to get the job done	60	78	90
Career Development			
Opportunity for advancement	65	51	42
Opportunity to improve skills	50	49	62
Opportunity to transfer	45	57	63
Recognition/Rewards			
Satisfaction with pay	48	73	82
Satisfaction with benefits	71	56	75
Better performers rewarded appropriately	30	49	50
Poor performance not tolerated	20	37	45
Employee efforts are recognized	26	41	77
Supervision			
Treats employees with respect	64	63	67
Encourages teamwork	74	79	82
Clear to me when I should work on my own	59	75	70

Source: Employee Opinion Surveys

devoted to these matters. This group not only analyzes the EOS data but also conducts benchmarking studies of recognition systems at RBOCs and independent telephone companies.

Perhaps the most revealing comments come from employees as part of their appraisals. Each employee is invited to respond in writing to his or her evaluation and to his or her supervisor's administration of the appraisal in particular and positive reinforcement in general. Copies of these comments are given to the supervisor's own manager and the human resource director.

4.5 Employee Well-Being and Morale

a.   One of the ongoing quality teams at AlphaTel is the Safety QIT. This group analyzes sources of employee discomfort and works to find solutions to them. The group is not simply reactive; that is, it does not simply study accident and injury reports. Rather, it actively solicits employee comments on all aspects of the work environment, from heating and lighting to the comfort of chairs and restrooms. Many of the findings of this team were used in the design and development of the new classroom building.

The surveys conducted by the Safety QIT are used in conjunction with their audits of accident and injury reports to determine, through Pareto methods, the most common causes of workplace accidents and injuries. Employees are encouraged to report all lost time to the Safety QIT, which pledges to keep all statistics anonymous and confidential. The statistics are used in analyses of tools, motor vehicles, test equipment, and building design. A new study asks employees who work with CRTs to record all discomfort, no matter how slight.

b.   One of the most common sources of employee discontent in the past has been the company's inability to accommodate employees who wished to move into more challenging jobs. AlphaTel has been able to address this problem with a job rotation system in which certain employees are given three-, six-, or twelve-month assignments as part of their overall training. Some technical employees, for example, may find their brief training stints with the marketing group to be to their liking. If they show an aptitude for marketing work, they are permitted to stay in the group, provided a position is available.

Other employees decide to leave the marketing track for technical work. The company's liberal tuition reimbursement plan permits these employees to acquire the appropriate college-level training, at the end of which the company will reassign them to technical positions.

Despite its best efforts, AlphaTel has not been immune to the economic pressures that have imposed corporate "right-sizing." The company feels it has a strong obligation to employees affected by resource redeployment, and it offers several outplacement and redevelopment options.

- Extended tuition reimbursement plans provide up to two years of full-time equivalent tuition to employees wishing to return to college.

- An occupational staffing system, available by toll-free telephone number, advertises available and future jobs throughout the corporation. Surplus employees receive first consideration in these jobs, and there is no time limit.

- Surplus employees who find jobs in another location are given limited relocation allowances. If the job is found through the company's outplacement efforts, AlphaTel pays all relocation costs, treating them as transfer expenses. The only restriction is that the employee must find the job within six months of being released by AlphaTel.

   c.   AlphaTel is committed to the physical and emotional well-being of its employees and provides a full range of services to support them. All major locations have exercise facilities, for example; where the offices are too small to permit an exercise room, the company purchases a corporate membership at a nearby health club. The company also sponsors a confidential counseling service, available by toll-free telephone number. To ensure the confidentiality of this service, this number does not show up on any of the company's telephone usage summaries. Employees who are judged by their counselors to need treatment are given time off, and payment for the treatment is provided by the company's insurance program. Among other support benefits are:

- Adoption assistance and extended maternity and paternity benefits for the parents of newborns with congenital defects.

- A flexible dependent-care spending account. The company has an on-site intergenerational daycare facility with a sliding fee structure.

- A company store where employees can buy such items as clothing, theater and museum tickets, and gifts at discount.

- AlphaTel Night at the local ballet company's annual performance of *The Nutcracker*. Employees may purchase two tickets at half price.

d.   The primary vehicle for determining employee satisfaction is the annual Employee Opinion Survey (EOS). Because timeliness of response is so critical to the company's quality improvement efforts, EOS is administered, wherever possible, during department-level presentations. Members of the CQO's staff and the human resources department detail each section, and employees are given two hours to fill out the short-answer portion of the survey; the open-ended questions may be answered outside the session, but the company requires all forms to be returned within a week. To facilitate the sessions, sample EOS forms are available for review prior to the administration of the survey.

EOS is a multilevel, multipurpose document that seeks employee input on the work environment, benefits, compensation, management, quality team activities, and company plans. Management uses the results to determine key sources of employee satisfaction and dissatisfaction, potential areas for process improvement, and evaluation of management personnel.

e.   AlphaTel has shown significant improvement in many of the key indicators of employee well-being and morale and compares favorably with industry and high-performance norms (Table 4.5).

Four principal measures of accidents are used to evaluate safety performance (Table 4.6). Total Occupational Injuries measures all work-related injuries and illnesses that require medical treatments or result in restriction of work motion. Total Nonoccupational Injuries measures all nonwork-related injuries and illnesses that result in lost work days. Occupational Lost Work Days measures the number of work days per 100 employees lost to occupational injuries. Motor Vehicle Accidents measures preventable motor vehicle accidents.

Table 4.7 shows that AlphaTel's incidental absenteeism for 1986–1990 is about half the national average for service firms, as compiled by the Bureau of National Affairs.

AlphaTel also tracks turnover data. Beginning in 1989, AlphaTel divided its measures into noncontrollable and controllable to better target programs to the specific causes of turnover. Table 4.8 shows AlphaTel's 1990 turnover rates with these new measures.

TABLE 4.5
Benchmark of Employee Opinion Survey: AlphaTel vs. Service 100

Satisfaction Criterion	1986	1988	1990
Overall job satisfaction	0	0	+
Use of skill/ability	−	−	0
Sense of personal accomplishment	0	0	0
Understand AlphaTel goals	0	0	+
Taking action	−	−	0
Getting opinions	0	0	+
Revealing problems	−	−	0
Information regarding pay	−	0	0
Information regarding benefits	0	0	0
Deals fairly	0	0	+
Solves people problems	0	0	0
Uses feedback	−	0	0
Solves job problems	0	0	+
Pay for performance	−	−	0
Poor performance not tolerated	−	0	+
Recognition	−	−	0
Benefits	0	0	0
Job security	0	0	−
Opportunity to advance	0	−	−
Opportunity to improve skills	0	−	0
Clarity of career paths	−	−	0
Training for job	0	0	+
Cooperation	0	0	+
Quality of work	−	−	0
Overall quality of service	0	0	+

Key: − = One standard deviation worse than Service 100™ average
    0 = Service 100™ average
    + = One standard deviation better then Service 100™ average

Source: Employee Opinion Surveys; MMH Service 100™.

TABLE 4.6
Safety Results (Per 100 Employees)

	1986	1987	1988	1989	1990
Total Occupational Injuries	0.87	0.85	0.87	1.10	0.90
Total Non-Occupational Injuries	1.88	1.81	1.78	1.83	1.90
Occupational Lost Work Days	0.54	0.50	0.47	0.69	0.54
Motor Vehicle Accidents					
(per 100 vehicles)	5.60	5.60	5.60	5.70	5.50

TABLE 4.7
AlphaTel Absenteeism

	1986	1987	1988	1989	1990
	AlphaTel				
Incidental	0.9%	0.8%	0.7%	0.8%	0.7%
Disability	1.7	1.5	1.5	1.7	1.6
Total	2.6	2.3	2.2	2.5	2.3
U.S. Service Firms					
(Incidental absenteeism					
only)	1.8	1.6	1.6	1.6	1.6

TABLE 4.8
Employee Turnover in 1990

Job Group	Average Total Employees	Noncontrollable[1]	Controllable[2]	Total
Customer services	12,226	4.9%	2.1%	7.0%
Network services	7,234	4.0	2.3	7.2
Marketing/sales	746	5.4	6.8	12.2
Finance and accounting	982	4.1	4.1	8.2
Support Services	735	4.5	3.5	8.0
Corporate staff (HR, External Affairs, Legal, and Executive)	345	3.0	2.0	5.0
Total	22,268	4.8%	3.5%	8.3%

[1]Noncontrollable turnover includes leave of absence, health leave, spouse relocation, education, or retirement.
[2]Controllable turnover includes terminations and layoffs, mutual termination, and other employment.

Source: AlphaTel Human Resources Management System.

EVALUATION

4.0 HUMAN RESOURCE UTILIZATION

4.1 Human Resource Management

Strengths

- AlphaTel's short-term human resource goals include sending every employee through the three-course, eight-day Quality Basic Training program. AlphaTel also has the goals of achieving a 75% job offer acceptance rate for technical and professional staff, and of reducing all staff turnover to 6% in the first four years and 3% thereafter.
- AlphaTel's human resource function has helped departments address critical personnel issues such as the aging of the work force, the education level of entry-level employees, and bilingual requirements.
- AlphaTel is active in creating partnerships with employees' unions.
- Data from the Employee Opinion Survey are used to determine areas and causes of employee dissatisfaction. Attrition are also reviewed.

Areas for Improvement

- The scope of the human resources management goals that are discussed is very limited. In addition, there is no discussion of how the goals link to the company's overall quality goals or what the plans and requirements for achieving the goals might be. There appears to be little in the way of a formal human resources planning process.
- No improvement methods for human resources practices such as hiring and career development are described.
- Exactly how the data from the Employee Opinion Survey are used to determine the primary cause of employee dissatisfaction and improve the effectiveness of all categories of employees is not clear.
- Other than the data from the Employee Opinion Survey, few other measures or data appear to be used.

Site Visit Issues

- While very few human resources goals are discussed in the text, all of the measures shown in Table 4.1 have goals listed for 1992.

Determine whether or not these goals are part of a well-developed human resource plan that are integrated with the overall quality plans, and exactly what the methods and strategies will be used to attain them.

- Examine the Employee Opinion Survey and determine how data from it are used to improve the effectiveness of all categories of employees.

4.2 Employee Involvement

Strengths

- AlphaTel's primary approaches to employee involvement are: teams, including interdepartmental teams and customer and supplier teams; participating management for installers and maintenance technicians; an on-line suggestion box.
- A joint union-management study team that analyzes unprofitable work performed by bargaining-unit employees has saved over $7 million.
- Customer-contact employees are given limited customer-oriented empowerment, which includes a discretionary fund. Use of current authority is encouraged and there is a goal for increasing the percentage of employees that use their authority from 26% now to 75% by 1992.
- A variety of employee involvement measures are used, including measures of departmental quality meetings, suggestions, customer focused acts, and quality improvement teams.
- There are significant improvements and sustained trends in the employee involvement data reported since 1986.

Areas for Improvement

- Except for brief mention of self-management groups among installers and maintenance technicians, there is no mention of employee-oriented empowerment. No further empowerment of employees is planned.
- Company actions to increase employee responsibility and innovation are not discussed.
- How the employee involvement measures are used in improving employee involvement is not indicated.

- The percentage of employees involved in QITs appears to be low.
- There is no indication of management or supervisor involvement. The focus of the discussion is entirely on the work force.

Site Visit Issues

- The suggestion system is not described in sufficient detail. Determine how the suggestion system works.
- There are very few customer-focused acts for the category "Other Personnel." Determine if this category includes all employees that are not front-line customer service representatives or installation and repair personnel. If so, why is the number so low?
- Obtain more details on exactly what the union-management teams do.
- Determine how much money is involved in the discretionary funds as an absolute amount, as an amount per empowered employee, and as an amount per compensated customer.
- Determine how to interpret the data listed in Table 4.1, especially the number of meetings, suggestion-box participation and implementation rates, and the number of customer-focused acts.

4.3 Quality Education and Training

Strengths

- Training is delivered through a well-developed and broad curriculum of courses.
- All employees receive some quality orientation. Nearly all employees have received training in basic quality tools. A large number of employees have been trained in SPC. On average, employees receive about 35 hours training per year.
- AlphaTel's goal is to provide 72 hours of training for each employee per year—40 hours of quality training and 32 hours of skills training.
- A high percentage of "Managerial and Above" employees have received quality training through the "advanced quality skills" level.
- AlphaTel assesses the effectiveness of its courses by course evaluations and questionnaires. Surveys are also sent to employees' supervisors. Evaluation is repeated six months after a course has been taken.

Areas for Improvement

- The application does not address how the company assesses needs for the types and amounts of quality training. In particular, how is the training curriculum adapted to address weaknesses in the company?
- There appears to be little in the way of a formal mechanism for ensuring that on-the-job reinforcement of knowledge and skills occurs. This is left up to employees' supervisors.
- There are no direct measures of the effectiveness of the training. The only measures are of the perceptions of the employees and their supervisors. In addition, no data are given about levels and trends in the effectiveness, or perceptions of the effectiveness, of the training.

Site Visit Issues

- It is impossible to interpret the data given concerning the percentages of employees that rate the training effective and very effective (51 percent and 37 percent, respectively). Examine the course evaluation questionnaires. Also examine how the course ratings change between the initial course evaluation questionnaire and the follow-up six months later.
- Determine if the percentage data given in Table 4.3 indicates the percentage of employees who have had one course in the course category or all the courses in the category.
- Determine if and how refresher, maintenance, and updating training is accomplished.

4.4 Employee Recognition and Performance Measurement

Strengths

- AlphaTel's reward and recognition programs emphasize teams and the use of quality tools and techniques.
- As part of the process of establishing performance objectives, employees specify their goals for recognition. This is an innovative way to increase the visibility of the recognition program and thus emphasize the importance of the things that the recognition program rewards.

- Department-level commendations or awards have increased from 90 to 816 since 1986; cash bonuses have increased from 535 to 6,015.
- Employee Opinion Survey results for "Employee efforts are recognized" have increased from 26 to 77 percent since 1986.
- The Employee Opinion Survey and written employee responses to performance evaluations are used to evaluate the reward and recognition process. There is also a QIT that analyzes the Employee Opinion Survey data and benchmarks the recognition systems of other telephone companies.

Areas for Improvement

- The scope of the reward and recognition programs appears to be very limited.
- The annual performance evaluation process is not addressed.
- Employee Opinion Survey responses to "Poor performance not tolerated" and "Better performers rewarded appropriately" are low. No strategies for addressing these areas of weakness are described.
- There is little evidence suggesting that approaches to rewards and recognition are effectively utilized or systematically improved.
- The recognition QIT benchmarks only other telephone companies. The benchmark data are not presented.

Site Visit Issues

- Determine how the annual employee performance evaluations are done, how quality is reinforced relative to other considerations, and how data are aggregated from the performance evaluations.
- Determine how long the recognition QIT has existed. Find out what it has done thus far and examine any benchmark data it has collected.
- Although awards and cash bonuses have increased in number, they still represent recognition of a very small percentage of the employees. Determine if this small percentage is a weakness or if it is consistent with a well-developed approach to recognition and reward.
- Examine the questionnaire that was used to obtain the satisfaction data. Make sure that the items reported are not selected from multi-response items in a manner that creates a biased impression.

- It is unclear how recognition and reward strategies are tied to AlphaTel's overall quality goals and plans.

4.5 Employee Well-Being and Morale

Strengths

- AlphaTel has a safety QIT that takes a preventive approach. It actively solicits employee comments and suggestions and pledges to keep the sources of all statistics and information confidential.
- AlphaTel has attempted to address its problems in the area of career development and satisfaction by developing a job rotation program and an occupational staffing system that gives surplus employees first consideration, tuition reimbursement, and plans concerning outplacement and redevelopment.
- The primary approach to measurement of employee satisfaction is the Employment Opinion Survey. This survey compares AlphaTel's performance to the comparison group of companies used by Service 100.
- Since 1986, AlphaTel has achieved an overall improvement in the employee satisfaction measures that are part of the Employee Opinion Survey.
- AlphaTel's absenteeism rate compares favorably with the average of U.S. service firms.

Areas for Improvement

- It is unclear how well-being and morale factors other than safety are included in the quality improvement activities.
- The Employee Opinion Survey is only administered every two years.
- The performance on the employee satisfaction measures listed in Table 4.5 are, for the most part, only average in comparison to the Service 100 benchmark.
- AlphaTel shows weak employee satisfaction results in the areas of "Job security" and "Opportunity to advance."
- All safety results appear stable; there is no improvement. In addition, no comparison data for safety are given. The absenteeism rates also appear to be stable but not improving.
- No trend data for turnover are given.

Site Visit Issues

- AlphaTel relies almost exclusively on the Employee Opinion Survey to assess human resources and management effectiveness issues. Thus, the survey is very important and should be examined in detail. This includes examination of the scope and validity of the questionnaire, its method of administration, and the validity of the comparison group of companies used by Service 100.
- Examine in detail some of the improvements made by the safety QIT. Ask for an explanation about why the overall safety data are not showing improvement.

SCORING

SCORING CONSENSUS SUMMARY WORKSHEET	Total Points Possible A	Percent Score 0–100% B	Score (A × B) C
4.0 HUMAN RESOURCE UTILIZATION 150 Possible Points			
4.1 Human Resource Management	20	40%	8.0
4.2 Employee Involvement	40	55%	22.0
4.3 Quality Education and Training	40	64%	25.6
4.4 Employee Recognition and Performance Measurement	25	46%	11.5
4.5 Employee Well-Being and Morale	25	50%	12.5
Category Total	150		79.6
	SUM A		SUM C

Category 4.0
HUMAN RESOURCE UTILIZATION

Percent Score

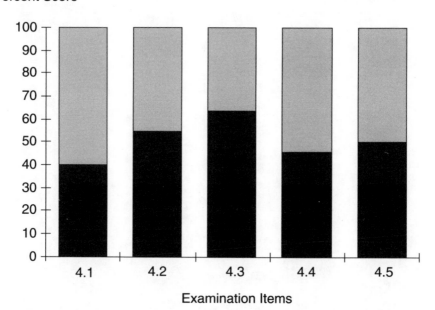

Examination Items

CHAPTER 10

QUALITY ASSURANCE OF PRODUCTS AND SERVICES: CATEGORY 5.0

You don't make a cultural change overnight. Total quality is a total process. When we first started the program, we looked just at manufacturing. Manufacturing is just a piece of our whole business cycle. What about the order entry? What about the collection? What about the engineering modifications that have to be made? So you have to look at the total process and to do that, it literally takes years.

John C. Marous, Chairman and CEO (1988–1990), Westinghouse Electric Corporation

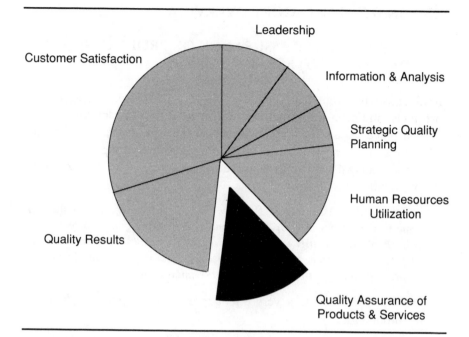

Examination Category/Items	Maximum Points
5.0 Quality Assurance of Products and Services	140
5.1 Design and Introduction of Quality Products and Services	35
5.2 Process Quality Control	20
5.3 Continuous Improvement of Processes	20
5.4 Quality Assessment	15
5.5 Documentation	10
5.6 Business Process and Support Service Quality	20
5.7 Supplier Quality	20

EXAMINATION CATEGORY OVERVIEW

5.0 QUALITY ASSURANCE OF PRODUCTS AND SERVICES (140 points)

Continuous improvement depends upon process control. Divisions, departments, and even individual workers must be able to monitor their respective processes and systems in a meaningful way if improvements are to be made. The use of scientific monitoring and measuring techniques is one of the principal ways employees are empowered to contribute to quality improvement.

> *The Quality Assurance of Products and Services category examines systematic approaches used by the company for assuring quality of goods and services based primarily upon process design and control, including control of procured materials, parts, and services. Also examined is the integration of process control with continuous quality improvement.*

- This category has a very strong process and systems orientation throughout.
- Processes may be carried out entirely by employees or largely by means of technology, or through a combination of the two.
- A company's quality assurance processes rating is based upon a number of factors such as size of the business, types of products and services, customer and government requirements, regulatory requirements, and the number of business locations.
- Evaluations take into account consistency of execution of quality operations that incorporate a sound prevention basis accompanied by continuous quality improvement activities. (Consistency of execution is taken to mean the existence of defined, suitably recorded processes with clear delineation of responsibilities.)
- Evaluations do not depend upon how responsibilities are distributed or organized or whether or not the company has a quality organization or officer. Moreover, in small businesses, one person might carry out two or more functions.

Items

5.1 Design and Introduction of Quality Products and Services (35 points)

Describe how new and/or improved products and services are designed and introduced and how processes are designed to meet key product and service quality requirements.

5.2 Process Quality Control (20 points)

Describe how the processes used to produce the company's products and services are controlled.

5.3 Continuous Improvement of Processes (20 points)

Describe how processes used to produce products and services are continuously improved.

5.4 Quality Assessment (15 points)

Describe how the company assesses the quality of its systems, processes, practices, products, and services.

5.5 Documentation (10 points)

Describe documentation and other modes of knowledge preservation and knowledge transfer to support quality assurance, quality assessment, and quality improvement.

5.6 Business Process and Support Service Quality (20 points)

Summarize process quality, quality assessment, and quality improvement activities for business processes and support services.

5.7 Supplier Quality (20 points)

Describe how the quality of materials, components, and services furnished by other businesses is assured, assessed, and improved.

INSTANT INDEX

CASE STUDY

5.0 QUALITY ASSURANCE OF PRODUCTS AND SERVICES

5.1 Design and Introduction of Quality Products and Services

a. AlphaTel delivers new or improved products and services through a mechanism called Process Management (PM), a three-level approach that combines the best elements of its predecessors with techniques specifically designed for the telecommunications environment. In essence, PM seeks to combine the traditional determinants of customer satisfaction—product quality, locations, and price—with the new criterion of service quality. In so doing, it ensures that when customers interact with the company at various moments of truth—such as service ordering, billing, inquiries, and complaints—and evaluate the company based on their expectations—such as ease of doing business, professionalism, courtesy, and responsiveness—they are satisfied with the company's performance at all levels. AlphaTel therefore regards a process as a discrete set of related activities that transforms specific measurable inputs into specific measurable outputs that meet customers' expectations.

The three levels of Process Management are described in Figure 5.1. While every element may not apply to a specific development project, PM provides a checklist of all elements and phases that should be considered.

The group that initiates all new products or improvements is the customer team (CT), which is responsible for conveying all requirements throughout the company. In essence, the CT is a QIT that comes together whenever the need for a new product or service has been identified (usually from customer interviews or focus groups, but also from competitive analysis). The CT includes a technical subteam, a group of vendor managers and technicians that performs a technical needs analysis (TNA). The TNA describes the needs in technical depth and identifies the roles of the various in-house and external suppliers. When all parties have signed off on the TNA, the CT develops a delivery plan that specifies all project goals and target dates, submits a budget to support the work, and incorporates it with the strategic plan developed by the department-level QMT. The process control plan for the production and delivery of products is described below.

b. Every customer team at AlphaTel is required to test all delivery plans in the company's proprietary Product Analysis and Modeling Program

FIGURE 5.1
Process Management Levels

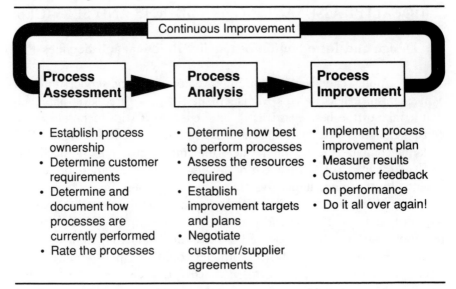

Continuous Improvement

Process Assessment → **Process Analysis** → **Process Improvement**

- Establish process ownership
- Determine customer requirements
- Determine and document how processes are currently performed
- Rate the processes

- Determine how best to perform processes
- Assess the resources required
- Establish improvement targets and plans
- Negotiate customer/supplier agreements

- Implement process improvement plan
- Measure results
- Customer feedback on performance
- Do it all over again!

(PAMPER), a chaos-based (i.e., nonlinear) scheme that allows several hundred variables to be input and modified along several dimensions. Recognizing that new introductions often have a "sensitive dependence on initial conditions," the algorithm permits the CT to build worst-case and what-if scenarios. For example, a one-day delay in the delivery of a vital part usually does not result in a simple one-day delay in the delivery of the final product; rather, the delay could have effects ranging from no time lost to month-late delivery and doubled product costs, depending on the sensitivity of all the other variables to the delay.

"Optimized" results from PAMPER then become the first inputs to the CT's new-product pilot, a localized introduction of the product or service in a demographically representative area of 10,000 to 50,000 people. AlphaTel uses this pilot as an opportunity to optimize inputs based on the reactions of real customers, using customer responses to identify and resolve any problems with the service or support processes.

The new product pilot usually lasts several months to a year. In that time, AlphaTel is able to determine when and where process upsets occur and to use Pareto analysis to find the critical few. These then become the key control characteristics, which are then input to PAMPER for further refinement. The company also evaluates the performance of customer-contact personnel in an effort to define where training in the product or service will need to be concentrated in the future.

c. AlphaTel has found that proper use of PAMPER is an effective means of minimizing new product introduction time, as the program simulates the effects of certain changes in supplier performance, market conditions, and even the prevailing economy. In fact, cross-correlation of PAMPER data with real-world results has shown that the simulation has a correlation coefficient of 0.6 or greater (on the basic cross-correlation scale of -1 to $+1$) about 50 percent of the time. Naturally, this also shows that PAMPER has room for improvement. The programmers are therefore taking steps to hone the algorithm with the results of actual introductions, to determine how dependent certain processes are on certain inputs.

5.2 Process Quality Control

a. For existing products and services (that is, those with established processes), AlphaTel's Process Management methodology provides strict procedures for controlling product- and service-producing processes. The Process Assessment (PASS) level includes six steps:

1. Identify key processes and establish responsibilities.
2. Define the process.
3. Assess customer requirements and performance.
4. "Walk the Process."
5. Complete and validate process documentation.
6. Certify the process.

As regards process control, Steps 1 and 2 require the PASS team to develop a hierarchical framework that shows the critical relationships between key processes; the team must then develop a process overview, establish a data collection plan, and then draft a process assessment plan.

Step 3 of PASS requires the process team to ask four questions:

- What are the key outputs of the process?
- What are the important performance characteristics of the output and how should the output be measured?
- How effectively are we meeting our customers' expectations for each of these performance characteristics?

• What are the priority areas for improvement?

Steps 4–6 of PASS call on team members to conduct a detailed walk-through of the process in preparation for rating its current condition. Team members see how the process is actually performed and the resources used in it, study existing performance standards and measures (and actual performance levels) for the key characteristics identified by customers, and look for opportunities to improve process performance. The team then documents all steps and results, and rates the current condition of the process. Improvement priorities are based on the process certification, with highest priority generally going to those areas with high impact on customer satisfaction and rated as being in critical to fair condition.

After the PASS teams have competed their work, the Process Management methodology moves to the process analysis (PANL) level, with new process teams working on evaluating measurement quality. (In general, PASS and PANL teams have significant overlap in membership; changes are made to take advantage of employees' specialized skills.) The first step in the PANL level is a benchmarking study performed along two principal dimensions: results benchmarking determines the levels of performance that can be achieved for the process; operational benchmarking identifies alternative approaches or best practices for performing the process.

The benchmarking phase is also intended to determine which functions represent the highest percentage of cost and would have the highest impact on margin; which processes differentiate AlphaTel from RBOCs and other telephone companies; and which functions can be improved.

b.   AlphaTel identifies root causes of poor performance using several quality improvement tools, including Pareto analysis, control charts, fishbone diagrams, and histograms. The analysis requires a definition of the problem, data analysis (using the methods mentioned above), and an identification of alternatives. The Process Management methodology then permits the design of measures to correct process upsets. These stem from the identification of alternative approaches for enhancing process performance. The PANL team evaluates these alternatives and develops a specific set of process improvement recommendations (see also Item 5.3).

The process team is responsible for testing these alternatives—whether through modeling programs or pilot programs—to verify that they achieve the required results and that they are sufficient for preventing future occurrences of the upset. In many cases, this is best done by inputting the proposed approaches to PAMPER, which has been found to be an effective predicator of process capabilities.

c.   In general, AlphaTel verifies the accuracy of its process measurements by using redundant technologies, the most important being a smaller-scale, linear version of PAMPER. This Limited Analysis Modeling Program (LAMP) works with fewer variables and models shorter time frames than PAMPER, but for many applications its results are as reliable as those from the larger program.

5.3 Continuous Improvement of Processes

a.   AlphaTel is constantly seeking to improve its processes and uses every means at its disposal to identify improvement opportunities. Many opportunities come to light in the PASS and PANL levels of the Process Management methodology (see Item 5.2). Just as many, however, come to light in discussions with suppliers and customers and through competitive analysis. In particular, the operational benchmarking module of PASS is used to identify best practices for performing specific processes.

AlphaTel's Product Analysis and Modeling Program (PAMPER; see Item 5.1) is the company's primary process optimization tool. This is used in concert with the process improvement plan that is developed as part of the final stages of the PANL level of PM. The process improvement plan includes a problem statement and objectives for each process improvement, steps and procedures to guide the implementation, measurement system requirements, and resources required for successful process operation.

b.   Improvements to processes are evaluated using the metrics defined above, as applied to a pilot effort or to PAMPER. If the process is not producing the desired results, the root-cause analysis or problem-solving approach is employed once again. This cycle continues until the results have been optimized and is repeated for all recommended process improvements. AlphaTel uses the LAMP algorithm to isolate the effects of individual or paired variables. The variables deemed most effective are then analyzed in various combinations by PAMPER. (Although it is true that two or more "good" variables do not always make a "good" combination, the company has found that "bad" ones never do.)

c.   Once the pilot efforts have demonstrated that the improvements do achieve the desired results, the improvements are standardized so that they can be introduced throughout the organization. The rollout process often takes several months, depending on the extent of the improvements and the pervasiveness of the process. In general, the process is piloted within the company by the work unit that would be most immediately and pervasively affected. The rollout involves:

- Creating and testing process documentation (see also Item 5.5).
- Training individual work units in the new process. This is most effectively done by the unit's technical experts, who know their own processes and are quick to learn which process characteristics need to be modified.
- Evaluating results from the company's pilot work unit and setting a schedule for deployment based on the results.
- Introducing the improvements companywide.
- Revisiting the new process in six months to evaluate its effect and also to make modifications necessitated by changing customer needs and expectations, the availability of new technology, and the basic continuous improvement mandates of the Process Management methodology.

5.4 Quality Assessment

a. AlphaTel had been assessing the quality of its products and processes for many years prior to the development of the company's quality initiative. The major change that occurred in 1986 was the introduction of customer perception data, deemed necessary because the customer is the final arbiter of quality attributes in the marketplace. The company still conducts its internal product and systems audits, but it uses third-party surveys to evaluate customer perceptions.

- Formal internal quality auditing is conducted twice a year by management personnel within specific line and staff departments and by quality auditors within the CQO's staff. It is conducted annually by the company's corporate audit staff. Assessments cover all aspects of product and service quality (see Items 6.1 and 7.7).
- The independent auditors retained by AlphaTel for annual financial audits incorporate a significant quality audit module in their work. Much of this work may be regarded as an audit of the company's own audit procedures and results.
- Because it is a regional telecommunications company, AlphaTel has

invited quality audits from the Federal Communications Commission and state PUCs during the past two years. These audits are used to verify internal measures of customer satisfaction and customer complaints.

- The company periodically contracts with knowledgeable personnel from groups such as BellCore and the National Communications Forum to audit various aspects of its process quality improvement and measurement systems.
- Finally, customer surveys and focus groups are conducted to verify the results of AlphaTel's various auditing and assessment programs.

b.   Because AlphaTel's Process Management methodology is a continuous improvement cycle, it requires the use of all audit findings concerning the company's efforts to improve existing processes or to develop alternatives. In particular, one part of the PANL team's efforts is directed toward negotiating customer-supplier agreements that incorporate those improvements. These agreements work both ways—with AlphaTel as the customer on the one hand and the supplier on the other.

The final stage of Process Management is process improvement (PIM). Essentially a continuation of the work described in Item 5.3, PIM requires continuous monitoring of all new processes even after they have been introduced throughout the company.

5.5 Documentation

a.   As a company that specializes in the transfer of information, AlphaTel maintains an extensive documentation system for all quality assurance efforts. The process improvement steps discussed in Items 5.1, 5.2, and 5.3 are all documented for future reference by the process teams involved in the evaluations. General information is provided to all employees, but specific and technical data are distributed to work groups or process teams as they require them.

In addition to process data, AlphaTel gathers information pertaining to personnel (e.g., job descriptions and performance appraisals); general company information (e.g., *AlphaBetics* and bulletin boards); quality policy and guidelines; training manuals; and technical documents, among others.

b.   Most of the documents cited above are produced by specific work groups, QITs, or process teams, and these parties are responsible for ensuring that the information is accurate, current, and accessible. Further, all teams that access existing data are required to record that access within the original document, so that readers of a file can know if it has been used in later work. Tracking of this sort enables users to determine if stated procedure and results have since been superseded.

Each of AlphaTel's management systems is integrated into its automated office communications network so that the entire AlphaBits system and its related data are easily accessible. All major departmental work standards and procedures are available within the same network; in effect, all employees have instant access to all aspects of the quality system library through the network.

5.6 Business Process and Support Service Quality

a.   AlphaTel uses the same comprehensive methodology to maintain process quality control and quality improvement in its support services and business processes as it uses for its primary products and services. This approach (described in Items 5.1, 5.2, and 5.3) is used by each service and support department (human resources, accounting, legal services, etc.) to assess process control and quality improvement opportunities in five steps:

1. Definition of the needs and expectations of the client (that is, primary company units served).
2. Translation of the customer's needs into process requirements and service standards.
3. Service design, pilot testing, and validation for support functions.
4. "Live" service implementation.
5. Conformance validation for performance requirements.

In addition, each business process and service and support department's process control standards, quality measures, and improvement goals are fully integrated into the quality management structure. Applying the same guidelines, each support unit and business process is also subjected to similar rigorous internal and external audit assessments (see also Item 5.4).

b.   Improvement of processes and services within the staff and support groups follows the same comprehensive framework as used in the line departments (see Item 5.3). The goals for each business process and each support unit include quality improvement, and all work groups and QITs are constantly challenged to analyze processes and improve quality.

AlphaTel's efforts to increase the participation of support departments in quality activities are coordinated with its efforts for line departments. Support staff are included in interdepartmental QITs, and support groups are required to assess the quality of the service they provide to their internal customers.

5.7 Supplier Quality

a.   AlphaTel's primary means of communicating its requirements to its suppliers is the vendor agreement, a binding and mutually beneficial statement of each party's rights and responsibilities. The agreement outlines the terms of delivery, invoicing and paying, and broad performance measures. Addenda to the agreement, drafted quarterly for a very active account (i.e., the supplier who makes monthly or more frequent deliveries) and annually for a less active account, detail specific performance measures. Agreements exist with 157 suppliers, providing more than 70 percent of AlphaTel's annual purchases. The company has notified all other suppliers that it wishes to enter into similar agreements with them; those who decline will be dropped from AlphaTel's supplier lists.

The vendor agreement specifies performance measures for AlphaTel's suppliers. Chief among these are:

- Material used in the company's core business of telecommunications must have an acceptance rate of 99.99 percent.
- Capital equipment must carry a two-year warranty, and service work must be completed within eight work hours of the call.
- Ninety-five percent of deliveries must be made by the time promised. Certain suppliers deliver according to a standing schedule, which permits them to build up a small backlog of supplies at AlphaTel; these vendors are permitted a 90 percent on-time delivery rate.

b.   Vendor agreements dictate that final users of supplier products will complete an annual product quality questionnaire covering 25 areas. AlphaTel provides summaries of user responses to all suppliers; in turn, suppliers must develop and present action plans to address areas needing improvement.

With or without an agreement, AlphaTel retains the right to audit all suppliers' production and business processes. Members of the CQO's audit staff visit key suppliers semiannually to verify that quality assurance procedures are in place and effective. In particular, the auditors ensure that suppliers adhere to the environmental protection measures defined in Item 1.4. These audits are in addition to those conducted quarterly by the Environmental Resources Defense Council.

c.   By requiring its suppliers to meet exacting standards of product and service quality, AlphaTel has reduced its supplier base 50 percent since 1985. Current and prospective suppliers must continue to meet standards; their performance in doing so is evaluated using the questionnaire cited above. Vendors with performance ratings below 90 percent are evaluated quarterly; those with ratings below 90 percent for four consecutive quarters are terminated unless they display significant improvement in each of those quarters. Vendors with ratings of 98 percent or more for four consecutive quarters are certified as Quality Suppliers. Quality Suppliers who pass AlphaTel's stringent audits with grades of A or A+ are named AlphaTel Quality Partners and given recognition in leading business journals and major metropolitan newspapers.

Former suppliers are encouraged to develop programs that will enable them to meet and maintain AlphaTel's quality standards. The company is prepared to provide whatever assistance, including training at AlphaTel's Quality Institute, that these vendors might need.

AlphaTel also encourages suppliers to comment freely about the company's own processes and practices. Some QITs and process teams even have supplier representation. In particular, those with union representation comparable to AlphaTel's are invited to use the company's union agreements as models for their own, should they wish to do so.

EVALUATION

5.0 QUALITY ASSURANCE OF PRODUCTS AND SERVICES

5.1 Design and Introduction of Quality Products and Services

Strengths

- All new products are developed by a customer team, which is a cross-functional team that includes a technical needs analysis sub-team.

- The customer team develops a delivery plan.
- Computer simulation is used extensively to test and optimize new products and their delivery plans. Pilot tests are performed.
- The computer simulation software is continuously refined and improved.

Areas for Improvement

- The customer team is convened when the need to develop a new product becomes apparent. New product development thus is not an ongoing process.
- Exactly how the customer team functions is not described. As a result, it is unclear if there are well-defined processes for design and introduction of new products, including a well-defined process for translating customer requirements into new product design requirements.
- How the delivery plan and the process control plan are developed in not described.
- The extent to which customers and suppliers are either involved in new product development or have direct input is not clear.
- The scope of new product development discussed in the Item appears to be limited to only AlphaTel's most basic product (telephone communications transmission). There is no mention of new products such as new billing options for businesses, new phone books or yellow pages options, etc.
- The process for test marketing and evaluating results is not described in detail.
- Other than refinement of the simulation software, there appears to be no new product development improvement process. Further, it is unclear how the design-to-introduction time is shortened.

Site Visit Issues

- Determine exactly what the customer teams do, who their members are, etc.
- Get detailed information about PAMPER and how it is used in the design and introduction process. Determine exactly how PAMPER is validated by correlating its results with real-world results.
- Determine how new products in areas other than basic telephone service are designed and introduced.

5.2 Process Quality Control

Strengths

- A well-defined process (PASS and PANL) for defining processes, anticipating potential areas where problems may develop, bringing processes under control, and developing process measures is described. The process appears to be prevention-based and includes both results and operational benchmarking.
- The approach taken to identifying root causes is the use of basic quality tools, such as control charts, by the Process Team.
- The results of the simulation software are validated by comparison with an approximation generated using a different approach.

Areas for Improvement

- How processes are controlled, how they are measured, and how out-of-control occurrences are remedied is described only in the most general terms. As a result, how AlphaTel addresses the issues in this Item cannot be assessed.
- There is no evidence given concerning the extent of deployment of the approach described.
- The application gives little sense that root cause analysis is well developed and extensively deployed.
- Issues related to measurement and measurement quality are addressed only in a rudimentary way.

Site Visit Issues

- Determine the extent to which the PASS and PANL modules of the Process Management process are deployed. Examine examples of processes that are managed in this way. Determine how they are controlled and how process upsets are corrected.
- Determine the extent to which process control occurs rapidly, in "real time." Much of the approach described appears to be manual and may not be very responsive.

5.3 Continuous Improvement of Processes

Strengths

- The PASS and PANL methodologies of the Process Management process are the primary approaches to continuous improvement. This includes analyzing the process to identify potential sources of defects, developing measures of the process and a plan for collecting data, and benchmarking the results and operations of the process.

- The computer simulation software is used to evaluate potential changes to the processes.
- The approach to standardization that is described is well developed. Improvements are integrated into operations by creating process documentation, training work units, evaluating results of the pilot implementation, developing an implementation schedule, and then revisiting the process six months later to ensure that the improvements are sustained.

Areas for Improvement

- The PASS and PANL sections of the Process Management processes are not described in sufficient detail to determine how AlphaTel addresses the areas listed in this item. In addition, there is little evidence given of deployment throughout the organization.
- Except for mention of benchmark data, the primary data used to drive continuous improvement are not described. In particular, it is unclear how customer data such as complaints or dissatisfaction expressed in surveys are used in identifying opportunities for improvement.
- The extent to which the described approaches to continuous improvement are applied to all important processes is not clear. The heavy reliance on the PAMPER software in the response suggests that the continuous improvement process is limited primarily to the basic telephone service.

Site Visit Issues

- Examine the PASS and PANL modules of the Process Management process in detail. Determine the extent to which they are deployed to all processes. Examine some examples of QITs using these methodologies. Make sure that a wide variety of data are used to identify opportunities for improvement and that the analysis of the possibilities does not ignore important areas such as customer data or new technology.

5.4 Quality Assessment

Strengths

- AlphaTel has an established internal quality audit process. Internal quality auditing is conducted twice a year by management personnel and by quality auditors within the CQO's staff.
- Quality audits are also sometimes performed by external auditors. This includes audits by BellCore and the National Communications Forum. In addition, during the last two years AlphaTel has invited quality audits from the FCC and the state PUCs.
- Audit results are validated by comparing them with data from customer surveys and focus groups.

Areas for Improvement

- Few details are given about the audit process. It is unclear what is assessed and how the assessments are made.
- There appears to be no mechanism for effectively using audit findings: 1) how audit findings are used in continuous improvement is not clear; 2) the mechanism for ensuring that audit findings will be responded to is not described.
- It is unclear whether or not all important processes are audited. AlphaTel claims to conduct audits twice a year, but it is not clear if this means that all important processes are audited twice a year or if only two audits per year are performed.

Site Visit Issues

- Examine the audit process and the training of the auditors.
- Determine whether or not all important processes are audited and how often they are audited.
- What is the nature of the quality module that is part of the financial audits?
- Request details on both the nature and frequency of the quality audits that are performed by external auditors such as those from Bellcore and the National Communications Forum.

5.5 Documentation

Strengths

- The Process Management process includes extensive documentation that is supported by the on-line data bases PROMISE and AlphaNumerics, to which employees have wide access.

Areas for Improvement

- The extent to which the Process Management process and its documentation activities are deployed to all important processes is unclear.
- Neither the nature of the documentation developed during the Process Management process nor how it is used is described. For example, the extent to which the standard operating procedure or similar documents are developed and deployed to training is not addressed.
- The nature of the information in the computer data bases is not clear. In particular, it is not clear the extent to which documentation is on-line.
- Improvement of the documentation system and disposition of obsolete documents is not addressed.

Site Visit Issues

- Examine the documentation produced as part of the Process Management process. Determine the extent of deployment.
- Access the documentation on the various computer data bases.

5.6 Business Process and Support Service Quality

Strengths

- AlphaTel's approach to business processes and support service quality is the same as for its primary products and services–the Process Management process.
- AlphaTel uses the internal customer/supplier idea to develop the requirements of business processes and support services. Quality

improvement goals are set for each business process and support unit.

Areas for Improvement

- There is little evidence given of deployment of the Process Management approach in the areas of business processes and support service quality.
- How often business processes and support service quality are measured and how assessments are made is not described.
- The quality improvement goals and activities for key support processes are not described.

Site Visit Issues

- Determine the extent of deployment of the Process Management process in support areas.

5.7 Supplier Quality

Strengths

- AlphaTel uses a vendor agreement to communicate required quality levels to suppliers. Agreements exist with 157 suppliers (out of 613) and cover over 70% of AlphaTel's purchases. Agreements are updated quarterly for active accounts.
- AlphaTel plans to extend its vendor agreement program to the rest of its suppliers.
- Principal quality requirements are specified and include an acceptance rate of 99.99 percent, two-year warranty on capital equipment, service work completion within eight hours for capital equipment, and 95 percent on-time deliveries..
- Final users of suppliers' products are surveyed annually about their satisfaction with the suppliers. This seems to form AlphaTel's primary approach to measuring supplier quality.
- Key suppliers are audited by the CQO's staff semiannually.
- AlphaTel has implemented a supplier certification program based on the internal supplier survey. Suppliers who achieve the highest level of certification are publicly recognized by AlphaTel in leading business publications and metropolitan newspapers.

- AlphaTel will give assistance, including training, to help suppliers meet and maintain AlphaTel's standards.
- Some AlphaTel QITs have supplier representation.

Areas for Improvement

- The provisions of the vendor agreements seem to be reactive rather than proactive, emphasizing inspection, warranties, and repair service rather than prevention.
- It is unclear the extent to which AlphaTel's relationship with suppliers is based on cooperation. There is some evidence that the degree of cooperation is limited.
- There is no description of how the measurement quality is ensured in the annual supplier product quality survey.
- The extent of direct measurement of supplier quality levels is unclear. The supplier audit process is not defined in sufficient detail to be evaluated.

Site Visit Issues

- Examine some vendor agreements to determine their content.
- Determine the extent to which AlphaTel's relationship with suppliers is based on cooperation.
- Determine whether or not the annual product quality questionnaires are an accurate measurement of supplier quality, and whether or not this process results in better communication between the suppliers and their customers.
- Determine if the reduction in AlphaTel's supplier base by 50 percent has resulted in any measurable quality improvement.
- Determine how many suppliers have been certified, how many have participated in AlphaTel's training, and how many participate on AlphaTel's QITs.
- Examine the plans to extend AlphaTel's supplier programs to the rest of its supplier base. Determine the degree of implementation.

SCORING

SCORING CONSENSUS SUMMARY WORKSHEET	Total Points Possible A	Percent Score 0–100% B	Score (A × B) C
5.0 QUALITY ASSURANCE OF PRODUCTS AND SERVICES 140 Possible Points			
5.1 Design and Introduction of Quality Products and Services	35	45%	15.8
5.2 Process Quality Control	20	39%	7.8
5.3 Continuous Improvement of Processes	20	45%	9.0
5.4 Quality Assessment	15	48%	7.2
5.5 Documentation	10	39%	3.9
5.6 Business Process and Support Service Quality	20	39%	7.8
5.7 Supplier Quality	20	43%	8.6
Category Total	140		60.1
	SUM A		SUM C

Category 5.0
QUALITY ASSURANCE OF PRODUCTS AND SERVICES

Percent Score

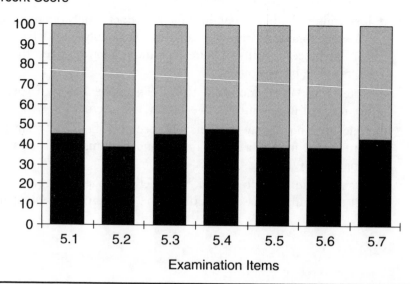

Examination Items

CHAPTER 11

QUALITY RESULTS: CATEGORY 6.0

What are the results of improved quality? One result of improved quality was increased business. . . . Another result of improved quality was lower costs.

Arden C. Sims, President and CEO, Globe Metallurgical Inc.

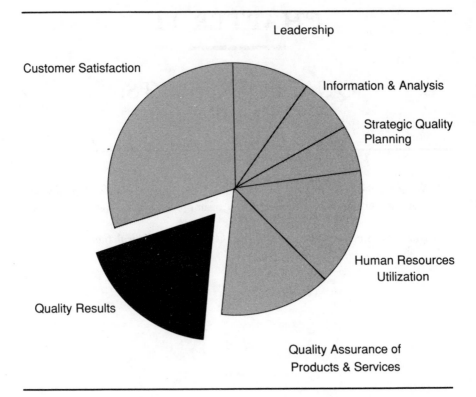

Examination Category/Items	Maximum Points
6.0 QUALITY RESULTS	180
6.1 Product and Service Quality Results	90
6.2 Business Process, Operational, and Support Service Quality Results	50
6.3 Supplier Quality Results	40

EXAMINATION CATEGORY OVERVIEW

6.0 QUALITY RESULTS (180 points)

Results! Lest we forget, the ultimate goal of quality improvement is measurably improved quality!

The Quality Results category examines quality levels and quality improvement based upon objective measures derived from analysis of customer requirements and expectations and from analysis of business operations. Also examined are current quality levels in relation to those of competing firms.

- This category examines the company's quality improvement and quality levels by themselves and in relation to those of competitors. Included are the quality of products and services, internal operations, and suppliers.

- As might be expected, evaluators look for documentable results of a company's quality improvement. Is the company's product more reliable? Have levels of defects, scrap, and rework decreased? Are services improved? Is efficiency improved? Has the company improved the quality of its suppliers as well as its own quality?

- Evaluators also look at the appropriateness of a company's measures of quality, depending on factors such as the company's size, types of products and services, and competitive environment. Are the measures sufficient to support overall improvement and to establish clear quality levels and comparisons?

Items

6.1 Product and Service Quality Results (90 points)

Summarize trends in quality improvement and current quality levels for key product and service features; compare the company's current quality levels with those of competitors and world leaders.

6.2 Business Process, Operational, and Support Service Quality Results (50 points)

Summarize trends in quality improvement and current quality levels for business processes, operations, and support services.

6.3 Supplier Quality Results (40 points)

Summarize trends and levels in quality of suppliers and services furnished by other companies; compare the company's supplier quality with that of competitors and with key benchmarks.

INSTANT INDEX

CASE STUDY

6.0 QUALITY RESULTS

6.1 Product and Service Quality Results

   a.   Table 6.1 details AlphaTel's historical and current performance in its major measures of quality of services. For all measures, performance in 1990 was better than that in 1986, in many cases by significant margins. For example, the responsiveness of the business office to customer installation inquiries—as measured by speed of answering calls and number of

TABLE 6.1
AlphaTel Major Measures of Service Quality

Service	Alpha Telco					Ave.[1]	Best[2]
	1986	1987	1988	1989	1990	1990	1990
Installation							
Business office speed to answer (average sec)	34	30	24	24	20	25	20
Business office access (percentage of calls abandoned)	17	15	12	9	8	10	5
Service offered 1–3 days (percentage of orders)	53	65	62	75	82	80	86
Service order due date (percentage completed)							
• Residence	95.8	97.9	99.4	99.4	99.2	98.0	99.3
• Business/special services	97.9	98.0	99.6	100.0	100.0	98.3	100.0
• Carrier access	96.2	97.2	698.6	99.7	99.8	98.9	100.0
Held orders (percentage of total orders)	0.08	0.09	0.12	0.07	0.05	0.07	0.04
Held orders more than 30 days (average daily number)	314	150	0	0	0	N/A	N/A
I reports (percentage in inward orders)							
• POTS	12.2	11.1	9.0	5.8	4.0	5.0	3.9
• Special services	5.0	4.1	2.9	3.0	2.1	2.5	2.0
Automated provisioning (percentage of inward orders)	0	0	5	45	60	60	90
Operations							
Operator services							
• Toll (seconds to answer)	3	3	2	3	2	2	2
• DA (seconds to answer)	7	8	6	5	6	6	5
Switching performance (H&O bands percent)	95	96	98	96	97	96	100
Switching downtime (minutes per switch per year)	12.0	9.0	5.0	2.5	2.0	2.5	2.0
Dial tone response (three second objective)	94.4	96.3	97.4	99.2	99.9	99.6	99.9
Transmission quality (percentage of calls meeting standard)	84.0	88.0	96.0	95.0	100.0	98.0	100.0
Maintenance and Repair							
Trouble reports (per 100 lines)	5.0	4.0	3.5	3.0	2.1	2.5	1.9
• CO troubles	0.8	0.5	0.4	0.3	0.4	0.5	N/A
• OSP troubles	2.5	1.5	1.0	0.9	0.8	1.0	N/A
• Other (inside wire, CPE, trouble not found)	1.7	2.0	2.1	1.8	0.9	1.0	N/A
Repeat reports (percentage of total reports)	15.3	13.1	11.9	7.1	2.0	5.0	2.0
Special services: Out-of-service cleared within eight hours (percent)	97.0	98.1	99.2	98.9	100.0	99.1	100.0
All customers: Out-of-service ≥ 24 hours (percent)	33.3	25.1	20.2	12.1	5.0	8.0	4.5
Missed appointments (percentage of total)	17.6	12.0	6.0	4.2	5.1	6.0	4.9
Average duration of outage (hours)							
• POTS	7.5	8.0	8.5	7.0	6.0	6.5	5.5
• Special services	4.5	4.9	4.5	4.0	3.5	4.0	3.0

[1]Represents average of all U.S. telcos.

[2]Represents best-performing U.S. telco.

Source: AlphaTel Performance Management System; State PUCs; Benchmation, Inc.

calls abandoned—has nearly doubled since 1986. AlphaTel has also completed all business and special service installations by the due date for two consecutive years; in fact, through December 1990, the installations have been completed for 31 months without a late order. Furthermore, all special service outages have been cleared in less than eight hours for 17 consecutive months.

b. Table 6.1 also compares AlphaTel's performance with that of both average and best-performing U.S. telcos in those areas for which benchmark and competitive data are available. The data—which show that AlphaTel is the industry leader or co-leader in more than half of the measures, and exceeds industry averages for all measures—are derived from four principal sources:

- Competitive data on service interruptions and outages are collected by the state public utilities commissions. These become available when the PUCs hold inquiries or hearings about the causes; all PUC transactions and proceedings then become a matter of public record.
- Competitive data on all other measures are provided by various third parties. Two of the states in AlphaTel's service area have active public interest research groups that monitor the performance of telcos, electric and gas utilities, and mass transit systems. Other data are developed and compiled on a for-hire basis by consulting groups and Benchmation, Inc., a nationally known opinion-analysis firm.
- AlphaTel benchmarks semiannually against the telco that receives the highest customer satisfaction rating as determined by an analysis of PUC data throughout the country. In all competitive comparisons, AlphaTel focuses on service measures that have historically been indicators of customer satisfaction.
- Internal data are compiled by the AlphaTel Performance Management System (PMS), which evaluates service performance in real and simulated situations.

6.2 Business Process, Operational, and Support Service Quality Results

a. Since the AlphaTel quality initiative began in 1986, internal operations have improved significantly (see Table 6.2). In particular:

TABLE 6.2
AlphaTel Operational Trends

Operation or Service	1986	1988	1990
Order entry processing time (hours)	26.0	7.5	0.8
Order entry processing unit cost[1]	1.0	0.6	0.4
Expense account reimbursement (days)	19	15	4[a]
Flexible accounts reimbursement (days)[2]		21	9
IXC billing disputes (percent)	17.5	10.4	3.3
Other billing errors (per thousand)	6.3	2.2	0.7
Supplier payment errors (per thousand)	2.0	0.2	0.08

[1]1.0 = 1986 unit cost.
[2]Flexible spending accounts were initiated 1/1/88.
[a]When reimbursements are electronically made to employee's bank accounts.

Source: AlphaTel Performance Management System; *AlphaNumerics*.

- Supplier payment errors have declined from one per 500 to one per 12,000.
- With assistance from its interexchange customers, AlphaTel's interLATA billing errors have declined from more than $8.9 million per month to less than $1.7 million.
- Automated order-entry procedures have enabled the company to reduce order processing time from 26 hours to 45 minutes, and to reduce the cost per order by 60 percent.
- By transferring certain accounting functions to third-party vendors, the company has reduced the dependent care reimbursement time from 30 days to two weeks.

b. In general, competitor data on internal measures are not available to the same extent as customer satisfaction and network quality data. Billing-error information from the state PUCs and the interexchange carriers, however, shows that:

- Among U.S. telcos serving the three largest long-distance carriers, AlphaTel's billing procedures have improved the fastest since 1987, and its billing errors are now the third-lowest of all local exchange companies.
- Billing errors are significantly below the industry average, and AlphaTel ranks fourth among the 10 largest telcos.

TABLE 6.3
AlphaTel Supplier Quality Trends

	1986	1988	1990
Equipment acceptance rate	96.0%	97.4%	99.9%
On-time delivery	63.5	77.8	89.7
Inspected lots	70.3	44.5	28.5
Repeat orders	16.5	11.5	4.3
Order completeness	71.3	81.5	92.0
Invoice accuracy	60.0	70.5	91.5

Source: AlphaTel Performance Management System.

6.3 Supplier Quality Results

a. Supplier product and service quality is evaluated by users in the company with annual vendor questionnaires (see also Item 5.7). The results (Table 6.3) show that the combination of reductions in the supplier base and imposition of strict quality standards has improved supplier quality significantly. For example, the percentage of returned equipment went from 4 percent in 1986 to 0.06 percent in 1990; indeed, seven of the company's suppliers had no rejects in the period 1987–1990.

b. AlphaTel has not researched supplier quality of competitors and world leaders, so comparative data are not available.

EVALUATION

6.0 QUALITY RESULTS

6.1 Product and Service Quality Results

Strengths

- AlphaTel has made substantial and sustained improvement in nearly all of the reported measures since 1986.
- The measures reported are broad in scope and include measures for installation, operations, and maintenance and repair.
- Comparisons are made to the industry leader and the industry av-

erage for nearly all measures. Data for comparison are drawn from a number of sources: public interest research groups, consulting firms, and benchmarks.

- AlphaTel is the industry leader in about one-third of the measures and is above average in virtually all of the measures.

Areas for Improvement

- No comparison data are presented over time. Thus, it is not possible to compare AlphaTel's rate of improvement with that of other telephone companies.

Site Visit Issues

- Determine if the scope of the measures presented captures all important aspects. Ask for explanation of all technical terms in Table 6.1, such as POTS. Try to determine how large the differences in service levels for the various items must be before they are significant (especially from the customer's point of view).
- Determine the extent to which the improvements in results are due to AlphaTel's quality improvement and quality management approaches. Be sure that improvement is not just due to other factors such as capital investment in new technology.
- Determine if trend data are available for comparison.

6.2 Business Process, Operational, and Support Service Quality Results

Strengths

- There are substantial and sustained improvements for all of the measures shown. These measures include order-entry processing time and cost, expense and flexible account reimbursement, IXC billing disputes, billing errors, and supplier payment errors.
- Billing errors are substantially better than average. AlphaTel ranks fourth among the 10 largest telephone companies.

Areas for Improvement

- The scope of the operational data presented is very limited.
- There is very little comparative data given for these measures. In

particular, no benchmark data (which other Items imply are collected for major processes) are presented. In addition, no attempt is made to make comparisons to similar processes in companies outside of the telephone industry.

- It is unclear how good fourth of 10 is for billing errors.

Site Visit Issues

- Determine the extent that improvements in results are due to AlphaTel's quality management and quality improvement approaches (as required by the note to the item.)
- Request more extensive data on operations.
- Examine relevant benchmark data.
- Request data for the missing odd years.

6.3 Supplier Quality Results

Strengths

- Results from the supplier surveys indicates that, for the measures shown, supplier quality has improved substantially since 1986 and that the improvement is sustained.

Areas for Improvement

- The data presented are only for a subset of AlphaTel's suppliers.
- The scope of the measures presented is limited.
- The extent to which the annual vendor questionnaires are direct measures of supplier quality is not clear. They may primarily measure internal perceptions of supplier quality.
- No comparisons are made.

Site Visit Issues

- Determine the extent to which the improvements relate to AlphaTel's quality management and quality improvement activities.
- Request data for missing years. Determine if more extensive supplier data are available.

SCORING

SCORING CONSENSUS SUMMARY WORKSHEET	Total Points Possible A	Percent Score 0–100% B	Score (A × B) C
6.0 QUALITY RESULTS 180 Possible Points			
6.1 Product and Service Quality Results	90	65%	58.5
6.2 Business Process, Operational and Support Service Quality Results	50	51%	25.5
6.3 Supplier Quality Results	40	40%	16.0
Category Total	180		100.0
	SUM A		SUM C

Category 6.0
QUALITY RESULTS

Percent Score

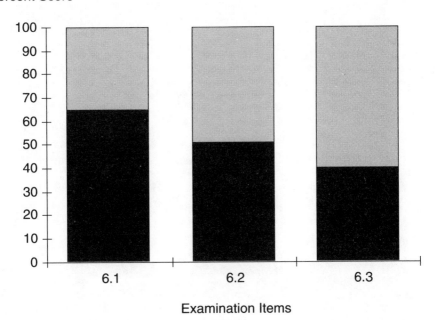

Examination Items

CHAPTER 12

CUSTOMER SATISFACTION: CATEGORY 7.0

Market-driven quality starts with making customer satisfaction an obsession and empowering our people to use their creative energy to satisfy and delight the customers.

John F. Akers, Chairman and CEO, IBM Corporation

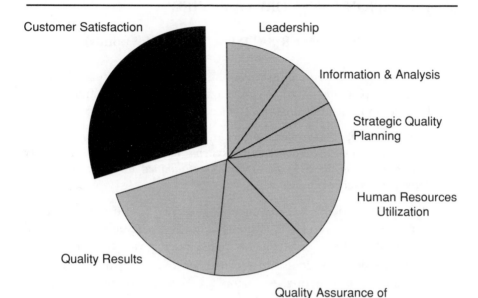

Examination Category/Items	Maximum Points
7.0 CUSTOMER SATISFACTION	300
7.1 Determining Customer Requirements and Expectations	30
7.2 Customer Relationship Management	50
7.3 Customer Service Standards	20
7.4 Commitment to Customers	15
7.5 Complaint Resolution for Quality Improvement	25
7.6 Determining Customer Satisfaction	20
7.7 Customer Satisfaction Results	70
7.8 Customer Satisfaction Comparison	70

EXAMINATION CATEGORY OVERVIEW

7.0 CUSTOMER SATISFACTION (300 points)

Ultimately, customers define quality and therefore are the final arbiters of quality. A company must look to its customers first in determining what it needs to do and last in evaluating its success at doing it.

> *The Customer Satisfaction category examines the company's knowledge of the customer, overall customer service systems, responsiveness, and its ability to meet requirements and expectations. Also examined are current levels and trends in customer satisfaction.*

- Evaluators focus on the company's knowledge of customer requirements, responsiveness to customer's needs, the levels of service, and the satisfaction results as measured through a variety of indicators.
- In assessing the scope and organization of a company's customer-related data gathering, evaluators take into consideration company resources, types of products and services, and geographical distribution of business units and customers. Evaluations are based upon the appropriateness and effectiveness of efforts in relation to these business factors.
- Also taken into account is whether or not a company utilizes all instruments at its disposal or within its resources to meet all the key requirements of an excellent customer service system.
- Evaluations do not depend upon how responsibilities are distributed or whether or not the company has separate departments for customer service, complaints, or other special purposes.

Items

7.1 Determining Customer Requirements and Expectations (30 points)

Describe how the company determines current and future customer requirements and expectations.

7.2 Customer Relationship Management (50 points)

Describe how the company provides effective management of its relationships with its customers and uses information gained from customers to improve products and services as well as its customer relationship management practices.

7.3 Customer Service Standards (20 points)

Describe the company's standards governing the direct contact between its employees and customers and how these standards are set and modified.

7.4 Commitment to Customers (15 points)

Describe the company's commitments to customers on its explicit and implicit promises underlying its products and services.

7.5 Complaint Resolution for Quality Improvement (25 points)

Describe how the company handles complaints, resolves them, and uses complaint information for quality improvement and for prevention of recurrence of problems.

7.6 Determining Customer Satisfaction (20 points)

Describe the company's methods for determining customer satisfaction, how satisfaction information is used in quality improvement, and how methods for determining customer satisfaction are improved.

7.7 Customer Satisfaction Results (70 points)

Summarize trends in the company's customer satisfaction and in indicators of adverse customer response.

7.8 Customer Satisfaction Comparison (70 points)

Compare the company's customer satisfaction results and recognition with those of competitors that provide similar products and services.

INSTANT INDEX

Examiner Evaluation

Consensus Scoring

CASE STUDY

7.0 CUSTOMER SATISFACTION

7.1 Determining Customer Requirements and Expectations

a. AlphaTel identifies customer needs by first categorizing business, interexchange carrier, and residential customers. The company identifies potential business customers by cross-referencing its toll-free directory with published lists of all companies operating in its service area with at least $1 million in annual revenues.

The needs of business customers are determined through the company's Customer Needs Assessments (CNAs). The decision makers of the Top 100 customers (as determined by billed revenue; see also Table 7.3 in Item 7.6) are interviewed in person semiannually with the CNA I vehicle. Representatives from the large, medium, and small companies are sampled and surveyed by phone on a quarterly basis with the CNA II and CNA III vehicles. All CNAs are administered by a third-party vendor to ensure confidentiality and objectivity; in no case is AlphaTel identified as the sponsor of the survey.

Interexchange carriers have very different needs from business and residential customers, and AlphaTel has a customer-supplier relationship with each one. The carriers and AlphaTel develop a list of access expectations that detail such aspects of the relationship as price, accounting, service performance, and transmission quality requirements. The expectations of residential customers are evaluated monthly through the Tel-Us surveys. These data are aggregated with unsolicited complaint and praise data and published monthly.

Local business offices also survey municipal building departments for information on preliminary architectural and building permits. This information is useful for determining the access needs of contracted or potential tenants of new buildings. Finally, AlphaTel relies on focus groups and findings from state-sponsored consumer attitude surveys.

Data collected from the surveys, focus groups, and state surveys are supplemented with internal AlphaTel data pertaining to transmission quality, major accounts lost, and new accounts won. Where the trend data are long enough, the company performs a cross-correlation of all "waveforms," seeking not only trends with high degrees of correlation but also the lag times between complaints and losses. By so doing, the company hopes to be able to predict trends and thus to slow losses by various countervailing methods.

b.   Each CNA and Tel-Us survey has several questions regarding the relative importance of current and potential offerings. These data, plus performance data from other portions of the surveys, are used in performance-importance charts to reveal where AlphaTel is falling short of expectations and where it can do better. Open commentary provided by the survey respondents is also studied for patterns among the various categories of users.

c.   All CNA and Tel-Us vehicles ask respondents to evaluate the survey with respect to relevance, completeness, and time. Open-commentary sections also provide opportunities for customers to answer unasked questions. Further, the company frequently monitors survey data retrospectively; for example, were service features that received low importance ratings in 1989 the source of major complaints in 1990? If so, it might indicate that the way the question was cast proved elusive or deceptive to the respondent. Analysis like this often leads to rephrasing of questions or even redesign of the survey.

In addition to analyzing the surveys, AlphaTel works closely with leading market research firms to develop new surveys that accommodate new tools and processes for analyzing customer needs.

7.2 Customer Relationship Management

a.   AlphaTel provides residential customers with one easy-to-remember toll-free number for all types of communication, whether complaint, billing inquiry, or request for information. By calling 1-555-HELP, callers reach the company's Customer Assistance Center (CAC), where employees are prepared to answer any and all questions. Switching software enables the company to route the call to the appropriate person in the CAC. Business customers have toll-free numbers that route them to their sales representatives. Interexchange carriers can make comments directly through the members of the appropriate customer-supplier team.

Customers can also comment in writing, a process AlphaTel facilitates by enclosing a postage-paid comment card with each invoice or notice. Cards are addressed not to AlphaTel's main office but to the regional or local business office that handles the account. There, inquiries are answered—in writing or by phone if the customer has included a phone number—by the same personnel who handle walk-in comments, questions, and inquiries.

In general, AlphaTel installation and service personnel can answer any question about a customer's level of service. Thus, an installer can explain billing details for a customer who is having a certain kind of service installed, and a repair person can detail options and prices for custom calling services. Even so, field personnel carry a supply of comment cards in case they cannot answer a question.

b.   AlphaTel has an on-line tracking system that permits customer-contact employees to see where a given product or service is at any given time. Each item is flagged with dates for completion and intermediate customer update. Once the service has been installed, the company calls the customer to determine satisfaction. CNA I and II accounts are contacted by the appropriate account executives. Three months after delivery, the company sends a customer satisfaction questionnaire. These standards also apply on all repair matters.

  c. AlphaTel wants its customer-contact personnel to be customer oriented, and all other considerations—including educational background and technical skills—are regarded as secondary. The company has several policies and practices that enable it to satisfy this focus.

- Job applicants are screened for basic courtesy, phone voice, and communication skills. Those who pass the first round of interviews then gather in small groups for role-playing and discussion.

- At AlphaTel, a customer-contact position is not considered to be strictly an entry-level job. Rather, the selection process and training are rigorous enough—and the compensation is high enough—that many current employees seek transfers to customer-contact openings. From there, they may qualify for supervisory or managerial positions in other parts of the company. For some employees, however, customer contact is a true career; while the average customer-contact employee transfers into another type of job within three years, some have been in their positions for more than ten years. These employees and AlphaTel find that customers appreciate the stability and experience they bring to the organization.

- New hires and transfers receive ten weeks of training before they are permitted customer contact. In addition to detailed classes that explain the company's product and service offerings, this training includes:

  1. Thorough discussions of AlphaTel's quality values and its commitment to meeting customer expectations.

  2. A strong focus on timely reporting of progress to customers and on escalation procedures.

  3. Special emphasis on listening skills and social sensitivity.

  4. A module on service recovery, which also details the employee's empowerment and decision-making authority and responsibility (see also below).

  5. Special drills on the fundamentals of grammar and letter writing,

because customer-contact employees are encouraged to write letters of apology or thanks as circumstances warrant.

The training continues beyond this 10-week period, with employees cycling through special seminars on new products and services, new rate structures, and special rulings and decisions from state PUCs and the Federal Communications Commission. In addition, personnel in Coastal receive training every August (prior to hurricane season) in the company's storm outage procedures.

- All AlphaTel employees recognize that the customer comes first. Therefore, billing personnel are allowed to adjust bills within certain amounts, depending on the customer's credit and payment history. All employees are permitted to take one hour of unapproved overtime per day to resolve problems.

- It is not AlphaTel policy to monitor employee conversations with customers or to impose contact quotas. Nevertheless, specific work groups of operators and installation technicians summarize particularly difficult calls or experiences. The group members discuss the contacts, evaluate the employee's response, and determine ways that the experience could have been improved (or at least not worsened) by both the employee and the company's support systems.

- Customer-contact employees, along with all other AlphaTel employees, fill out the company's annual Employee Opinion Survey (see also Item 4.5). In addition, supervisors review all letters and calls of praise and criticism with employees on a quarterly basis. These reviews provide an appropriate forum for employee discussions of matters related to attitude and morale, particularly as they are affected by the special pressures that are often brought to bear on customer-contact personnel.

- As noted above, customer-contact employees are apprised of all favorable reviews that are given by customers. Personnel who receive exceptional commendations or especially large amounts of "fan mail" are eligible for AlphaTel's Good Call Award, which comprises a parchment certificate and up to $1,000 in cash. Customer-contact personnel are, of course, also eligible for other awards (Item 4.4).

- AlphaTel analyzes turnover of customer-contact employees the same way it does that of the employee population at large.

d.   Customer-contact workstations have instant access not only to the Numbers, but also to a complete data base of AlphaTel's customer offerings and services. In particular, customer-contact data are input and updated after every call or letter, so that the employee has ready access to the history of a complaint or a customer. Customer letters are also available on this system, having been digitally scanned and input upon receipt.

Installation technicians do not have the same degree of access to AlphaTel's computer systems. Instead, they carry laptop computers into which they have copied pertinent customer data at the beginning of each day, based on their installation agendas. Should they require more information or greater detail, the computer's built-in modem permits them to call up the data as necessary. At the customer's request, they can also print transaction summaries for the customer's records.

e.   The cross-correlation process described in Item 7.1 is used with complaint data, customer gains and losses, and lost orders to determine what lag time exists between a complaint and a customer defection.

f.   AlphaTel's continuous improvement process is described in Items 5.2 and 5.3. The same methodology is used in the context of customer relations, where it helps determine the efficacy of the company's hiring and training practices for customer-contact personnel. In particular, the PASS and PANL modules described earlier are useful in relating AlphaTel's training courses with personnel performance along such dimensions as response time, escalation rates, and the costs of resolving customer complaints. These, in turn, are measured against overall customer satisfaction.

7.3 Customer Service Standards

a.   As a telephone company, AlphaTel is required to meet certain minimum standards imposed by the state PUCs (Table 7.1). The company exceeds all of these standards, including Smoky Mountain's requirement of 100 percent out-of-service clearance in 24 hours. (AlphaTel achieves 100 percent clearance in less than 21 hours.)

In addition to the state-mandated standards, AlphaTel develops its internal standards to reflect and directly translate customer expectations. Thus, because meeting installation due dates is one of residence customers' most important requirements, the company developed its internal interval

TABLE 7.1
AlphaTel Residential Performance (State PUC standards in parentheses)

State	Orders completed in five working days (percent)	Installation commitments met (percent)	Troubles per 100 access lines	Out of service clearing time (percent/time)
Woodland	98% (90)	99% (88)	2.0 (7.5)	99/24 hours (95)
Smoky Mountain	95 (90)	99 (88)	1.5 (8.0)	100/24 hours (100)
Rocky Mountain	99 (85)	99 (95)	2.0 (10.0)	99/24 hours (95)
Coastal	95 (75)	98 (88)	2.5 (8.0)	96/24 hours (80)
Central	99 (95)	99 (90)	1.8 (6.0)	99/8 hours (95)

standard to be "installations completed by promised due date" rather than "installations completed within five days of order." And because customers want knowledgeable, courteous, and helpful employees, AlphaTel expects its employees to be able to answer all questions posed, to smile, to keep a moderate tone, and to offer unsolicited advice on service offerings.

Customer-contact standards are also developed after rigorous reviews of the best practices of leading service companies. In addition to those noted above, the most important standards developed from customer expectations and service benchmarking are as follows:

- Incoming calls should be answered before the third ring, and employees should identify themselves immediately.

- Employees accepting calls should determine the caller's phone number to facilitate calling back if a disconnection occurs.

- Except in cases where the information requested is complex or specialized, employees may not transfer customer calls. Rather, the call recipient is expected to secure the requested information and call the customer back within two hours. This two-hour limit is in force even for calls received near the end of the business day.

- If a transfer is required, the employee must first determine that the caller wants to be transferred, explain why a transfer is necessary, give the name and title of the person to whom the call is being transferred, and then announce the caller and the nature of the inquiry. In any case, the original call recipient is still the person responsible for satisfying the customer and should be the one making any follow-up calls to the customer.

- Customers may not be put on hold unless employees must leave their stations to find the answers to questions. Otherwise, the employee who needs to access the Numbers, for example, does so with the line connected. AlphaTel has found that customers prefer the sound of the keyboard to silence.
- If a customer is put on hold, it may not be for more than 45 seconds. If the employee expects the search for an answer to take longer, he or she must offer either to transfer the call or to call the customer back within two hours.

   b.   A detailed booklet containing AlphaTel's customer service standards is provided to all new customer-contact employees during the initiation process. To ensure that all standards are deployed throughout all company units, initiations take place at every major location. The standards are among the few areas of company business for which employees receive—and are evaluated on—written examinations. Furthermore, all support personnel who exist in a supplier-customer relationship with customer-contact employees are made aware of the service standards. They are expected to provide customer-contact employees with all the assistance they require; for their part, customer-contact employees are expected to make it known when the support they require has been lacking.

   c.   AlphaTel uses customer interviews to determine if employees have met the stated standards. In addition, the company's phone system records the use of the transfer and hold buttons and also records the length of each hold. Employees also keep track of this information, so that they may be able to explain each circumstance to their supervisors.

   Supervisors occasionally observe operators during phone conversations and review written material intended for the customer. Supervisors and managers also review with employees the circumstances that led to escalation of a complaint or service problem.

   The Process Management methodology is the primary mechanism for evaluating the company's service standards. This work is supplemented with frequent customer interviews (see also Item 7.1) and follow-up calls to customers no more than a month after resolution of the problem. In these interviews, AlphaTel seeks information on how the customer-contact experience could have been improved. Company personnel also use their experiences as customers to their suppliers. Employee teams that work with vendors record favorable experiences and seek to apply vendors' approaches to the company's own status as a supplier to its customers.

AlphaTel's Process Management methodology also allows for employee input in the development and improvement of customer service standards. The mechanism is similar to that used for processes that produce the company's services. Indeed, customer contact is among the most tangible of the company's services. Employee efforts usually come during the assessment and analysis stages of a process team's work. The company is also eager to receive comments regarding service standards through the suggestion box.

7.4 Commitment to Customers

a.   AlphaTel makes the following guarantees to residential customers:

- Installers will arrive within a two-hour window either in the morning or in the afternoon.
- If a customer experiences a service difficulty within 30 days of installation, the company will provide one month of service free of charge, regardless of the reason for the problem.
- For a nominal charge, AlphaTel will assume all service and repair responsibilities for the wiring in a customer's residence, even if the wiring was installed by another party.

For WATS and special services customers:

- AlphaTel has provisioning guarantees that provide monetary credits whenever installation is late.
- In the event of an outage, the company guarantees restoration of service within one to three hours, depending on the class of service.

Service guarantees to interexchange carriers are part of the customer-supplier agreements. In all cases, the guarantees noted above are unconditional. They may also change from time to time, depending on customer responses regarding what service factors are important to them.

AlphaTel has several policies that make life easier for its business and residential customers.

- The company has always given instant credit for wrong numbers.
- The company has several WATS programs for business customers and makes every effort to provide each customer with the right

program. In the event an AlphaTell billing review shows that a business customer could benefit from another plan—even a less costly one—the company will offer to revise the service at no cost.

- AlphaTel offers residential customers the option of blocking outgoing calls to 900 numbers. This service is free to all customers and is summarized on bills every three months.

- Although AlphaTel is investigating Caller ID–type services, the company has made clear to each of the states in its service area its intention to provide alternatives to callers who do not wish to have their phone numbers appear on the receiver's screen. Most of these alternatives would make the ID block free to the caller.

- Whenever the company includes important billing or rate information in a monthly bill, that information is provided in English, Spanish, and Chinese. Further, a notice that the information is important and should be translated is written in 12 other languages. A toll-free number is provided for each language, so that customers may call and hear the message in their native languages.

- By request, and upon verification of age or disability, AlphaTel guarantees uninterrupted phone service to the elderly and the handicapped, regardless of payment history. The company makes every effort to help these customers budget their payments.

b.   Whenever AlphaTel feels it has made a significant gain in product or service quality, a study team analyzes the company's performance along all design parameters. When it is clear that the gains are resulting in improved customer satisfaction and better financial performance, the team recommends changes to the guarantee structure of the product or service. Thus, quality improvements enabled the company to strengthen its WATS and special services provisioning and restoration guarantees. Improvements in switching have also made it possible to provide service alternatives during outages: Customers have a choice of redirecting 800-service to a local number or to a test number, or of using a customized recording for the duration of the outage.

Similarly, the company analyzes its progress toward its short- and long-term quality goals to assess when warranty modifications are appropriate. Because each set of goals implies enhancements to both quality and profits, achievement of those goals is a sufficient condition for the strengthening of AlphaTel's commitments to its customers.

7.5 Complaint Resolution for Quality Improvement

a.   AlphaTel's goal is to resolve 95 percent of customer complaints within 48 hours. To this end, customer-contact employees are given ownership of the complaints they receive. They understand that other employees and management will support their efforts because all work groups have customer satisfaction goals as well as profit goals, and no bonuses are distributed unless the former have been met, regardless of the profit.

Very often, the employee hearing a complaint is not connected to the department responsible for it. AlphaTel ensures that complaints are directed to the appropriate personnel through the use of postage-paid comment cards. All field personnel (who hear 95 percent of these informal complaints) carry a supply of these cards and help customers in phrasing the problem correctly and addressing the card to the correct department.

Whether formal or informal, all complaints are recorded in AlphaBad, the company's problem log. This online system, which is arranged by department and includes the name of the recipient and the date and time of the complaint, is updated daily. Once an employee has solved a customer complaint, he or she records all pertinent information in AlphaBad so that others who receive similar complaints can use it as reference.

b.   Once an employee receives a complaint call, he or she acknowledges receipt of it and promises to call back with an update in two hours, and if the problem remains, again in 24 hours. To minimize handoffs, employees are permitted to work one hour of unapproved overtime each day to solve problems, and billing employees are permitted to make adjustments within certain amounts. If the problem has not been solved by the time of the second update call, the employee and the customer negotiate a mutually agreeable resolution time. Escalation procedures go into effect if the problem cannot be resolved in another 24 hours. If the resolution is regarded by the customer as unsatisfactory, he or she has the right to file an appeal, a copy of which is forwarded to the state PUC. AlphaTel's overall complaint management trends are shown in Table 7.2.

c.   AlphaTel performs Pareto analysis on all complaints along several dimensions to determine common sources of problems and geographical trends, among other factors. For example, one complaint QIT found that a particular exchange had an unusually high outage rate not because of

TABLE 7.2
AlphaTel Complaint Handling

Measure	1986	1988	1990
Median Resolution Time (days)	4.8	3.7	1.2
First-Contact Resolution (percent)	37.0%	55.3%	66.4%
48-Hour Resolution (percent)	61.4%	84.2%	96.2%
Handoffs per Complaint	3.2	1.4	0.5
Escalated Complaints (percent)	10.3%	6.6%	1.8%
Appeals per Thousand Complaints	8.2	6.6	3.5

frequent lightning, as had been previously thought, but because of crossfeed from a nearby electrical transformer. This led to the development of supplier-supplier partnerships in which electrical, telephone, and cable-TV installers work together in providing service to an area. These partnerships have the added benefit of giving real-estate developers one primary contact for most utility work in a new subdivision.

AlphaTel has also found that many complaints are due to faulty inside wiring. This can often be determined by a customer check of the network interface on the premises. As many older homes do not have network interfaces, however, the company has embarked on a campaign to install them in older homes and apartment complexes. The customer pays a nominal fee for the installation and is given the inside-wiring guarantee at no charge for the first two years.

Using Pareto and Ishikawa analysis, AlphaTel is able to determine how many complaints are related to what the customer regards as inadequate training of customer-contact and support staff, misleading product or service information, and low service standards. The complaint QITs assess the relative merits of these comments and work with the appropriate departments or teams to recommend refresher courses or to develop stricter standards. Such analysis led to the standard that customers put on hold remain connected to the call recipient instead of being forced to listen to silence or music.

d.   All escalated complaints are reviewed by the supervisor and the office of the CQO to determine their root cause. If the analysis shows that problem resolution could have been accelerated by further employee empowerment, then plans for that increased authority are developed.

7.6 Customer Satisfaction Determination

a.   AlphaTel's customer groups are described in Table 7.3.

AlphaTel uses these vehicles, as well as surveys inserted with bills, third-party telephone interviews, and focus groups, to determine customer satisfaction. In addition, the company evaluates customer satisfaction as soon after providing a product or service as possible, and then follows up three, six, or twelve months later. Customer-contact personnel ask customers if they would like a callback a few days after the service or repair; those who agree are asked a few questions to determine whether the company performed to expectations and how the company can improve. The company combines these data with data from the FCC and state PUCs.

In administering the CNA and Tel-Us vehicles, AlphaTel assures confidentiality and objectivity by using a third-party opinion-analysis firm. Telephone interviews are conducted with randomly selected customers. The company also regards mailed-in cards as representing a cross section of opinion; in general, however, more cards are returned by dissatisfied customers than by satisfied ones, a fact supported by most opinion analysts. AlphaTel does not seek to balance these viewpoints with more favorable ones on the theory that attending to the needs of unhappy customers will increase the satisfaction of all.

Designed with a significant amount of customer input, all CNA and

TABLE 7.3
AlphaTel Customer Groups

Survey	*Segment*	*Definition*	*Survey Mode and Frequency*
CNA I	Top 100 Businesses	> $1 million/yr	In person semiannually
CNA II	Large Business	> $100,000/yr	By phone quarterly
CNA III	Medium Business	< $100,000/yr, 3–9 lines	By phone quarterly
CNA III	Small Business	< $100,000/yr, 1–2 lines	By phone quarterly
Tel-Us	Residential		Various methods monthly
Partnership	Interexchange Carriers		By partnership agreement

Tel-Us surveys ask customers to rank service features in order of importance to them, and then to rate AlphaTel's performance for each of these features. These data are used to develop importance-performance matrices: Areas in the high-importance/low performance quadrant represent key sources of existing or potential customer dissatisfaction. They are targeted for improvement, and process teams and QITs are deployed to address these issues.

b.   AlphaTel serves 90 percent of the population and 70 percent of the area of its five-state service market. In general, AlphaTel relies on PUC data for customer satisfaction measures of the telephone companies serving the rest of the region, and FCC data for comparisons with RBOCs and other telephone companies outside the region.

c.   The cross-correlation techniques described in Items 7.1 and 7.2 are used to evaluate the relationship of customer satisfaction data with such adverse indicators as complaints and defections. Where the correlation coefficient is low, the company reevaluates the customer satisfaction measure for validity, objectivity, and accuracy. (Statistically, AlphaTel regards low correlation to be between -0.5 and $+0.5$ in the correlation scale of -1 to $+1$.)

d.   AlphaTel's Process Management methodology is the primary agent for assessing and improving customer satisfaction methods. The first step is to ensure that the data are both relevant and revealing; this is done by asking customers to rate the quality of the survey and to suggest ways it can be improved. Process teams then work on improving the surveys, as was done in 1986, when AlphaTel's entire approach to customer measurements was changed.

Prior to 1986, the company used the traditional "satisfied or dissatisfied" approach. Customer satisfaction as measured on this scale was quite high, for both AlphaTel and the RBOCs. In AlphaTel's view, however, the system overstated customer satisfaction; partially satisfied customers were not upset enough to claim they were dissatisfied, but the system was unable to account for their reservations. The system did not focus on whether AlphaTel was meeting expectations, nor did it measure whether AlphaTel was superior to companies that customers defined as comparable. Consequently, the system was redesigned to maintain, largely for regulatory reasons, the traditional satisfaction measures, but to allow customers to qualify their comments (for example, satisfied with the overall installation, but not the installer's courtesy) and to ask customers whether AlphaTel was superior overall and in comparison with a customer-defined set of comparable service providers.

The effect (Table 7.4) has been to make satisfaction harder to achieve; initially discouraging, the new vehicle has nevertheless allowed AlphaTel to aim for higher targets, using the 1986 data as a baseline.

7.7 Customer Satisfaction Results

a.   AlphaTel's customer satisfaction trends for key customer segments are shown in Table 7.5. The company has exhibited improvement in all customer segments and major improvement with respect to interexchange carriers.

Table 7.6 shows trends in residential customer satisfaction with respect to direct contact with the business office. Again, the company has exhibited clear and significant improvements since the inception of the quality initiative.

b.   Historically, AlphaTel's performance with respect to adverse indicators has been quite good. For example, only 350 of the company's 3 million residential customers file official PUC grievances in any given year.

TABLE 7.4
Comparison of Customer Measurement Systems

| | *Old System* | *New System* | | | |
| | | *Met Expectations* | | *Superior*[1] | |
Customers	*Satisfied (percent)*	*Unqualified (percent)*	*Qualified (percent)*	*AlphaTel (percent)*	*Best Other (percent)*
Residential	93	80	85	53	59
Business	94	81	92	43	50
IXC	95	84	96	22	34
Overall[2]	94	82	91	42	54

[1]Percentage of customers giving a 1 rating, where 1 = excellent and 5 = poor.
[2]Weighted by revenue.

Source: AlphaTel CNA and Tel-Us.

TABLE 7.5
AlphaTel Customer Satisfaction Trends (Percentage stating that AlphaTel met expectations)

	Unqualified Response			Qualified Response		
Customer	*1986 (percent)*	*1988 (percent)*	*1990 (percent)*	*1986 (percent)*	*1988 (percent)*	*1990 (percent)*
Top 100	80	82	85	90	90	91
Large Business	83	85	85	93	93	92
Small Business	81	81	83	92	93	94
Residential	80	83	86	85	87	89
IXC	84	88	90	96	96	97

Source: AlphaTel CNAs and Tel-Us.

TABLE 7.6
Residential Customer Satisfaction with the Business Office (Percentage of responses that were favorable)

Performance Measure	*1986 (percent)*	*1987 (percent)*	*1988 (percent)*	*1989 (percent)*	*1990 (percent)*
Call-answering time	75	77	82	86	90
Courtesy of the service representative	92	94	97	100	98
Knowledge of the service representative	82	81	94	97	96
General quality of business office contact	90	92	92	95	97

Source: AlphaTel Tel-Us.

AlphaTel recognizes, however, that each person who complains speaks for many who do not, and regards even one complaint as excessive. Analogously, each person who seeks a refund represents many who cannot (or wish not to) take the time to do so. Therefore, the company has placed major emphasis on reducing all adverse indicators and has been successful in doing so (Table 7.7).

7.8 Customer Satisfaction Comparison

a.   Tables 7.8 and 7.9 show overall customer satisfaction data for AlphaTel and RBOCs for the last five years; they also show AlphaTel's

TABLE 7.7
Trends in Customer Satisfaction Adverse Indicators

Adverse Indicator	1986	1988	1990
Complaints per 10,000 Lines	0.80	1.30	0.80
Warranty Costs/$Million Revenue	1541	1201	811
Refund Requests per 10,000 Lines	0.06	0.07	0.05
Repair Repeat Rate (percent)	15.3%	11.9%	2.0%

Source: AlphaTel Tel-Us.

TABLE 7.8
Benchmark of Residential Customer Satisfaction (Percentage satisfied or very satisfied)

	1986	1987	1988	1989	1990
AlphaTel	92.0%	93.6%	94.1%	95.6%	96.6%
Atlantel	92.8	94.0	92.4	94.2	93.6
Dixietel	92.4	93.0	90.2	92.1	93.3
Eastel	92.0	92.8	94.0	93.6	93.2
Midwestel	93.7	92.9	93.6	94.0	94.1
Mountel	94.1	94.4	96.1	95.7	96.0
Omegatel	97.6	95.5	95.8	96.3	96.4
Westel	91.9	92.4	94.1	93.3	91.4
Composite	93.5	93.6	93.8	94.2	94.0

Source: FCC; AlphaTel CNA and Tel-Us.

rank each year. The data show that where the company was well below the industry average in 1986, it now ranks at or near the top for the customer groups listed. Only with respect to large businesses did another company make gains as significant as AlphaTel's.

Table 7.10 compares important adverse indicators for AlphaTel and other groups of telcos. AlphaTel has consistently outperformed the industry average in all measures, and it is the industry leader in two of the four measures. As important, the company responds to PUC-filed complaints almost twice as fast as peer-group companies.

b.   AlphaTel has received several state achievement awards as well as customer recognition for excellence among service companies:

• The Coastal PUC gave AlphaTel its ServicePlus award for the third

TABLE 7.9
Benchmark of Business Customer Satisfaction (Percentage satisfied or very satisfied)

	1986	1987	1988	1989	1990
		Small Business			
AlphaTel	89.9%	92.7%	94.2%	94.2%	94.8%
Atlantel	90.6	93.8	93.3	93.9	94.0
Dixietel	89.9	91.7	90.7	92.0	93.7
Eastel	92.0	93.3	94.5	94.8	94.7
Midwestel	91.6	91.5	92.2	92.6	92.8
Mountel	94.2	93.4	94.0	94.1	95.3
Omegatel	97.1	94.6	95.0	95.6	95.5
Westel	89.4	91.1	93.5	92.4	89.9
Composite	92.1	92.7	93.3	93.6	93.7
		Large Business			
AlphaTel	91.2%	94.0%	95.0%	95.4%	96.3%
Atlantel	89.1	90.2	92.0	93.6	94.7
Dixietel	93.1	94.0	95.0	95.7	96.0
Eastel	89.9	94.2	94.9	93.9	94.1
Midwestel	94.8	97.0	91.6	92.0	93.5
Mountel	90.4	95.9	93.3	94.7	95.0
Omegatel	91.3	92.3	94.4	95.4	94.0
Westel	92.2	95.1	96.3	95.5	89.0
Composite	91.5	94.1	93.9	94.4	93.8

Source: FCC; AlphaTel CNA and Tel-Us.

year in a row in 1989 (the 1990 award has not been announced). This award is given to the utility or company overseen by the PUC that provides the fastest and most effective responses to PUC complaints or filings; the significance of the award is that it is not mandated every year. In the 1989 award presentation, the PUC director lauded AlphaTel for "consistently presenting rate requests that demonstrated sensitivity to the public," citing in particular the rate decrease made possible by the company's quality programs.

- The Smoky Mountain state legislature gave AlphaTel its 1990 Gold Seal for excellence in service to government institutions. This award is given every year to the public or private company that provides superior service to the state in the conduct of its business. (As a measure of the award's importance, the state evaluates more than 500 service providers in naming the recipient. The 1989 award

TABLE 7.10
Comparisons of Adverse Indicators (1990)

Adverse Indicator	AlphaTel	RBOCs	Independent Telcos	U.S. Telco Average
PUC Complaints per 10,000 Lines	0.8	1.1	1.0	1.1
Response Time (days)	8.0	14.0	16.5	14.6
Warranty Costs/$Million Revenue	$811	$1200	N/A	$1200
Refund Requests per 10,000 Lines	0.05	0.06	N/A	0.06
Repair Repeat Rate (percent)	2.0%	5.0%	7.1%	5.5%

N/A = not available

Source: State PUCs; FCC; AlphaTel analysis.

went to Commonwealth Medical for its innovative HMO service to the state.)

- JCN Corporation, the largest computer manufacturer in AlphaTel's service area, named the company a winner of its 1990 Big Blue Ribbon. Fewer than 1 percent of JCN's suppliers are named each year.

In addition, AlphaTel was the only regulated company cited in E.O. Donaldson's book *Now THAT's How You Run A Company!* and was acclaimed by a leading consumer magazine for its sensitivity to employees.

c.   AlphaTel's pricing and service policies have enabled more small businesses to install WATS lines than ever before, with twice as many subscribers in 1990 as in 1986. AlphaTel serves 90 percent of the residents in its five-state service area and has experienced no significant declines in market share since 1986. This is especially notable because after the 1984 divestiture of the local telephone companies, most RBOCs lost market share, some significantly.

d.   The growth in AlphaTel's customer base is reflected in the number of customer lines in service, which has grown from 4.7 million in 1986 to 5.1 million in 1990. This compares favorably with the growth experienced by other regional phone companies, even though much of AlphaTel's region has shown slow economic growth in the same period.

EVALUATION

7.0 CUSTOMER SATISFACTION

7.1 Determining Customer Requirements and Expectations

Strengths

- Customers are stratified into business, residential, and interexchange customers.
- AlphaTel uses three major kinds of surveys to assess top large, medium, and small business customers. The surveys are administered by a third-party vendor to ensure confidentiality and objectivity.
- AlphaTel's approach to determining the needs and expectations of the interexchange carriers relies on the customer-supplier relationship with each one. Lists of expectations are developed.
- Tel-Us surveys, focus groups, response cards, data from state-sponsored surveys, and data from municipal building departments are also used.
- The primary approaches to determining product and service features and their relative importance are:
  1. Survey questions about the importance of both current and potential features and offerings.
  2. Open commentary questions and focus groups.
- The survey data are cross-compared with transmission quality, major accounts lost, new accounts won, complaints, etc. Attempts are made to understand time lags between complaints and losses.
- The surveys are improved by:
  1. Asking survey respondent to evaluate the survey.
  2. Retrospective analysis of the surveys to ensure consistency and validity.

Areas for Improvement

- Stratification of customers appears to use very coarse segments. For example, it is hard to believe that all residential customers are about the same and do not require further stratification by income or other variables.

- There is little distinction made between assessing customer satisfaction and determining customer needs and requirements (Item 7.6). Without more detailed information, it is difficult to assess the extent to which the survey vehicles described specifically address assessment of customer needs and expectations.

Site Visit Issues

- Examine the survey instruments in detail to assess the degree to which they address customer requirements and expectations. Also determine if the surveys and surveying methodologies used are valid.
- Determine the extent to which "exploratory" customer needs and expectations analysis occurs to uncover latent customer desires.
- Request more details on how cross-comparisons of the survey data with other information and data are made.
- Assess the extent to which integration of data from a variety of sources occurs and whether or not data from all relevant sources (e.g. the sales force) are used.
- It is unlikely that the views of the decision makers of the top 100 customers represent the experience of the real AlphaTel customers within those organizations. What efforts are made to assess the needs of those customers?

7.2 Customer Relationship Management

Strengths

- AlphaTel residential customers have easy access via a toll-free number to customer service representatives who can handle almost all types of requests. Business customers have toll-free access to their sales representatives.
- Field personnel can answer questions about any aspect of the customer's service (billing, etc.).
- Customers are called after service has been installed. Follow-up occurs again after three months, when a customer satisfaction questionnaire is sent. In addition, response cards are carried by field personnel and are enclosed with each invoice or notice.
- Customer-contact personnel are screened for suitability before hiring

and are trained for 10 weeks. Customer-contact positions are not considered to be strictly entry-level jobs.

- Billing personnel have the authority to adjust bills up to certain amounts depending on the customer's credit and payment history.
- Customer service representatives do not have contact quotas. In addition, they can take up to one hour of overtime per day without approval to resolve customer problems.
- The Good Call Award is a special award for customer service representatives.
- Technological support of customer-contact employees appears to be substantial. Customer service representatives are supported by workstations that have immediate access to the Numbers data base and to customer letters, which are scanned in. Field personnel have laptop computers that are preloaded with customer information based on their service or installation schedules.
- The Process Management method is used to improve customer service standards.

Areas for Improvement

- The ease of access for business customers (especially small accounts) is unclear. Availability of an account representative obviously depends on the number of accounts that the representative services. No indication is given of how service levels in this area are maintained.
- Response cards are addressed to local service offices, suggesting that aggregation of this data for policy decisions may not occur.
- The extent of empowerment of the customer service representative is unclear.
- Little or no analysis of customer data to improve customer relationship management is described.
- No specific improvement of customer relationship management is described. The extent of deployment of the Process Management method to this area is unclear.

Site Visit Issues

- Are installers and repairers considered part of the customer-contact group and given 10 weeks of training? What is the basis for the claim that installers can answer questions about all aspects of service? Are they specifically trained?

- Hours of operation for the toll-free numbers and customer service centers are not mentioned.
- A basis is needed for assessing the average three-year stay for customer-contact employees. Determine if comparison data are available.
- What is the compensation level for customer-contact employees, and how does it compare to compensation for similar positions in other companies and industries?
- Examine the capabilities of the customer representatives' workstations.
- Determine how often the customer service representatives take the additional hour of overtime to solve customer problems and how this correlates with customer needs rather than their own schedules.
- What are the rules for adjustments made by billing personnel? How much of an adjustment can they make? Are billing personnel different than the customer service representatives, and if so, to what extent are the customer service representatives empowered?

7.3 Customer Service Standards

Strengths

- AlphaTel exceeds all state PUC standards.
- AlphaTel has developed a number of explicit customer service standards: calls are to be answered before the third ring; calls should not be transferred; customers should not be put on hold; all holds should be for less than 45 seconds.
- AlphaTel claims to benchmark the best practices of leading service companies.
- Customer service standards are documented in a manual. Customer-contact employees are trained in the standards and evaluated on their knowledge of the standards by examinations.
- Service standards are tracked down by customer interviews. In addition, transfers and holds are tracked automatically by the telephone equipment, and supervisors occasionally observe telephone representatives and review written material intended for customers.

- The customer service standards are improved using the Process Management methodology. Customer service representatives can have input into the development of the standards through the process teams or through the suggestion box.

Areas for Improvement

- While a number of customer service standards are listed, no well-defined process or rationale for developing the customer service standards is described.
- The focus of the responses in this Item is entirely on the telephone service representatives. Thus, it is unclear the extent to which appropriate customer service standards also are applied to the field service personnel and the extent to which they are deployed and measured.
- The scope of the customer service standards seems narrow. For example, no standards concerning knowledge, friendliness, or clarity are discussed.
- Except for automatic tracking of transfers and holds, there is little direct measurement of the customer-contact process. Thus, it is unclear how the process is controlled.
- The extent to which the Process Management method is deployed to develop and assess customer service standards is not clear.
- AlphaTel's system seems to allow but not encourage customer service representatives to help develop and improve customer service standards.

Site Visit Issues

- Determine the process for improving the standards. What is involved? How are the changes deployed to all customer-contact personnel?
- Review the manual that documents the customer service standards.
- Determine what customer service standards are supposed to apply to other customer-contact employees such as installers and repairpeople.
- Determine the extent to which the customer service standards are fully deployed, both customer service representatives and to all other

customer-contact employees, such as repair people, installers, and business account representatives.

- Determine how the customer service standards have been improved over the last few years.

7.4 Commitment to Customers

Strengths

- AlphaTel makes a number of guarantees to customers: service difficulties within one month of installation result in a free month of service for residential customers; for a nominal charge, AlphaTel will assume responsibility for residential inside wiring; instant credit will be provided for wrong numbers; late installation results in monetary credits for WATS customers; WATS service customers get guaranteed three-hour restoration of service.
- In addition, AlphaTel makes a number of commitments: to scheduling installation within a two-hour window; to a residential option to block 900-number calls; to uninterrupted service for the elderly or handicapped.
- The range of guarantees and commitments is quite extensive.
- AlphaTel makes considerable effort to ensure that important information is available for customers in several languages.
- Quality improvements have enabled the company to strengthen its WATS and special services provisioning and restoration warranties.

Areas for Improvement

- For most of the commitments listed, such as the two-hour installation window, it is unclear what compensation customers receive when the commitment is violated.
- Commitments are not compared to those of other similar companies.
- Exactly how quality improvement has led to changes in the commitments is not clear. For example, what analysis is done to determine when and how to change the commitments?

Site Visit Issues

- Determine the extent to which the commitments listed are required by regulation.

- The extent to which guarantees are made in response to customer expectations and desires is not clear. Do the guarantees really address the customers' principal concerns? What data are available to assess this?
- Determine the extent to which the company ensures that customers are aware of the guarantees.
- Obtain more details concerning how commitments are changed in response to quality improvement.
- Obtain comparison information for commitments. Commitments such as outage credits, which are common in this industry, are not mentioned.

7.5 Complaint Resolution for Quality Improvement

Strengths

- A major approach to capturing informal complaints is the response cards that are carried by field personnel. The field personnel can aid customers in phrasing the problem description correctly and in directing the card to the appropriate department.
- A procedure for handling complaints exists. All complaints are recorded in the on-line problem log AlphaBad. A commitment is made to call the customer back within two hours and, if the problem remains, again in 24 hours. Escalation procedures begin if the problem is not resolved in another 24 hours.
- Customer service representatives can work up to one hour overtime each day without approval to resolve customer problems.
- For all measures shown, trends in complaint handling appear to have improved since 1986. The improvement appears sustained.
- Complaints are analyzed using quality tools and techniques, including Pareto analysis, geographic areas, etc. Complaint analysis has led to improvements. Examples include the development of supplier-supplier partnerships with electric utilities and cable-TV installers, and the customer service standard that discourages putting customers on hold.

Areas for Improvement

- The mechanism described is inadequate to ensure that informal complaints are captured. There is no discussion of how customer service representatives determine what constitutes an informal complaint, or how AlphaTel ensures that these complaints actually are logged.

- The response card approach is not likely to capture informal complaints about the field service personnel, since they are involved in directing the cards.
- No direct measurement of the complaint handling process is described. For example, there is description of a mechanism to measure if all complaints are logged or if all informal complaints are recognized as complaints. There is also no mechanism to determine if complaints that are listed as resolved have been resolved from the customer's point of view.
- The complaint handling process described seems focused almost entirely on the telephone customer service representatives.
- Complaint escalation procedures are mentioned but not described.
- The degree of deployment of root cause analysis of complaints is not fully described. Further, how complaint data are systematically used in continuous improvement is not clear. While a couple of anecdotes are given, there is little evidence given of full deployment.
- There appears to be little continuous improvement of the complaint handling process. This is especially true of complaints made to areas other than the Customer Assistance Center. There is no mention of how business customer complaints are handled or how account representatives are included in the complaint handling process.
- No benchmarking of the complaint handling system is mentioned.

Site Visit Issues

- The data shows escalated complaints at 1.8 percent for 1990 and appeals per thousand complaints at 3.5 percent. Are these data consistent with one another? Ask for clarification.
- Determine how complaints are handled by parts of the company other than the Customer Assistance Center.
- Data are needed more frequently than every two years to aid in assessment of variability.
- Comparison or benchmark data are required to aid in interpretation.

7.6 Determining Customer Satisfaction

Strengths

- Customer satisfaction is determined using the same surveys described in 7.1a to determine customer needs and expectations. Customer follow-up occurs as described in 7.2b.
- Customer satisfaction data are cross-correlated with complaint and performance data.
- Customer satisfaction determination is improved using the Process Management process. Customers are asked to rate the surveys they receive and suggest ways the surveys can be improved.
- Table 7.4 provides evidence that AlphaTel is trying to improve and refine its customer satisfaction measurement process.

Areas for Improvement

- As indicated for Item 7.1, more stratification of the customer groups appears necessary.
- AlphaTel relies on the PUCs for customer satisfaction comparison data. No other approaches to customer satisfaction comparison that validate the PUC comparison data are indicated. No comparison or benchmarking outside the telephone industry is mentioned here. This contrasts with what is stated in Items 2.2 and 3.1.

Site Visit Issues

- It is important to ascertain whether or not the surveys that are done are valid.
- Find out if the last change to the surveys was in 1986 (the date of the major change addressed in Table 7.4) or if the improvement is ongoing.
- Determine what AlphaTel's process for cross-comparison is. Their interpretation and use of correlation may be inappropriate.
- Determine if AlphaTel's integration of customer satisfaction indicators of various types (surveys, complaints, lost business, etc.) is adequate.
- Assess the extent to which "exploratory" analysis occurs to uncover

latent areas of customer dissatisfaction or opportunities for improving satisfaction.

7.7 Customer Satisfaction Results

Strengths

- There seems to be overall improvement in customer satisfaction since 1986 for all of the customer groups except large businesses. For large businesses, there appears to be no trend.
- There seems to be an overall improvement in customer satisfaction with the business office in all listed categories since 1986.
- Warranty costs and the repair repeat rate have improved since 1986.

Areas for Improvement

- No data are given for installation or repair (except repeat rate) or for other major areas of AlphaTel's business. Data are given only overall and for the business office.
- The data need to be refined into more segments. All residential customers are not likely to be the same.
- There appears to be little or no improvement for large businesses.
- Complaints per 10,000 lines and refund requests per 10,000 lines appear to be stable, not improving.
- The absolute levels of satisfaction in Table 7.5 may be low. It is difficult to interpret the absolute level of satisfaction without some basis for comparison.

Site Visit Issues

- The survey instruments must be examined. Further, it must be explained exactly what the data presented in Tables 7.5–7.7 are. It is not clear what "percentage starting that AlphaTel met expectations" or "percentage of responses that were favorable" really means.
- Data should be requested for intervals smaller than two years.
- Determine the number of interexchange carriers. Such small percentage changes as those shown in Table 7.5 are unlikely if there are only a few.
- Determine if there are data on customer satisfaction with the complaint handling process.

- Determine if all of the adverse indicators that are appropriate were actually reported.

7.8 Customer Satisfaction Comparison

Strengths

- AlphaTel ranks number one in aggregate customer satisfaction for residential and large business customers, having improved from number six and number five since 1986. For small businesses, AlphaTel has improved from number six to number three.
- AlphaTel has won several awards: the Coastal PUC ServicePlus award for the last three years, the Smoky Mountain 1990 Gold Seal, and JCN's 1990 Big Blue Ribbon. AlphaTel was also cited in E.O. Donaldson's book *Now THAT's How You Run A Company!*
- Unlike other telephone companies, AlphaTel claims not to have lost residential market share after divestiture. AlphaTel has doubled the number of small business WATS lines.
- AlphaTel's customer base has grown from 4.7 million to 5.1 million since 1986, in spite of slow economic growth in the regions served.

Areas for Improvement

- Comparison of adverse indicators in Table 7.10 is only to industry averages. In addition, no trend data for the comparisons are given.
- Insufficient data are given on the gains and losses of customers. AlphaTel defines loss of a customer as total loss rather than loss of just an aspect of service to a customer (e.g. call waiting).
- No market penetration comparison with other telephone companies has been given. These are appropriate data for a monopoly to provide. For example, did all telephone companies double the number of small business WATS lines?

Site Visit Issues

- Determine if all relevant comparisons have been made. Are there any other independent telephone companies that should be among the companies listed?
- Make sure that the reason the numbers in Table 7.8 do not match

those in Table 7.5 is the change in the customer measurement system described in section 7.6.

- Determine comparison of adverse indicators to best in class.
- Determine comparison trends for adverse indicators.
- More market share and market penetration data are required. Determine the market penetration for all product types and compare this with other telephone companies and utilities.
- Insufficient data have been given to determine if AlphaTel is world-class. Benchmarks and comparisons, including companies outside the telephone industry, that address this issue are necessary.

SCORING

SCORING CONSENSUS SUMMARY WORKSHEET	Total Points Possible A	Percent Score 0–100% B	Score (A × B) C
7.0 CUSTOMER SATISFACTION 300 Possible Points			
7.1 Determining Customer Requirements and Expectations	30	64%	19.2
7.2 Customer Relationship Management	50	65%	32.5
7.3 Customer Service Standards	20	50%	10.0
7.4 Commitment to Customers	15	58%	8.7
7.5 Complaint Resolution for Quality Improvement	25	65%	16.3
7.6 Determining Customer Satisfaction	20	66%	13.2
7.7 Customer Satisfaction Results	70	59%	41.3
7.8 Customer Satisfaction Comparison	70	65%	45.5
Category Total	300		186.7
	SUM A		SUM C

Category 7.0
CUSTOMER SATISFACTION

Percent Score

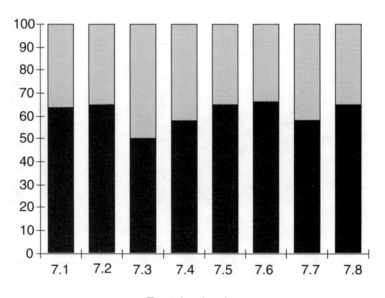

Examination Items

ALPHA TELCO SCORING CONSENSUS SUMMARY

Categories	Possible Points	Consensus Score	Percentage
1.0 LEADERSHIP	100	55.9	56%
2.0 INFORMATION AND ANALYSIS	70	31.8	45%
3.0 STRATEGIC QUALITY PLANNING	60	29.0	48%
4.0 HUMAN RESOURCE UTILIZATION	150	79.6	53%
5.0 QUALITY ASSURANCE OF PRODUCTS AND SERVICES	140	60.1	43%
6.0 QUALITY RESULTS	180	100.0	56%
7.0 CUSTOMER SATISFACTION	300	186.7	62%
	1000	543.1	54%

ALPHA TELCO SCORING CONSENSUS SUMMARY

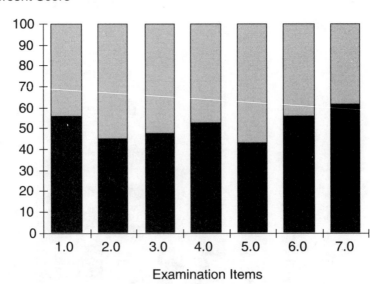

Percent Score

Examination Items

PART 3

THE WINNERS: PROFILES OF WORLD-CLASS COMPANIES

Malcolm Baldrige National Quality Award Winners

1988

    Globe Metallurgical Inc.
    Motorola Inc.
    Commercial Nuclear Fuel Division
        of Westinghouse Electric Corporation

1989

    Milliken & Company
    Xerox Business Products and Systems

1990

    Cadillac Motor Car Company
    IBM Rochester
    Federal Express Corporation
    Wallace Co., Inc.

1991

    Marlow Industries
    Solectron Corporation
    Zytec Corporation

THE WINNERS:
ROLE MODELS FOR QUALITY ACHIEVEMENT

Since its inception, the Baldrige Award has become a nucleus for the rapidly expanding quality movement. Award recipients provide tangible models of Total Quality Management. What follows is an overview of the strategies used by actual Baldrige Award winners. These profiles highlight specific improvements that led to companies receiving the Award. Since winning, the Baldrige companies have continued to progress in their quest for excellence.

Responding to the information-transfer requirement of the Award, the winners have opened the doors to the executive offices and factory floors, allowing the opportunity to scrutinize the Total Quality Management revolution-in-process. That the accounts are publicly available is, in itself, remarkable. At no time before has such a wealth of information on key business practices been accessible for sharing from one company to another.

The importance of this knowledge to the growth of the quality movement in the United States could hardly be overstated. Reading these chronologies provides insights far beyond what can be achieved purely through an academic discussion of the elements of TQM.

In seeking a philosophy to guide their futures, the needs of companies are very similar to the needs of individuals on a similar sort of quest. In the end, each company must find its own way. But just as role models provide individuals with ideas and actions to emulate, these world-class companies provide us with benchmarks to illuminate our path as we seek our way down the road to total quality.

You would be hard-pressed to find better corporate role models than these. Although the Baldrige is a national award, each of the winners has aspired to and achieved world-class quality. Baldrige winners have attained the highest levels of quality management excellence, and the story of how that excellence has been attained can be studied in much the same way that an art student might analyze the sketches of great artists or an aspiring physicist might explore the works of renowned scientists.

These are stories of struggle. At such high levels of achievement, winning is never simply an accident of greatness. To be the best requires unflagging determination to excel. Like an Olympic gold medal, the Malcolm Baldrige Award is not an honor that is likely to be achieved simply by the natural application of talent and determination. The Award symbolizes quality accomplishments that were deliberately and thoughtfully worked toward.

In reading the following stories, you will see that all of the Baldrige Award recipients underwent the most fundamental of changes in their corporate structure. Each of these companies devoted itself to the single-minded pursuit of the goal of creating a total quality culture. In the winners' stories, the key elements of change necessary to create an environment of continuous quality improvement emerge: visionary leadership, quality strategy, employee participation, fact-based actions, and customer-driven quality.

Visionary Leadership

Clearly, responsibility for quality cannot be delegated. Those companies that have attained the greatest success in quality improvement are those whose top echelons have articulated the quality vision and led the quality charge.

Quality leadership means creating a clear, concise concept of change that can be understood at every level of the company; setting aggresive goals based on only the highest level of excellence possible; and following through with a commitment of resources to effect change.

Quality Strategy

Out of the vision created by effective leadership must come a strategy that is both aggressive and long term. Quality strategy and planning start with such "stretch" objectives as magnitudes of improvement and moves on to involve every employee, department, division, and area of the company, external customers, and suppliers in the process.

Baldrige-winning companies have discovered that the business plan and the quality plan are one and the same thing. Beyond meeting the current needs of the marketplace, strategic quality planning anticipates future needs and reaches for standards above and beyond present expectations. Baldrige companies have made remarkable improvements in quality by forging close, long-term relationships with suppliers who can then be integrated into the planning process.

Employee Participation

Employee participation means empowering employees. Those who are responsible for quality improvement must also have the power to execute quality improvement. Before employees can be empowered to construct changes, they must have the tools necessary to evaluate problems and make decisions. Training is broad based, including but not limited to job training, cross-training, and, of course, training in quality.

Employee participation incorporates the concept of employees as internal customers. Quality products and services are dictated by the external customer, but quality processes are executed and improved by internal customers.

Fact-Based Actions

The science of collecting and analyzing appropriate, meaningful data is key to quality improvement. Quality information and analysis refers to constant internal monitoring of all processes and a systematic means of acting on results to effect quality improvement.

Fact-based actions depend on having a coherent, company-wide vocabulary for quality and a comprehensive process for quality analysis. Constant monitoring of customers, suppliers, and best-practicing companies (competitors and others), as well as having systems in place to react to that information are essential. Accurate and timely data are needed to ensure fast response and continuous quality improvement.

Customer-Driven Quality

No definition of quality is valid except the definition provided by the customer. Any attempt to improve quality without first asking the customer to define it is, for all practical purposes, an exercise in futility and a waste of resources.

A customer-driven company has a dynamic, fact-based dialogue with customers. Through surveys, complaint monitoring and follow-up, and tracking of sales, service, and other customer-contact areas, quality companies know a great deal about customer requirements and are constantly moving in a forward direction to meet or exceed those requirements.

Clearly, the winners disscussed here have set the standard for American business today. In that sense, winning the Malcolm Baldrige Award is much like winning an Olympic gold medal. Yet, for amateur athletes, winning the gold typically represents the pinnacle of a lifetime achievement. For winners of the Baldrige Award, however, the recognition is simply an important signpost near the beginning of a journey that has no end.

CHAPTER 13

1988 AWARD WINNERS: THE BEST OF THE BEST

We salute three corporations that reflect American industry's dedication to quality. Each of them and thousands of others help keep America strong by making American products the best products available. They and others like them exemplify the belief that quality counts first, foremost, and always. The one trait that characterizes these winners is a never ending process, a company-wide effort in which every worker plays a critical part. They realize that America's economic strength and future depend more and more upon the quality of its products.

Ronald Reagan
November 14, 1988

GLOBE METALLURGICAL INC.:
HOW GOOD IS "GOOD ENOUGH"?

> *Three years ago [1985], Globe refused to accept the gloom spreading over America's smokestack industries. We refused to be swamped by a flood of cheap imported commodity-grade metals. Other companies in our business closed their doors. At Globe we raised our sights. We aimed to become the lowest-cost, highest-quality producer in the world. We hit that mark.*

Arden Sims,
President and Chief Executive Officer,
Globe Metallurgical Inc.

Business Overview

Globe Metallurgical Inc. manufactures ferroalloys and silicon metals. A privately held company since 1987, Globe has 230 employees at two plants, one in Beverly, Ohio, and the other in Selma, Alabama. Annual production of alloys is approximately 100,000 tons. Globe in 1988 was this country's largest producer of silicon metals. General Motors, Ford Motor Company, and Dow Corning are major customers. Annual sales in 1990 were $120 million, up from $100 million in 1987.

How Quality Began

Globe can trace its origins back to 1873, and it has had a long record as a quality producer of commodity products for the steel, aluminum, and foundry industries. At Globe, the 1950s through the mid-1970s were prosperous years of operating at full capacity, with any cost increases passed on to customers. Then, in the latter half of the 1970s, South American companies began penetrating several of Globe's markets, using the advantages of cheap labor and lower operating costs. A strong U.S. dollar also contributed to the company's difficulty in staying competitive with foreign producers. In the early to mid-1980s, many of Globe's customers—such as the aluminum, steel, and foundry industries—also experienced rust-belt declines. That, combined with rising labor costs and increasing electrical power rates, began to erode profitability. Electricity costs were 25 percent of Globe's product costs, and 20 percent power-rate increases were looming.

On top of everything else, Globe faced the uncertainties of an imminent sale by its parent company, Moore McCormick Resources.

Threatened by imports, costs, and a probable change of ownership, Globe began to look to quality improvement as an effective means of staying competitive in a changing marketplace. Globe produced more specialized goods to strengthen its business. Since a number of customers had unique needs, Globe utilized the advanced analytical equipment in its chemical laboratories to grade out special products to meet specific customer requirements.

Quality Turnaround

Like many American companies, Globe did not turn to quality management entirely of its own accord. In early 1985, some of Globe's major customers, American auto makers, began to focus on the shift from detection to prevention of quality problems. Ford Motor Company had initiated a quality certification program for its suppliers called Q-1. In order to continue as a Ford supplier, Globe needed to meet the auto manufacturer's Q-1 requirements for basic quality levels. Globe's leadership decided to build a total commitment to quality throughout the company. The goal was not only to pass Ford's test but also to become a recognized quality leader in its industry.

To secure the Ford Q-1 rating, Globe's first step in the program was to undergo the Q-101 audit. The results of Globe's self-assessment revealed some primary inadequacies: detection-based systems as opposed to preventative ones, no statistical process-control implementation, limited quality planning, and little employee involvement in quality improvement. Globe's response to the deficiencies began in three areas: providing Statistical Process Control (SPC) training for all employees, developing a quality manual and methods for a quality system, and educating its own suppliers in quality, including SPC.

Quality-Efficiency-Cost

Globe quickly built a comprehensive quality system using the Q-101 criteria as its foundation. The Quality-Efficiency-Cost (QEC) Committee was created to establish this system. Fortunately, the company commanded the needed muscle: good products, good equipment, good people, and good customer relations. With these strengths, Globe accomplished the change to Total Quality Management in a condensed time frame.

Globe also began in-house training in SPC fundamentals to provide all employees with skills to read, interpret, and maintain control charts. To maximize the usefulness of the training, actual job-site data were incorporated into the instruction. In the Beverly plant, an outside trainer helped with the sessions; Selma employees were trained by the QEC Committee.

As the quality implementation progressed, the QEC Committee evolved into the QEC Steering Committee, with president and CEO Arden Sims as chair, and the top officers as members. They met monthly to review the company's overall quality system activities. These meetings alternated between the Beverly and the Selma plant sites. Much time was spent talking to line workers about problems and solutions. The QEC Steering Committee had the responsibility of establishing the company's quality goals, and it gathered input from the people on the factory floor.

Plant managers in Beverly and Selma began to chair their own QEC committees. The membership at each plant consisted of the heads of all the departments: accounting, maintenance, purchasing, raw materials, production, and shipping. These multidisciplined groups worked on implementation issues. At daily meetings, each plant's QEC monitored control charts, discussed any out-of-control conditions, and took the necessary corrective actions. The aim was to build a systematic, prevention-based process.

Quality Manual

In the development of a standard quality manual for the purpose of identifing correct methods to assure consistent work practices, five key segments were addressed: procedures, job-work instructions, critical process variables, product parameters, and failure mode and effect analysis. A manual was assembled for each department and located in work areas for employees' reference. Each department also contained a quality information center that displayed its control charts, quality circle status, upcoming customer audits or results, and recognition for employee contributions.

Supplier Quality Training

Globe worked with suppliers to assure the consistent quality of incoming materials. Beginning in October 1985, Globe provided quality training for five of its major suppliers. This effort was later expanded to all suppliers.

In some cases suppliers traveled to Globe's facilities, and in others QEC members took the training on the road. Hourly employees learned SPC fundamentals in order to construct control charts to track critical process variables. A major benefit of Globe's sharing was that the quality systems its suppliers designed precisely met the QEC Committee parameters. The net result was that suppliers produced more consistent raw materials, which led to record production in Globe's furnaces. Starting in 1988, Globe installed a certification program in which suppliers could earn preferred-supplier status and benefit from longer-term contracts.

Strategic Quality Plan

Globe's Continuous Improvement Plan contains the company's quality improvement goals, objectives, and individual implementation projects, as well as specific accountabilities. The QEC Steering Committee develops the plan's goals, while the plant QEC committees have responsibility for specific projects. The plan also includes employees' input and quality circles' recommendations that call for sizable capital expenses. Globe has quarterly meetings with all employees—about 20 people at a time—to hear their views on how the company is approaching its plans and what could be done to solve any problems.

An innovative aspect of the Globe plan is its calendar format. In this calendar plan, project responsibilities are posted on specified dates, along with the names of the employees accountable to meet specific goals. The calendar, backed up by a vigorous follow-up system, has become a critical component in keeping Globe's quality implementation on track.

Customers also provide input into the planning process. Globe's quality planning teams visit customers prior to developing new products. The plant QEC committees then use various techniques, such as Pareto diagrams, storyboarding, and Failure Mode and Effects Analysis (FMEA), to translate this voice of the customer into the product design.

Quality Teams

To achieve increased employee participation in quality improvement, Globe launched quality circle teams (QCs) in 1986. The company has four formats for these QCs: departmental, interdepartmental, project, and interplant teams. Over 60 percent of the company's employees are participating on teams, and an average of 70 ideas a week are generated for improving quality, efficiency, and/or cost. All participation is voluntary, and employees are paid for their time working on teams.

Globe initiated a profit-sharing plan that applies to all employees, hourly and salaried. Each quarter, workers receive a dividend check: The average annual per-employee payout totals $5,000.

Results

The quality system Globe initiated in 1985 has brought clear, positive results. In June 1986, Ford presented a Q-1 award to Globe, the first ferroalloy company to be so recognized. General Motors awarded Globe its first Mark of Excellence Award.

Productivity improved over 50 percent in some areas of the operation. Market share for one high-end foundry product went from 5 percent to 50 percent in 1988.

In 1985, there were 44 customer complaints, with 49,000 pounds of product returned. By 1987, complaints were down to four, with no product returns—a 91 percent improvement overall. Figure 13.1 depicts those improvements.

Baldrige Award

In 1988, Globe became the first small business to win the Malcolm Baldrige Award. After this triumph, Kenneth E. Leach, Globe's vice president of administration commented, "What makes us stand up above our competitors for the National Quality Award? I think it's our keen focus on the customer, a very visible commitment from the leadership in our company to the total quality system, and our never-ending pursuit of the subject of continuous improvement."

Since winning, Globe continues to maintain its competitive quality advantage. Its U.S. market share has risen, and there has been an increase in European and Canadian sales. Overall business has grown 10 percent. Globe's commitment to quality is recognized by buyers in the United States and abroad, who stipulate that alloy materials they are purchasing must be "Globe Quality."

The most recent success for Globe has been the receipt in 1989 of the first annual Shigeo Shingo Prize for manufacturing excellence. This is a productivity-based award requiring that companies attribute cost savings to their quality initiatives. Based on $100 million in sales, Globe could

FIGURE 13.1
Globe Metallurgical Complaint/Returned Product History

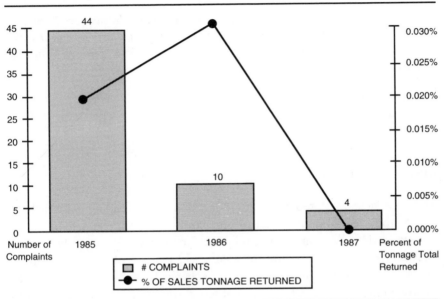

Source: Globe Metallurgical Inc.

attribute $10.3 million in savings to its quality process. The Shingo formula revealed that from 1986 through 1988, Globe improved productivity 367 percent. Globe has clearly reached the goal it set: that of becoming a leading world-class company.

MOTOROLA INC.: QUALITY ON A GRAND SCALE

We always knew that the customer was important. But now we know that the customer demands perfection. We can achieve perfection, and it's that higher expectation level that's probably been the single greatest thing that has happened to our company in the last ten years.

Robert W. Galvin,
Chairman of Executive Committee,
Motorola Inc.

Business Overview

Motorola, headquartered in Schaumburg, Illinois, is a leading manufacturer of electronic equipment, systems, and components in the United States and worldwide. Two-way radios and pagers account for 36 percent of annual sales; semiconductors account for another 32 percent of sales; and cellular telephone systems, defense and aerospace electronic systems, and automotive and industrial electronic equipment result in the remaining revenues. Sales, in 1987, were $6.7 billion.

In 1928, Paul V. Galvin founded the business that was responsible for the commercialization of car radios under the brand name Motorola. The company went on to become a leader in the electronics industry. In the 1960s, with the guidance of master-strategist Robert W. Galvin, Paul Galvin's son, the company moved away from consumer electronics and into high-tech industrial, commercial, and government fields.

During the mid-1970s, Motorola was hit hard by Japanese competitors. NEC, Hitachi, and Toshiba pushed Motorola out of some global electronics arenas. As the Japanese dumped higher quality products into the market, Motorola ceased production of televisions, stereo equipment, and car radios and eventually abandoned some semiconductor markets.

The Quality Crusade Begins

At an officers' meeting in 1979, Art Sundry, who headed the company's best division (two-way radios), bravely stood up and said, "Our quality stinks!" At the time, Motorola was number one in the industry, with over 50 percent market share. But customers weren't satisfied with delivery time, product reliability, and scores of other factors.

Bob Galvin describes this event as his "epiphany." He set Motorola in motion to challenge formidable Japanese competitors on the quality battle field. Under Galvin's visionary leadership, the company launched an almost evangelical crusade and began to put in place a range of quality improvement techniques, including agressive business objectives, statistical methods, and massive quality training.

In 1981, Motorola's Operating Policy Committee (made up of the company's highest echelon of executives) set a five-year goal for tenfold improvement in the quality of all products and services. To reach this stretch objective, Galvin recognized the company had to be overhauled. Like most American corporations, Motorola's existing culture accepted a certain level of imperfection as a normal part of doing business. The bulk of the then-50,000 employees thought that trying to reach near-perfect output would require so much additional time that products would be too costly and unaffordable to customers. This conventional "wisdom" was at the root of what needed to be changed in order to restore the company's competitive strength. If Motorola was to reach its 1986 objective of tenfold improvement, it had to transform itself on a grand scale and adopt new ways to run the business.

Total Customer Satisfaction

The transformation in thinking was propelled by top management. Motorola's fundamental objective became "Total Customer Satisfaction." Motorola's managers carry a business card in their pockets as a constant reminder of the corporate objective. Refer to Figure 13.2.

Corporate officers and managers donned pagers so that they would be instantly available to customers. Likewise, officers scheduled regular visits to customers' businesses to learn firsthand what customers liked and disliked about Motorola products. Customer surveys, complaint hot lines, field audits, and other customer feedback measures were integrated with planning for quality improvement and product development.

Common Culture, Common Language

It was critical to maximizing all efforts that the company have a common quality culture and language. Creating this was a monumental challenge in an enterprise as diverse and decentralized as Motorola. In the past, it generally had been accepted that each division knew best how to measure

FIGURE 13.2

OUR FUNDAMENTAL OBJECTIVE
(Everyone's Overriding Responsibility)
Total Customer Satisfaction
MOTOROLA, INC.

KEY BELIEFS—How We Will Always Act
  • Constant Respect for People
  • Uncompromising Integrity
KEY GOALS—What We Must Accomplish
  • Increased Global Market Share
  • Best in Class
    —People
    —Marketing
    —Technology
    —Product
    —Manufacturing
    —Service
  • Superior Financial Results
KEY INITIATIVES—How We Will Do It
  • Six Sigma Quality
  • Total Cycle Time Reduction
  • Product and Manufacturing Leadership
  • Profit Improvement
  • Participative Management within and Cooperation between Organizations

Source: Motorola, Inc.

its own quality levels. However, the net result of these dissimilar measurement systems was that it was virtually impossible for top management to assess and compare quality levels across the corporation, much less work toward common quality objectives.

Then, in 1986, the primary manufacturing plant, Communications or Comm Sector, cut through this Gordian knot by adopting a single metric for quality, *total defects per unit*. For the first time, all divisions within the sector could measure and compare their quality improvement rates. This common vocabulary enabled the Comm Sector to apply the defect reduction goal uniformly to all operations. Almost immediately, there was a substantial increase in the rate of improvement. These dramatic results influenced the entire corporation to adopt this uniform metric.

Motorola now had a common quality language, defects per unit of work, which gave people in all operations—manufacturing and business processes, operational and support services—the ability to talk to one another in the same terminology and have a common level of understanding. Defects are those things that cause customer dissatisfaction. Units are the output of an organization, such as a circuit board assembly, a material request, a line of software code, or a technical manual. The goal was to reduce the level of defects. The methodology that represented this common quality metric was Six Sigma, and it became one of the company's key initiatives deployed in order to reach its overriding objective of Total Customer Satisfaction.

Having met its 1981 target for a tenfold improvement in all products and services by 1986, Motorola's next goal became an additional tenfold improvement by 1989, and then a one-hundredfold improvement by 1991. The ultimate goal is to eliminate all defects in the corporation through achieving Six Sigma capability by 1992.

Six Sigma

Perfection is Motorola's goal. Six Sigma represents virtual perfection. Sigma is statistical parlance—an indicator of variation outside acceptable limits. The higher the sigma number, the less variation outside acceptable limits and the better the quality. When Motorola reaches Six Sigma, a customer will have to buy one million of its pagers or cellular phones to find three or four that do not work, have a cracked case, or have some other fault. The aim of achieving Six Sigma translates to 3.4 defects per million parts (ppm) or 99.9999998 percent perfect products, as shown in Figure 13.3.

FIGURE 13.3

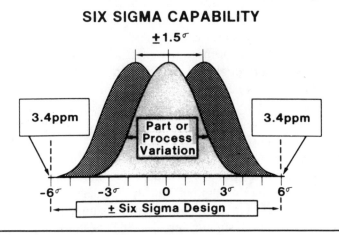

Source: Motorola, Inc.

Total Cycle Time Reduction

Another key initiative of Motorola is total cycle time reduction. Cycle time is the elapsed time from the placement of an order to delivery of the product to the customer. In the case of the company's custom-made Bravo pager, what used to take 13 weeks to manufacture was shortened to just two-and-one-half hours. Reengineering the pager brought down its defect rate. Motorola achieved a 30-to-1 reduction in factory time in its cellular telephone operation, with an accompanying 90 percent reduction in defects per unit over the previous model. The company cut the time required to fill a portable radio order from 55 days to 15; its 1991 goal is to go from 15 to 7 days.

This passion for quality and speed has spread beyond the manufacturing departments. Previously, Motorola's patent lawyers took 19 to 36 months to write and file a patent claim. That pedestrian pace has been cut to 2 months. The legal department's eventual Six Sigma goal: one-day service to get information about an invention from the engineers and file the claim.

Leadership

In the beginning of Motorola's quality initiative, the company's leadership reconstituted its monthly operating committee meeting to include quality.

Bob Galvin, Motorola's chairman, was scheduled to come in for the quality portion of the meeting. Quality was slotted on the agenda after the operations segment. However, the operating people repeatedly took the majority of the time discussing budgets and working over figures and quotas. Frustrated after four or five months of little, if any, time left for quality, Galvin decided things were upside down. He put quality first on the agenda. His belief was that if the quality was right, the profits would take care of themselves.

Motorola's management demonstrates its quality leadership in a variety of other ways. The Participative Management Program (PMP) is a system Motorola designed for organizational development. PMP teams involve employees in assessing progress toward quality goals, identifying new initiatives, and working on problem resolution. Through the PMP system, there is a sharing of the financial benefits of high-quality work. Team bonuses average three percent of Motorola's payroll.

Motorola knows what levels of quality its products must achieve to top its foreign and domestic competitors. The firm's six major groups and sectors have benchmarking initiatives to analyze all aspects of a competitor's products. Manufacturability, reliability, manufacturing cost, and performance of each competitor's products are assessed.

Education and Training

During a time when many companies were conducting huge layoffs and closing down entire operations to cut costs and stave off the competition, Galvin pioneered a massive corporate education and retraining effort. His actions were predicated on the belief that to be competitive for the long term requires an educated and trained work force. His foresight led to the development of one of the most comprehensive companywide programs in the United States. Today, Motorola offers employees more than 100 different quality-specific courses, ranging from Statistical Process Control (SPC) to design for manufacturability to the technical aspects of Six Sigma in manufacturing.

Between 1983 and 1987, the company spent more than $170 million for worker education to ensure that its employees had the necessary skills to achieve the company's quality and performance objectives. In 1989, Motorola invested $60 million for education, in 1990, it was $130 million, and in 1991, the amount reached $150 million. In excess of 40 percent of the total training is devoted to quality.

Despite this substantial dollar amount, Galvin has said the training hasn't really cost Motorola a penny—meaning the expense has more than paid for itself in benefits to the company. An independent audit verified this statement. The study revealed there was a 30-to-1 return for Motorola's education investment: For every dollar spent on education, there was a $30 improvement gain. At this point, Motorola does not require any further education audits because it has no need to justify the expenditures. Training has been institutionalized and enjoys the total support of management.

Supplier Partnerships

In 1982, Motorola initiated a program called Partnership for Growth, involving suppliers and Motorola purchasing people. The focus was on reducing adversarial relationships and entering into true partnerships. The results of the program have been dramatic. As a Baldrige winner, Motorola has done the most by far to spread the word on quality to suppliers. In an early 1989 letter, Motorola told 3,600 of its larger suppliers—vendors and distributors, including banks and insurance companies—that they, too, must be prepared to compete for the Baldrige Award. The 200 that refused were subsequently dropped as Motorola suppliers.

Results

In 1988, Motorola received the first Malcolm Baldrige National Quality Award in the manufacturing category. While Motorola officials cannot quantify precisely how much additional business has resulted from the Baldrige Award, they are convinced its benefits will continue to accrue over the long term. Calculations indicate that before Motorola raised its quality levels, it spent at least 5 to 10 percent, and in some cases as much as 20 percent, of its sales dollars on poor quality. From 1983 to 1989, defects at Motorola were reduced from 3,000 to less than 200 per million products. Striving toward Six Sigma has not only reduced defects and led to greater customer satisfaction, it has saved the company at least $250 million annually in production costs. The company continues its march to near perfection.

As a 1988 winner of the Baldrige Award, Motorola is eligible to compete again in five years. The company has announced it will apply for a second award.

Today, the company's products are the best in their class. Motorola now claims a major share of the Japanese pager market, and it is one of a number of high-tech manufacturers in the United States to successfully sell products in Japan. Also consider that in 1987, Motorola had 99,000 employees worldwide and $7 billion in sales; by 1990 there were 105,000 employees with sales of $11 billion.

George Fisher, Motorola's current chairman and CEO, said winning the Baldrige is a real accomplishment, but tougher challenges lay ahead on Motorola's path to achieving total customer satisfaction. His resolve is clear: "We intend to be the best manufacturer of electronics hardware in the world."

COMMERCIAL NUCLEAR FUEL DIVISION OF WESTINGHOUSE ELECTRIC CORPORATION: TURNING ON QUALITY

> *Total Quality is . . . our most powerful strategy for winning in the world marketplace. It results in value creation for our shareholders, personal pride and satisfaction for our employees, and quality performance for our customers.*

John C. Marous,
Chairman and CEO (1988–1990),
Westinghouse Electric Corporation

> *A major turning point in our history was the day in 1979 that our corporate management decided we would compete on the basis of quality. They knew the concept of continuous quality improvement transcended the quality assurance department, and it was much more than a cost reduction tool. They realized that it would be a powerful fundamental strategy for running the entire corporation, and that took vision.*

Mead D'Amore,
General Manager, Commercial Nuclear Fuel Division,
Westinghouse Electric Corporation

Business Overview

The Westinghouse Commercial Nuclear Fuel Division (CNFD) engineers, manufactures, and supplies fuel-rod assemblies for electrical utilities operating nuclear power reactors. CNFD was established in 1969 as a division within the Westinghouse Nuclear Fuel Business Unit. CNFD fabricates pressurized water reactor (PWR) fuel assemblies. There are more than 2,100 employees in CNFD, located at four sites: the Western Zirconium Plant near Ogden, Utah; the Specialty Metals Plant in Blairsville, Pennsylvania; the Fuel Manufacturing Plant in Columbia, South Carolina; and the headquarters and engineering facilities, both in Monroeville, Pennsylvania. Since 1969, the Specialty Metals Plant has produced over 120 million feet of zircalloy tubing, and the Columbia plant has fabricated over 28,000 nuclear fuel-rod assemblies. The company estimates that seven percent of the electricity consumed in the United States in 1987 was produced by Westinghouse nuclear fuel rods. Estimated 1990 sales for the CNFD were $350 million.

The quality of CNFD's products and services has led to a market leadership role: The company commands 40 percent of the U.S. light water reactor fuel market and 20 percent of the rest of the free world market. Quality requirements for nuclear fuel-rod assemblies are demanding in a production process involving thousands of variables in chemical and mechanical operations.

The fuel-rod assemblies CNFD manufactures form the core of a nuclear power reactor. A typical 1,100 megawatt electric nuclear plant houses approximately 51,000 fuel rods containing over 18 million uranium dioxide fuel pellets. All components must reliably operate for up to five years in a highly corrosive, high-temperature, high-pressure environment. Error could be catastrophic. Quality is crucial.

A Quantum Leap in Quality

From the time CNFD was established in 1969, quality efforts focused on meeting regulatory requirements through inspection-based systems, detailed procedures, extensive documentation, and frequent auditing. In a critical area, where quality standards have always been of the utmost importance, the CNFD quality assurance program was a model for its own and other industries.

Then, early in the 1980s, the marketplace forced changes in the company's quality approach. A virtual moratorium on nuclear power plant construction flattened demand. As the bottom fell out of the fuel-rod assembly market for new reactors, CNFD shifted its focus to providing reload fuel to existing power plants. Competition increased domestically as firms targeted the finite number of free-world nuclear power reactors; it increased globally as more foreign firms entered the nuclear fuels market.

Suddenly, simply meeting the standards (albeit very high standards) wasn't enough. In a shrinking market, only the best companies would survive. CNFD realized that a commitment to total quality would provide it with a clear competitive advantage. Acting on this, the division initiated its quality program in 1983. Continuous quality improvement became CNFD's strategy, and its annual Quality Plan became the primary communications tool. This plan was provided to employees, customers, and key suppliers.

Knowing quality goals would not be achieved overnight, the Quality Plan documented the actions to be taken to achieve continuous improvement. Every year after 1983, CNFD sharpened the program's focus and direction. In each year, the company selected a new theme that reflected its progress and the maturation of its quality culture. From 1983 to 1988, when the company won the Baldrige Award, the themes were:

- 1983—Increase general employee awareness of the importance of quality to its business.
- 1984—Track and report the quality failure costs.
- 1985—Establish the first divisionwide quality goals and accompanying first-level measurement system to monitor progress.
- 1986—Create a divisionwide mission statement and add second-level (department) and third-level (group) quality measures.
- 1987—Focus on customer orientation and include satisfaction rating to first-level measurement system.
- 1988—Achieve Total Quality in the Division.

Total Quality Culture

In order for CNFD to hold its market leadership position, the company's quality strategy was to add value for customers, improve productivity, and lower costs. In 1984, CNFD's goal was to be recognized as the world's highest-quality supplier of fuel-rod assemblies. To succeed, top management needed to be tangibly involved. Instead of delegating quality to one individual or a department, the decision was made to initiate a quality council to manage the quality improvement process. This quality council comprised the division's general managers, who were given key responsibilities to direct and coordinate quality improvement initiatives. Attainment of that goal required a transformation of the work environment into a quality-driven, quality-obsessed culture. This direct involvement of the people who daily managed the business, coupled with the resources provided by the corporate Productivity and Quality Center, became the foundation to support the quality initiative. From this base, quality was integrated into all activities in design, production, and customer service functions.

Starting slowly at first and then gaining momentum, members of the management team bought into the quality vision. Awareness of the company's quality mission gradually spread to employees, and the foundation was laid for a Total Quality culture. Westinghouse defines Total Quality as "performance leadership in meeting customer requirements by doing the right things right the first time." The company's commitment to Total Quality has been driven to all facets of the business, from engineering to information systems to human resource management. Customer satisfaction is the focus of Westinghouse's Total Quality culture.

Productivity and Quality Center

CNFD used the Total Quality model designed in the Westinghouse Productivity and Quality Center. This model is based on four key imperatives for continuous improvement: management leadership, product and process leadership, human resource excellence, and customer orientation. Twelve conditions of excellence are applied to the four imperatives, as displayed in Figure 13.4.

Pulse Points

CNFD's annual Quality Plan identifies the division's short- and long-term goals and translates them into measures called Pulse Points. The CNFD Pulse Points system was created in 1985 to track eight vital areas of the division. The Pulse Points are the key measures of customer satisfaction and internal performance. They include error-free software, on-time soft-

FIGURE 13.4
Total Quality Requires a Total Quality Culture

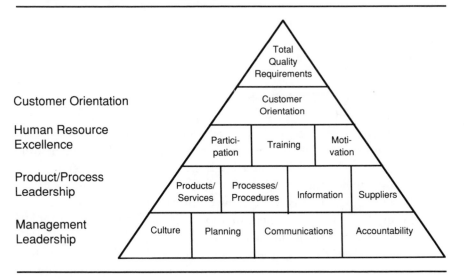

Source: CNFD, Westinghouse Electric Corp.

ware, on-time hardware, fuel reliability, once-through assembly yield, once-through cladding yield, total quality costs, and customer satisfaction. To accomplish the division's objectives, each department developed supporting, quantifiable goals that cascaded down to each worker.

Using statistical techniques and evaluation methods, hundreds of performance areas are monitored and analyzed. On a monthly basis, vital information for quality improvement is reviewed in a teleconference by the Quality Council, which checks progress on 55 division and department pulse points. Progress is also communicated to employees in workgroup meetings, and the top-level Pulse Point measures are posted at all CNFD locations.

Human Resource Excellance

Participative management became the cornerstone of CNFD's Total Quality culture. Each department manager established Total Quality improvement goals that were reviewed with employees. All management and professional employees set personal quality improvement objectives through a performance management system (PMS). In 1987, the division had 175 Quality Teams in place that involved more than 1,400 employees. From 1985 to 1988, approximately 90 percent of all employees participated in quality training. Employee quality improvement suggestions increased from 425 in 1985 to 2,000 in 1988.

Results

CNFD's Total Quality approach has produced significant results. From 1984 to 1987, reductions in scrap and rework, as well as improved manufacturing cycle time, led to enhanced yields on first-time-through fuel rods, increasing from less than 50 percent to 87 percent. On-time delivery of finished assemblies and related hardware reached 100 percent. Total quality costs, which included internal and external failure costs and prevention and appraisal costs, were reduced by 30 percent.

From 1985 to 1988, nuclear fuel-rod reliability improved from 99.95 percent to 99.995 percent, and it is approaching 99.9995 percent. In 1987, the value of CNFD's new orders reached a decade high, and more than 90 percent of the orders were from existing customers. Productivity has also shown dramatic increases. From 1982 to 1987, the corporation's net income per employee more than doubled, from $3,100 to $6,600. CFND's customer-satisfaction rating increased six percent from 1987 to 1988.

In 1988, the first year the Baldrige Awards were presented, the Commercial Nuclear Fuel Division of Westinghouse was one of three recipients. After CNFD received the nation's top quality prize, General Manager Mead D'Amore remarked, "We have made significant progress since we embarked on our quality quest eight years ago. We have transformed our organization into a Total Quality culture. Virtually every quality goal we established for ourselves in past quality plans has been achieved or exceeded—in some cases, years ahead of schedule." Then, in 1988, Mead D'Amore was awarded the Westinghouse Order of Merit—the corporation's highest individual honor for his notable contributions to the division.

Westinghouse Quality Award

To further spread total quality management throughout the entire Westinghouse corporation, Chairman John Marous expected the 90 corporate divisions to compete for the annual George Westinghouse Quality Awards Program. There are two prizes: best unit overall and most improved. The Westinghouse internal award process parallels Baldrige. In 1989, the best unit was Thermo King Truck Trailer division, which automatically became the Westinghouse candidate to apply for the 1990 Baldrige Award.

The success of CNFD's quality process is due in part to Westinghouse's efforts in a number of areas. While Westinghouse has a corporate-wide approach, it also provides for customization to accommodate local needs. The goal is that each division take control in establishing a strategy tailored to meet its unique needs. This is an important idea that many more U.S. corporations could take to heart.

CHAPTER 14

1989 AWARD WINNERS: WHAT IT TAKES TO WIN

All American firms benefit by having a standard of excellence to match and perhaps, one day, to surpass. For 1989 there can be no higher standard of quality management than those provided by the winners of the Malcolm Baldrige National Quality Award—Milliken & Company and Xerox.

George Bush
November 2, 1989

MILLIKEN & COMPANY:
IF AT FIRST YOU DON'T SUCCEED

We . . . work very hard empowering people to shut down the machinery if they find it making a defect or creating a safety hazard. And more and more we are finding that instead of thousands and thousands of pounds going through with a defect, the production associate will find it right off.

Roger Milliken,
Chairman and Chief Executive Officer,
Milliken & Company

Business Overview

Milliken & Company is a privately owned textile and chemical firm established 126 years ago and headquartered in Spartanburg, South Carolina. The company's 28 various businesses manufacture over 48,000 textile and chemical products for 8,500 worldwide customers. The majority of the company's 14,300 associates, as Milliken refers to its employees, are in the company's 47 manufacturing facilities scattered across the United States. In 1989, annual sales exceeded $1 billion.

Through most of the 1970s, Milliken was regarded as the undisputed textile technology leader. Milliken was a company known for being financially strong, having good people, leading in textile research, and manufacturing quality products with state-of-the-art technology. However, as the textile industry began to change, what once was good was no longer good enough.

In the late 1970s and early 1980s, Milliken began to feel the tremendous threat of foreign competition. Pacific Rim companies were assaulting the U.S. textile market with lower-cost, higher-quality imports. Milliken officials knew they had to do something. In searching for ways to improve, the company conducted benchmarking trips to Japan. Milliken teams discovered something unexpected. With less sophisticated equipment, the Japanese were turning out higher-quality products and were more productive. A principal reason for this was that on average, 22 percent of all Japanese manufacturing management was devoted to process improvement. Milliken officials recognized that Japanese success grew out of management methods, including quality systems and the handling of human resources. The impact of this discovery initiated the quality revolution at Milliken.

Pursuit of Excellence

Led by Roger Milliken, whose grandfather founded the company, the pursuit of excellence began. In 1980, Milliken's top several hundred management members participated in what became the first annual four-day, off-site meeting to zero in on quality. Roger Milliken fostered a spirit of commitment and cooperation. The company's goal became to match Milliken's human capabilities with its technical strengths. To meet the challenges of industry changes and the competition, Milliken initiated a total commitment to customer satisfaction and, in 1981, launched its Pursuit of Excellence (POE) program.

As a way to move forward, there was initial interest in starting quality circles to involve the production people in quality improvement. Fortunately, a wise adviser interceded, asking management if it had the conviction to support the tremendous change quality circle involvement would bring. Understanding that it had to change first, management began its quality journey by learning how and what to change. Managers and administrative associates attended courses in quality fundamentals; the company began measuring the cost of quality; a quality vice president was appointed; and the senior management team was given a key role.

Leadership Excellence

From the beginning, Roger Milliken and Thomas J. Malone, chief operating officer, led the revolution. Fully half their time was devoted to the POE process. As a major part of their commitment, they set aside the first four-and-a-half hours in the monthly policy meeting for quality. Every month in this mandatory meeting they heard quality task force summaries and reports on customer visits, went over quality measurements, and reviewed where the company stood in its pursuit of excellence.

Human resources became a pivot point for Milliken's revolution. In fact, Tom Peters dedicated *Thriving on Chaos* to Roger Milliken for his genius in responding to the competition with "unparalleled quality attained largely through people." Associates at Milliken were regarded as more than employees; they were an important part of the total process. The company took action to make every Milliken associate an autonomous, self-managed worker.

The organizational configuration at Milliken was made considerably flatter by taking 700 manufacturing and administrative managers and reassigning them to new positions as process improvement specialists. This spread the span of control (number of subordinates a manager supervises). The ratio of production to management associates was increased by 77 percent. Instead of relying on management to make changes, associates now worked directly to improve work processes themselves. Self-managed work teams were empowered to conduct scheduling and set performance objectives, and all employees were given the authority to stop the production line for quality and safety reasons. Associates received cross-training so they could rotate jobs.

Consistent with its valuing of people, the company removed artificial barriers that could make associates feel unimportant. As one way to emphasize open communications, the company established the ultimate in open-door policies: There were no doors. There were no executive dining rooms. The company did not believe in reserved executive parking places, which meant Roger Milliken parked his car and walked. Measures such as these served to emphasize the importance of associates in the company's quality process.

Milliken's Pursuit of Excellence encouraged team involvement by establishing three team approaches to quality participation: Customer Action Teams, Supplier Action Teams, and Corrective Action Teams. Corrective Action Teams became the most common team practice, and the company had 1,597 such teams in 1988. That same year there were 200 Supplier Action Teams working in partnership with suppliers to meet Milliken's expectations, and 500 Customer Action Teams that dealt with problems directly affecting customers.

Customer-Driven Quality

Customer satisfaction drove the Milliken planning process. The company's intent was to compete on the basis of quality, service, and innovation. Strategic planning input came through a variety of sources, including annual customer surveys. Additionally, Milliken conducted extensive benchmarking (at more than 400 companies worldwide!), seeking the best methods, systems, technologies, and techniques in every area of operation. Milliken looked to such companies as Hewlett-Packard, which gave Milliken the idea for open offices; Xerox, which taught Milliken to benchmark; Motorola, which set standards for education; and IBM, which excelled at customer surveys.

In Customer Action Teams (CATs), Milliken associates worked with customers, resolving problems and finding ways to be more responsive to special customer needs. Each CAT was chaired by the sales associates responsible for those customers. Insights gained in CATs were then fed into the planning process.

The requirements of customers' customers also became more important to Milliken. In one case, to learn firsthand the needs of a hospital supplied by a Milliken carpet dealer, a Milliken manager worked the third shift at the hospital. While on the job, the associate checked for ease in rolling equipment on the carpet and was alert for any special carpet-cleaning problems. (Milliken later recognized this noble effort by presenting the associate with a "Bed Pan Award.")

Time is now used as a competitive advantage by communicating to customers and suppliers in real time—electronically. Electronic Data Interchange (EDI) connects Milliken with customers and suppliers. Through its MIDAS data access system, customers can check an order's status, including the carpet rolls' shade category, size, and position in the truck. Milliken is teaching customers and suppliers to routinely use EDI. Customers can even electronically access Milliken's design system, which shortens product development cycle-time.

10-4 Objectives

Milliken first applied for the Baldrige Award in 1988, received a site visit, but did not win. Among areas cited for improvement by the Baldrige examiners was Milliken's need for more aggressive objectives. Milliken's response was to dismiss its complacent seven percent annual improvement goal and adopt what it called its 10-4 objectives in April 1989. The company's new strategy became to gain a tenfold improvement in all functions over the next four years.

Education and Training

Constant education was required to bring about continuous total quality improvement. Milliken placed special interest in five education areas: cross-training and self-management, Statistical Process Control (SPC), presentation and self-confidence, engineering courses, and health education and safety awareness programs.

Milliken's commitment to associate education is extensive. In 1988, the company spent $1,300 per associate and in 1989, over $1,800 per associate. In-house courses number over 400 and range from the economics of international trade to advanced Statistical Process Control. New hires take part in Leadership Training, a six-week orientation program. While all management people are required to take at least 40 hours of professional education annually, these minimums are routinely superceded. The actual average number of hours spent on education in 1989 was 99 per management associate.

Milliken's 1988 Baldrige Feedback Report indicated that an area of improvement was the use of Statistical Process Control. Milliken took action and had first management and then all associates trained in SPC tools. Milliken also provided training for customers and suppliers.

OFI

Milliken discovered early on that something as simple as choosing the proper phrase can sometimes make a big difference in involving employees in quality improvement. In trying to use an Error Cause Removal (ECR) method to identify problems, the newly formed task forces ran into trouble. People had difficulty believing that management truly wanted to hear their suggestions to on-the-job problems. A site manager came up with an idea that turned things around. By renaming the ERC process Opportunity for Improvement, any stigma of admitting a personal error was removed, and employee resistance dissipated.

The Opportunity for Improvement (OFI) process has been an enormous success. The first year of OFIs yielded an average of one-half suggestion per associate. In year two, there was one per associate; year three brought two; year four had four; year five bore eight; and then, in year six, there were 17. And on it went. In 1989, there was an average 19 OFIs per associate, and in 1990, 39.3. That totalled 472,884 OFIs for one year. The 1990 completion rate was 85 percent. While OFI stands for Opportunity for Improvement, it could just as well mean Opportunity for Involvement, because that seems to be the message. The involvement people feel in making suggestions and seeing them adopted not only contributes to a sense of ownership by being a part of improvement, it also shows people their tangible contribution to the company's progress. Within 24 hours, associates submitting an OFI receive a written acknowledgment; within 72 hours, either a completion or a plan for finding a solution is created. Figure 14.1 gives excerpts of Milliken's OFI data. Figure 14.2 shows a sample form.

Recognition

Milliken believed recognition was the great motivator and went to great lengths to recognize both individuals and teams. Top achieving associates became presenters at both Policy Committee meetings and at quality meetings. The company compiled feedback logs of recognized associates and posted their photographs. Associates who obtained patents were honored in the Innovators Hall of Fame. There were hero success stories, awards banquets, measurement scoreboards, and thank yous.

"Sharing rallies" became one of the company's most effective means of recognition. A sharing rally is a two-day series of presentations from production, administrative, and management associates. Rallies are held every quarter in the three major headquarters locations, where 300 to 400 associates hear four-minute presentations of improvement ideas and results.

FIGURE 14.1
Milliken & Company Opportunities for Improvement Process (OFIs)

1989 RESULTS	*1990 RESULTS*
• 262,000 OFIs submitted.	• 472,884 OFIs turned in.
• 19 per Milliken associate.	• 39.3 per Milliken associate.
• 87% completion rate.	• 85% completion rate.

WHAT THE MILLIKEN IDEA PROCESS IS
- Simple.
- No approval committee required except for major expenditure.
- A vehicle for associate involvement.
- A method to capture everyone's ideas.

WE USE NO FINANCIAL REWARD
- Financial rewards tend to focus people on big changes. We want the many little ideas—not just the few big ones.
- Financial rewards tend to work against "Teams."
- Less than half of our OFIs are for cost reduction.
- We believe that ideas and continuous improvement should be a part of every job, every day, and hence should not have a separate financial reward system.

Source: Milliken & Company

FIGURE 14.2
Sample OFI Form

OPPORTUNITY FOR IMPROVEMENT	No.
MILLIKEN	

Submitted By: Phone No: Mail Stop No:	Supervisor:	Date:

Opportunity/Obstacle/Optional Recommendation	TYPE
	Quality Improvement ☐ Cost Reduction ☐ Innovation ☐ Safety ☐ Energy ☐

Supervisor Action: (Please Acknowledge Within 24 Hours)   Date:

Final Action: Date:

Source: Milliken & Company

Individual and team accomplishments are recognized. Top management is always there. Recognition is given in the form of prizes, certificates, and, in true Milliken style, applause, applause, and applause. One of the ideas that scored a major hit was from an accounts payable department associate who had discovered the company lost $800,000 a year by not taking discounts for on-time payment. Follow-up revealed a lag from the time the plant received materials to the time accounting was notified. Improvement in the cycle time of reporting led to reducing losses the following year to $14,000, and in a savings of nearly $800,000.

Empowered people working together to make improvements was a cornerstone of Milliken's success. As Thomas J. Malone, Milliken's president and chief operating officer remarked, "If I had to say one word that summarizes what's made it possible, it's teamwork."

Results

For the South Carolina–based company, the wisdom of a customer-driven, quality-focused, associate-teamwork approach to improvement is verified by its success. From 1982 to 1988, Milliken reduced the cost of nonconformance by 60 percent. One yield from the company's supplier initiatives is that since 1981 there has been a 72 percent reduction in the number of suppliers. When benchmarking revealed that Milliken's deliveries were behind its competitors', a new goal was established, resulting in an improvement to the industry's best in 1988: 99 percent on-time deliveries, up from 77 percent in 1984.

The rest, as they say, is history. Having first applied for a Baldrige Award in 1988, a keener and stronger Milliken came back to win the Baldrige in 1989. The company's strength is evidenced in its growth: In 1989, sales were approximately $1 billion, by 1990, sales were estimated at $2 billion.

XEROX BUSINESS PRODUCTS AND SYSTEMS:
A RACE WITH NO FINISH LINE

If you are thinking about applying for the National Quality Award, go for it. It will change you and it will positively change your company more than you can possibly imagine. Two or three years from now your expectation levels and what you will realize is possible will pale by anything that you are currently thinking about.

David T. Kearns,
Chairman and Chief Executive Officer (1982–1991),
Xerox Corporation

Business Overview

Xerox Business Products and Systems (BP&S) is one of two Xerox Corporation businesses, the other being Financial Services. Xerox corporate headquarters are located in Stamford, Connecticut. BP&S has over 83 U.S. locations and 50,200 employees. It produces more than 250 types of document-processing machines. In 1988, U.S. sales were $6 billion. Copiers and other duplicating equipment generated nearly 70 percent of its revenue. The rest was split between typing equipment, electronic printers, workstations, networks, and software products.

Xerox created the world's plain-paper copier industry with the introduction of the 914 model in 1959. In its first 15 years, the company experienced explosive growth: Revenues jumped from $33 million in 1959 to $176 million in 1963, and to $4 billion by 1975.

However, by the mid-1970s, Xerox experienced two signal changes. The first blow came when the company was required by Federal Trade Commission settlements to open international access to its key patents. Xerox no longer enjoyed the protection of exclusive use of the reprographic process. Additionally, competition—both foreign and domestic—was invading the copier industry. Aggressive Japanese firms struck first at the low-end equipment market. IBM directed its blows to the middle, and Eastman Kodak hit the high-end market. Initially, competition was largely ignored by Xerox, and its market share eroded to less than 50 percent by 1980. From the mid-1970s to the early 1980s, revenue growth dropped to an average annual rate of approximately 16 percent (down from 23 percent per year in the mid-sixties through the mid-seventies), and profit growth fell to 14 percent per year (down from 20 percent the previous decade).

Japanese companies were selling copiers of similar or higher quality in the United States for what it cost Xerox to *make* its copiers, that is the unit manufacturing costs alone, not distribution costs. Also, Xerox took twice as long as Japanese competitors to develop products. In short, the Japanese brought more reliable products to market faster and retailed them for less than Xerox could manufacture its products.

Xerox initiated a series of changes to combat the growing crisis: The organization restructured itself into strategic business units; a customer satisfaction management system was developed; resizing reduced the number of employees worldwide. In 1979, employee involvement started in manufacturing, and Xerox people participated in improvement efforts. Also starting in 1979, Xerox developed competitive benchmarking to measure its products and services against the world's best. In 1981, benchmarking efforts expanded to cover the entire corporation.

David Kearns, Xerox chairman and chief executive officer, stated, "Xerox was in a battle for survival." During 1981 and 1982, Kearns made 23 trips to affiliate Fuji Xerox in Japan. The information gained on those visits proved invaluable. Competition had hammered Fuji Xerox, causing market share losses and declining profits. By focusing on quality, the company engineered an extraordinary turnaround and in 1980 was awarded Japan's Deming Prize for quality.

Kearns observed that Japanese business leaders' higher expectations for quality, relative to those of Americans and Europeans, were their prime strength. To meet the challenges of cost and competition, Kearns determined to use quality as the means to initiate a cultural revolution at Xerox. The question then became how to effectively implement quality in a megacorporation.

Leadership through Quality

Survival required fundamental changes in managing the business. In 1982, the Corporate Management Committee headed by Kearns resolved to implement quality throughout the corporation. Starting in late 1983, the senior leadership team began to develop Xerox's total quality initiative: Leadership Through Quality. This team of the 25 top operating executives developed the quality policy, strategy, and implementation plan. The foundation was laid in this policy statement:

Xerox is a quality company. Quality is the basic business principle for Xerox. Quality means providing our external and internal customers with innovative products and services that fully satisfy their requirements: Quality improvement is the job of every Xerox employee.

There were five major change mechanisms in the Leadership Through Quality initiative to support the transformation of the company:

- *Management:* Commit to attainment of strategic quality goals. Serve as role models for implementation of Leadership Through Quality.
- *Standards and measurements:* Provide tools and techniques to quantify quality improvement. This includes a six-step problem-solving process, a nine-step quality improvement process, and benchmarking.
- *Training:* Educate every employee in the Leadership Through Quality process. Starting with the training of top managers, have them participate in training their subordinates.
- *Recognition and reward:* Ensure both individuals and groups are motivated and recognized for practicing and improving quality.
- *Communications:* Inform employees consistently and effectively of the corporate priorities and objectives and progress toward meeting these goals.

To address the magnitude of the cultural change required to become a quality company, a quality implementation team was established to manage the transition. The team consisted of 15 field and staff managers. Kearns formed a corporate quality office and appointed a corporate quality vice president. Senior Xerox managers served as role models for quality through their active involvement in quality teams and quality presentations to other companies and groups, including government agencies. Strong emphasis was given to management behavior and action. Managers were expected to demonstrate competencies in quality goal setting, teamwork, and recognition for quality initiatives.

Quality Strategy

Leadership Through Quality's unifying goal was satisfying the customer. To meet this, the focus of the company's strategic planning was on knowing the customer, meeting his or her needs completely, and providing process measurements and mechanisms for continuous improvement. Supporting the planning process were the company's customer orientation, employee involvement, and benchmarking.

Xerox's Benchmarking Process

In the drive for world-class status, Xerox developed a benchmarking process to compare its functions with similar functions of other companies. Benchmarking is the continuous search for the best practices that lead to superior performance. It is a systematic way to measure performance capabilities of competitors or recognized leaders, and then develop plans to meet or exceed those levels. Xerox's outline for its competitive benchmarking process is illustrated in Figure 14.3. In benchmarking the toughest competition, the benchmark is not based on the competitors' current achievements but the projection of where that competitor will be in the coming years. This enables Xerox to compete against competitors' furture performance.

Xerox benchmarks both results and, more importantly, the processes that lead to the results. While the company used only 14 benchmark measurements in 1984 to compare such items as product quality, delivery, and costs, by 1989 that had expanded to about 240 separate comparisons of the company's products, services, and practices. Eventually, benchmarking became so pervasive that Xerox no longer counted all the areas of comparison.

As would be expected, Xerox BP&S benchmarked competitors such as IBM, Canon, and Kodak. But it also benchmarked the best practices of others, including L.L. Bean for distribution networks, American Express for billing systems, and Cummins Engine Co., for daily production schedules.

Quality Training

Starting with the six senior Xerox people, including David Kearns, the Leadership Through Quality course cascaded down until all employees were trained. The exact same training program was used throughout the entire company. This helped build the desired shared vocabulary and unified quality process.

Each year Xerox spends 2.5 to 3 percent of its revenue on education. From 1984 to 1988, an additional $125 million was spent exclusively on quality training. All Xerox Business Products and Systems employees have received at least 28 hours of quality-specific training.

FIGURE 14.3
Competitive Benchmarking: Key Process Phases

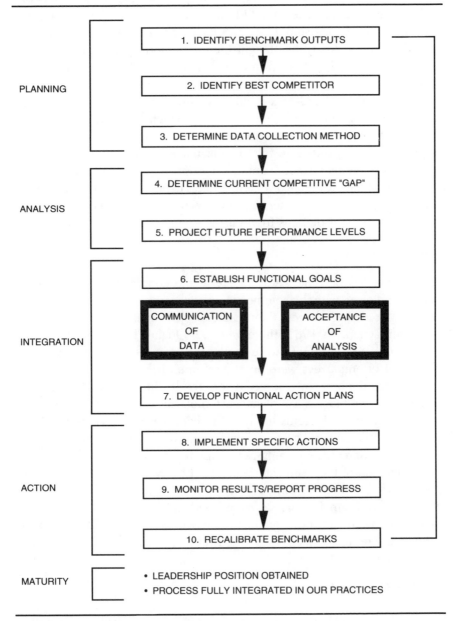

© Copyright 1987 Xerox Corporation

To produce the desired behavioral change, the company's strategy was to have managers become role models for quality. The method used was the learn, use, teach, inspect (LUTI) approach. This meant that managers first learned the Leadership Through Quality process and tools, then used them themselves. Next, they taught them to subordinates and, finally, inspected the outcomes—their own and their groups'—for utilization of the training.

Communication at Xerox is enhanced through the common language of the Leadership Through Quality process, which has furthered the positive impact of quality on the company's performance and has been a key means to embed quality into the organization's culture.

In 1980, Xerox formed a unique union-management partnership and put in place an employee involvement process to benefit both the employees and the business. This partnership has grown over the years to become a model for other corporations to emulate.

Team Xerox

Team Xerox has become a way of life at the company. The drive is to provide employees with the common language, common skills, and common processes needed to harness their assets to push quality and achieve customer satisfaction. In 1981, there were 31 Quality Improvement Teams (QITs). In 1983, 105 QITs were in place, and in 1986, 2,500. By 1988, 75 percent of employees were on at least one of the 7,000 QITs.

Teamwork Day showcases teamwork results throughout the company. In addition to employees, suppliers, customers, and consultants are invited. Each year since 1984, Xerox has held this companywide recognition event to celebrate its quality successes. Units from throughout the company nominate quality improvement teams. Senior management is active in the review and recognition of the team achievements. The event has grown from one location to four across the United States. There are a number of recognition vehicles: The Team Excellence Award and the Excellence in Customer Satisfaction Award acknowledge the most outstanding work of Xerox teams. Individuals are recognized with the President's Award and the Xerox Achievement Award.

Supplier Certification

In 1982, eight percent of parts supplied to Xerox were defective. To reduce that defect rate, Xerox instituted a certification process that required suppliers go through an ordered procedure to analyze their processes. Suppliers that met the requirements were awarded Certified Supplier status. Suppliers were also invited to take part in the Product Delivery Process, which allowed them to be significantly involved in product design and manufacturing. Additionally, Xerox began training suppliers in total quality, Statistical Process Control, and just-in-time delivery.

Results

Results of working with suppliers included thinning the supplier base from more than 5,000 in 1980 to about 400 in 1989. By improving the quality operations of suppliers, Xerox reduced incoming inspections from 85 to 15 percent; the need for inspectors has been lowered 85 percent.

Market share increased to 25 percent in 1988, up from 10 percent in 1984. As a result of qualifying suppliers, there has been a 73 percent reduction in defective parts. Defects per 100 machines have decreased 78 percent. Unscheduled maintenance has been minimized 40 percent. Service response time has dropped 27 percent.

Xerox designed more predictable, systematic approaches with Statistical Process Control and reduced the variability of its manufacturing and service practices. As an example, the number of bookkeeping errors for supplier payments has been abated from one for every 100 to one per 1,000.

Between 1984 and 1988, customer satisfaction increased 38 percent; materials overhead was lowered 40 percent; and labor overhead was reduced 50 percent. Since 1983, average manufacturing costs have been cut by 20 percent despite inflation; cycle time for new product introduction has been shortened by 60 percent; revenue per employee has been increased 20 percent. In 1984, BP&S revenues were $8.7 billion; by 1989, revenues climbed to $12.4 billion

In 1989, Xerox Business Products and Systems was honored for its achievements in manufacturing excellence with the Malcolm Baldrige Award. By 1990, revenues reached $14 billion. Xerox now has the industry's highest customer satisfaction ratings for mid- and high-volume copiers, and it is one of the first U.S. companies ever to win back market share from Japanese competitors.

CHAPTER 15

1990 AWARD WINNERS: WINNING IS JUST THE BEGINNING

The men and women of these four firms have . . . proven that quality management is not just a strategy. It must be a new style of working, even a style of thinking. Dedication to quality and excellence is more than good business, it's a way of life.

George Bush
December 13, 1990

CADILLAC MOTOR CAR COMPANY: RECLAIMING A LEGACY OF QUALITY

At Cadillac, our road map to a new way of doing business was crafted some five years ago, when in 1985 we stopped ourselves long enough to realize that we were going down the wrong track. Our heritage of excellence is both a blessing and a responsibility. Our owners demand a great deal from their cars and the company with which they do business—as well they should. The buying public today is unforgiving, and we knew back in the mid-1980s that we needed to make some changes if we were going to remain their carmaker of choice.

John O. Grettenberger,
General Manager,
Cadillac Motor Car Company

Business Overview

Cadillac, founded in 1902 by Henry Martin Leland, is the flagship of the General Motors (GM) operation. John O. Grettenberger is general manager of the Cadillac division, which is responsible for producing nine luxury car models: six Cadillac models, two Buick models that are marketed by Buick (GM), and one Oldsmobile model. The nearly 10,000 Cadillac employees are located in the Detroit-area headquarters, four manufacturing plants in Michigan, and 10 sales-zone and service offices in the United States. Cadillac's franchised dealership network covers 1,600 sites. Sales in 1990 were estimated at $8 billion.

A New Definition of Quality

The American auto industry has been besieged for the past two decades by foreign competition. While Cadillac had long been a symbol of quality, competition began to erode its market share in the early 1980s. The company made a number of strategic errors, notably the downsizing of its luxury cars, which met with consumer disappointment. Likewise, its longstanding reputation for quality was being eroded by less luxurious but more reliable imports. Cadillac recognized that improved quality and customer satisfaction were central to its survival into the next century.

The company's turnaround focused on three strategies: cultural change emphasizing teamwork and employee involvement; constant customer focus; and disciplined strategic planning. Integration of these strategies laid the foundation for Cadillac's total quality retooling. Four key initiatives involved employees in the total quality process: Simultaneous Engineering, supplier partnerships, the UAW-GM Quality Network, and Cadillac's People Strategy.

Simultaneous Engineering

The challenge to change the organization began in 1985 with a product development process called Simultaneous Engineering (SE). SE turned around traditional design and engineering methods. It also turned around the company's organizational structure (see Figure 15.1). The executive staff was placed at the base of a pyramid, demonstrating its role as leading in the creation and support of systems focused on the pinnacle of customer satisfaction. Success with this new structure and Simultaneous Engineering required teamwork.

FIGURE 15.1
The Cadillac Simultaneous Engineering Pyramid

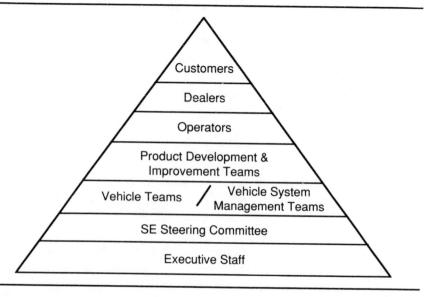

Source: Cadillac Motor Car Company

Unlike the past, when designers threw plans "over the wall" to engineers, who then threw them to suppliers and manufacturing, Simultaneous Engineering integrates all aspects of the product development and improvement process. Executive staff members and the SE steering committee support the SE team structure of vehicle teams, vehicle system management teams, and product development and improvement teams. These teams are responsible for quality, cost, timing, and vehicle system and component technology. Cross-functional integration is used to transfer knowledge from design to manufacturing and on to the market. Simultaneous Engineering is transforming Cadillac's culture. There are 69 SE teams with 750 employees representing both hourly and salaried workers. SE team improvements include a cycle-time reduction in implementing major styling changes from 175 weeks to 50–85 weeks.

In 1987, transformation was accelerated with a reorganization that resulted in Cadillac becoming an integrated car company. As a single business unit, Cadillac had total responsibility for engineering, manufacturing, and marketing. This change further emphasized the need for integration and teamwork.

The company's leaders asked employees, dealers, suppliers, journalists, and industry experts for feedback to a newly drafted mission statement. The resulting statement added fuel to the company's new quality direction:

> The mission of the Cadillac Motor Car Company is to engineer, produce and market the world's finest automobile known for uncompromised levels of distinctiveness, comfort, convenience and refined performance. Through its people, who are its strength, Cadillac will continuously improve the quality of its products and services to meet or exceed customer expectations and succeed as a profitable business.

Supplier Partnerships

Supplier partnerships are critical to the success of Cadillac's Simultaneous Engineering Process. Since 1985, Cadillac has extended the product development responsibilities of suppliers. To minimize variation, the supplier base was reduced. Not only has this action cut waste and improved the quality of materials supplied, since 1986 it has enabled a 425 percent increase in the number of suppliers shipping on a just-in-time basis.

To advance its suppliers' quality efforts, GM established Targets for Excellence. This program identifies five key areas in which suppliers must show evidence of continuous improvement: leadership, quality, cost, delivery, and technology. Cadillac also has included over 640 suppliers in its own quality-training programs.

UAW-GM Quality Network

Since 1973, Cadillac and the United Auto Workers (UAW) have worked jointly to improve both product quality and the quality of work life. Cadillac has 7,500 hourly employees who are UAW members, and 2,500 salaried employees. To succeed, everyone needs to be on board. In 1987, management and the union formed a UAW-GM Quality Network to improve competitiveness through partnering in quality improvement. This UAW-GM partnership has been integral to Cadillac's change.

Top union and management leadership hold quarterly manufacturing forums on business and quality. Throughout the company and at all levels of the organization—corporate, group, division, and plant—the Quality Network has joint union and management councils. Cochaired by a shop committee person and a plant manager, these councils develop and implement quality plans and support 471 functional work teams involving 4,000 employees, and 11 cross-functional teams of 800 people. The company and the union work together to beat the competition.

Cadillac's People Strategy

Cadillac's success depends on teamwork and employee involvement. The company regards its people as its greatest strength. People Strategy Teams develop and improve the company's people systems. These cross-functional teams have both hourly and salaried workers. People Strategy teams work on employee development, selection, communication, education and training, rewards and recognition, environment, and wellness.

The company's People Strategy approach includes a strong commitment to education. There is a Training Priorities Committee at each plant and staff unit. The needs of individual employees determine the content of a training program. Since implementing its People Strategy, Cadillac has increased worker education and training to an average of 40 hours per employee per year. Team participation is up 600 percent since 1985, and Cadillac's employee turnover is one of the industry's lowest.

Customer Focus

Customer satisfaction drives Cadillac's master plan. Functional barriers have been broken down in order to concentrate on external as well as internal customers. Cadillac's Design For Manufacturability (DFM) system is a prime example of meeting the needs of internal customers. Simultaneous Engineering teams use DFM to assess the products' manufacturing requirements throughout the development process. This method promotes the input of internal customers into the system.

With external customers, Cadillac's objective is to promote satisfaction with the total ownership experience. This process includes understanding customer needs and expectations, translating them into products and services, and finally, providing after-purchase support. The voice of the customer is integrated into product development through the use of a market-assurance process and market research. A quality function deployment approach is used to incorporate customer requirements into product specifications. Simultaneous Engineering teams use this information in product development and improvement.

Customer-focused improvement initiatives have integrated Cadillac's suppliers and dealers into the quality process: Suppliers make up 75 percent of the membership of the 55 product development and improvement teams.

Disciplined Planning

Cadillac's business plan is its quality plan. The business planning process reviews the company's mission and strategies to ensure alignment with corporate and business directions; guides internal processes, including the UAW-GM Quality Network and Simultaneous Engineering; and establishes a disciplined process to reach quality improvement goals. Employees at every level have input into the plan's development, and the finalized plan is communicated to all employees at the annual state-of-the business meeting, complete with a question-and-answer session.

By utilizing more than 50 data bases, information is analyzed and detailed quality plans with measurable actions are put in place for plants and staff units. Competitive analysis, comparative product and process data, and other vital planning information is gathered from a wide variety of sources. These include the GM proving grounds, which tests Cadillacs against competitors' cars, surveys of owners of all car makes, suppliers (through Partners in Excellence conferences), and dealers (through the National Dealer Council).

In the past, Cadillac tended to regard dealers as product distributors. Dealers often didn't see the product until it was introduced to the public. In 1984, Cadillac implemented a Dealer Quality Improvement Process with its 1,600 independent dealers. Now Cadillac's leadership listens at dealer council meetings for dealer suggestions about marketing strategies and current and future products. Dealership variation has been reduced by setting contractual agreements that spell out the dealer's role in achieving customer service requirements. Customer problems have been reduced 67 percent since 1985. Cadillac provides training to support dealers in achieving customer service excellence.

At Cadillac, continuous improvement in manufacturing and in service have gone hand in hand. At the same time warranty coverage has gone up, warranty costs have gone down. Warranty coverage in 1991 was a minimum of four years or 50,000 miles. While deductibles have been eliminated on all car warranties, warranty-related problems have been reduced more than 60 percent, and warranty claims dropped 29 percent from 1986 to 1989.

In 1991, Cadillac was the only automobile manufacturer with a 24-hour, 365-day-a-year customer assistance toll-free telephone number. Cadillac owners of any model or year can call any time for roadside service. This type of responsiveness has resulted in service satisfaction improving 17 percent since 1989. In achieving this, Cadillac equalled the benchmarked international competition.

Results

Cadillac's major product reliability and durability road test program simulates 100,000 miles of customer use. Since 1986, test results of the combined product line show product reliability and durability have improved 67 percent, which meets or exceeds world-class performance levels.

The Customer Oriented Vehicle Evaluation (COVE) is a comprehensive audit that checks fit-and-finish as well as performance dimensions. Results, since 1986, show improvement in all car lines. In the case of the Eldorado, Seville, Toronado, and Riviera models, discrepancies decreased 57 percent.

Reducing build combinations (the combinations of options a customer can order) by 90 percent has reduced variation and simplified designs. The previous combination possibilities numbered into the thousands, not including the varieties of color. Few customers have been dissatisfied with the reduction in choices, yet all customers appreciate the better quality. A more stable assembly process has meant that since 1987 there has been a 47 percent improvement in response time from customer order to delivery.

Engineering change orders have been reduced by 56 percent, proving that more is being done right and indicating that there are fewer mistakes and less rework. Process capability has improved, as evidenced by reduction of assembly hours: The division has shown a 58 percent productivity improvement since 1986 at its Detroit /Hamtramck Assembly Center. Die transition time has improved 75 percent since 1986.

In the auto industry, imports still set the standard for quality, dominating customer surveys. But Cadillac is leading the field among American auto manufacturers, recapturing its reputation as a leader in quality through its innovative and comprehensive quality culture. According to the J. D. Powers and Associates Customer Satisfaction Index, an industry standard rating, Cadillac has ranked as the top domestic automaker for the past four years in terms of overall customer satisfaction. During that same four-year period, the GM Customer Satisfaction Index increased eight points to the highest level ever achieved by domestic luxury car manufacturers.

In 1990, Cadillac became the first automobile company to win the Malcolm Baldrige Award. The company's quality improvement efforts have paid off: Since 1987, repurchase loyalty has increased 24 percent, and Cadillac now tops the list for having the most loyal car owners in the industry.

IBM ROCHESTER: MARKET-DRIVEN MANUFACTURING

As a proud recipient of the Malcolm Baldrige National Quality Award, we regard it as a promising signpost rather than an end in itself. Our work only begins here. No matter how well we may think we do something, we know it can always be better.

John Akers,
Chairman and Chief Executive Officer,
International Business Machines Corp.

Even in receiving the Malcolm Baldrige National Quality Award, we know that our continued success is dependent on being better tomorrow than we are today.

Larry Osterwise,
IBM Rochester Site Manager (1985–1990)

Business Overview

IBM Rochester, located in Rochester, Minnesota, is a manufacturer of intermediate computer systems: International Business Machine's flagship midrange business computer, the Application System/400, the AS/Entry Systems, and hard-disk storage devices (DASDs). More than 8,100 people are employed at the 3.6 million-square-foot Rochester facility. IBM Rochester is also a major research and development center with the capability to design, build, and test prototypes. Sales in 1990 were estimated at $14 billion.

Quality Strategy

IBM Rochester has undergone a significant cultural change. Its corporate orientation has been transformed from technology-driven to market-driven. The focus has shifted from just delivering products to involving customers and suppliers in the process of delivering solutions. IBM Rochester's leadership is committed to total quality and total customer satisfaction.

IBM Rochester's journey is one of continuously expanding the role of quality. In 1981, the focus was on the cost of quality with a goal of zero defects. By 1984, the quality initiative widened to include process management and cycle-time reduction. Involving the customer and supplier, as well as benchmarking, were incorporated into 1986 efforts. Beginning in 1990, the company launched a five-year program to increase employee involvement in quality improvement. Figure 15.2 shows the evolution of quality at IBM Rochester.

IBM Rochester's dedication to quality improvement produced two significant results:

1. Improved quality was a major factor in the success of the AS/400.
2. Rochester had reached such an outstanding level of quality that it received a Baldrige site visit in 1989.

This palpable evidence of quality improvement influenced corporate IBM to reinvigorate its quality effort with a customer-focused emphasis.

FIGURE 15.2
The Quality Journey Continues . . .

THE QUALITY JOURNEY CONTINUES...   **Q**   **1990-1994**

	1981	1984	1986	1989	1990-1994
Vision	Product reliability	Process effectiveness and efficiency	Customer and supplier partnerships Competitive and functional benchmarks	Market-driven customer satisfaction Total business process focus Closed loop quality/management system	Customer-The final arbiter Quality-Excellence in execution Products and services-First with the best People-Enabled, Empowered, Excited, Rewarded
Initiatives	Product performance improvement Cost of quality PRIDE	Process management Manufacturing cycle time improvement QFBP-Quality focus in business processes	Customer and supplier involvement Benchmarks Development cycle time improvement	Total cycle time to market Prevention based process Functional integration Extending customer involvement	Clinical success factors - Education - Requirements - Product strategy - 6-Sigma strategy - Cycle improvement - Employee involvement Proactive customer satisfaction processes
Goals	Zero defects	All processes rated	Best of competition	Total customer satisfaction	Undisputed leadership in customer satisfaction

Source: IBM Rochester

Market-Driven Quality

In January 1990, John Akers, IBM's chairman, launched a massive attack on quality problems. Under the banner of Market-Driven Quality, or MDQ, the corporation's quality efforts have been redoubled. The objectives are clear: improved product quality and greater customer satisfaction. The company's goal is virtual perfection. The target is to be defect free, that is, to reach Six Sigma by 1994. MDQ is grounded by four principles: "Make the customer the final arbiter, understand our markets, commit to leadership in markets we choose to serve, and deliver excellence in execution across our enterprise."

IBM Corporation's Market-Driven Quality forms the foundation for IBM Rochester's quality approach. Rochester's strategic goal is to be the "undisputed leader in customer satisfaction." To reach this target, the Rochester site identified six factors essential to its success:

1. Enhance total product strategy and plans,
2. Improve the requirements definition process,
3. Implement a Six-Sigma defect-level quality strategy,
4. Develop and implement an excellence in education plan,
5. Enhance and enable employee involvement,
6. Develop and implement reductions in total cycle time.

To carry out these actions, Rochester executives spearhead cross-functional teams assigned to each critical success factor. Key measurements were insituted to support improvement.

A Baldrige self-assessment was valuable in Rochester's continuous improvement. The Rochester Baldrige team, in preparing the Baldrige application, compiled a "wart" report. (They used Xerox's term for areas for improvement.) The Rochester team uncovered 71 warts (quality problems): 34 high-priority items and 37 not as urgent. Strategies and action plans were put in place to address each quality problem.

Additionally, feedback from IBM Rochester's 1989 Baldrige site visit helped with the company's quality restructuring. Areas for improvement included the need for more consistent education, focused leadership, and functional benchmarking.

Benchmarking

IBM Rochester's benchmarking process has been central to setting its strategic targets and establishing its five-year and annual operating plans. Rochester's 1989 Baldrige feedback reported that while the company was strong in traditional benchmarking of competitor's products and organizations, it had not adequately benchmarked practices and processes in noncompetitive areas such as financial systems, distribution systems, and so on. IBM Rochester tackled this issue, in early 1990, with a benchmarking plan to systematically measure the best of the best in functional areas. By June, at least one critical benchmark had been completed in each area; by August it was part of the company's ongoing operation.

An improvement was made in the company's competitive benchmarking as well. There was a shift from examining U.S., Japanese, and European competitors by dismantling and evaluating their equipment, to understanding competitors' business direction. There was a change from technical-competitive analysis to understanding the investments and alliances competitors were making and how they were positioning products.

Human Resources Strategy

To achieve Market-Driven Quality goals, IBM human resources strategy uses a four-pronged approach. Success depends upon employees who are "enabled, empowered, excited, and rewarded." Employees have become part of the process to establish objectives and requirements. They originate the majority of plans for the achievement of quality targets, with cross-functional teams identifying resources needed.

Long considered one of the best employers in America, IBM's strong heritage of good people management practices, which rests on its basic respect for the individual, gave it a head start in employee involvement. Added to this long-standing ethic is a new emphasis on teamwork as the cornerstone of quality improvement. At IBM Rochester, employee involvement is regarded as the greatest lever for enhancing quality improvement. Teams are trained to make process improvements. In 1990, there were 4,000 operating teams.

Excellence in Education

Education and communications are key elements in converting a technology-driven company to one that is market and customer driven. The IBM Rochester commitment to education is substantial, representing five percent of its payroll.

The cultural shift from product focus to market focus meant management had to learn to shift from managing to leading, and from directing employees to empowering them. To effect this change, the Management College was recast as IBM's Leadership College, and twice a year, sessions are held for managers and key team leaders. All employees take the Transformational Leadership course that covers the new market-driven culture.

IBM Rochester had used a course catalog approach, in which employees made selections based on their needs. There was no expectation that all employees would share a common core of basic quality principles. As a result, certain gaps existed. The Malcolm Baldrige assessment led IBM Rochester to focus more intently on a consistent educational format. One measure taken in 1990: The company, starting with its leadership, cascaded a uniform quality course through the organization. The general manager taught his or her people, and they taught theirs.

Communicating

IBM Rochester has 11,000 terminals and PCs connecting its 8,100 employees across its site and around the world. This gives global access to data bases, design and analysis tools, and communication capabilities. Face-to-face communication occurs in weekly departmental meetings covering the state of the business, quality, and measurements. IBM has a communications network with TV monitors throughout the Rochester site, providing real-time information. For example, employees saw the live broadcast of John Akers accepting the Malcolm Baldrige National Quality Award from President Bush.

Educating, communicating, and involving employees with customers has enhanced employee satisfaction. The annual opinion survey shows that Rochester's 94 percent participation rate in this corporate measure is the highest in the entire IBM company. The survey was put on-line three years ago to increase the response rate. Annual independent surveys show that employee morale is high compared with levels at 34 U.S. companies. In absenteeism, turnover, and safety, IBM Rochester employees have better attendance, are more loyal, and are more safety conscious than the industry average.

Customer Satisfaction Focus

The quality process at IBM Rochester provides a continuous loop with the customer, from the product-planning process through production and on to delivery. In 1986, the company began emphasizing involvement of customers in the development and manufacturing process. A variety of methods have been devised to facilitate involvement, including advisory councils, roundtables, information systems, and prototype trailing.

In the case of the development of the AS/400 midrange computer, its basic architecture was the result of customer input. Customers from a variety of businesses worked with Rochester on such things as setting design priorities, making recommendations to coordinate software codes, and testing equipment usability. To secure feedback after installation, the company conducts a quarterly marketing and customer satisfaction survey of approximately 2,200 AS/400 customers.

The Customer Satisfaction Council involves people from all functional areas. It meets monthly to agree on the top 10 customer issues. These become the month's action items. As items are resolved, they are crossed off the list and new ones are added. There are always 10, and it is the job of the Customer Satisfaction Council to monitor and manage the issues.

Supplier Partners

IBM Rochester's approximately 700 suppliers are its partners in continuous quality improvement. In 1986, IBM instituted a defect-free supplier program. Then, in 1989, IBM strongly encouraged suppliers to meet the quality objectives of the Malcolm Baldrige National Quality Award. Rochester uses a three-stage selection process to evaluate suppliers. There is a certification process, with quality awards for excellence. IBM Rochester has trained over 1,000 supplier employees in quality.

Results

As might be expected of a division of the world's largest computer manufacturer, IBM Rochester has a technically sophisticated work environment that has helped accelerate the continuous improvement process. In an effort to prevent problems rather than merely detect them, Rochester tooled up its information systems and processes at a cost of $300 million. One payoff for this investment was a 55 percent reduction in write-offs for scrap and excess inventory from 1984 to 1990.

Since 1983, cycle time has been reduced by more than 50 percent on the product development of new midrange computer systems, and by 60 percent on manufacturing. Productivity improved 30 percent from 1986 to 1989. Service costs have dropped despite increased warranty coverage (from 3 to 12 months), principally because of the company's threefold improvement in product reliability. The company's market share in mid-range computers, one of the world's most intensely competitive industries, is increasing a half a point each year. In revenue growth, of six leading competitors only Rochester grew faster than the industry rate.

In 1990, IBM Rochester won the Baldrige Award. That same year, with approximately 2 percent of the worldwide IBM Corporation's work force of 380,000, IBM Rochester produced 8.5 percent of the corporation's revenues. Quality improvement has clearly given IBM Rochester an edge in maintaining its position as a world leader in many computer markets.

FEDERAL EXPRESS CORPORATION:
A LICENSE TO PRACTICE

> *Since we were awarded the Malcolm Baldrige National Quality Award, I have been asked many times if this means we have now achieved the ultimate level of quality. My answer is that the receipt of the award is simply our "license to practice." We have recognized since the beginning of this company that the key to our ultimate success would be quality service. What set us apart from the very earliest days was an absolutely zealous approach to quality and customer satisfaction. Customers chose us for that reason in 1973, they choose us for that reason today.*

Frederick W. Smith,
Chairman, President, and Chief Executive Officer,
Federal Express Corporation

Business Overview

Since Memphis, Tennessee-based Federal Express began express transportation operations in 1973, its fleet has grown from 8 small aircraft to 419 planes, the world's largest air cargo fleet. There are 94,000 employees at more than 1,600 sites worldwide, processing 1.5 million shipments a day. These packages are tracked through a central information system, sorted at various facilities, and delivered by a decentralized distribution network. Revenues in fiscal year 1990 were $7 billion. Nearly 75 percent of total revenues is from domestic overnight and second-day delivery; the remaining revenue (approximately 25 percent) is from international shipments.

The technology revolution of increased automation, mechanization, and computerization that began in the mid-1960s spawned markets that would need reliable, time-sensitive distribution systems. In 1965, while an undergraduate student at Yale University, Fred Smith wrote a term paper describing the concept for an air-express business. Before FedEx set up operations, two market research studies were conducted to see if demand was sufficient to support air-express transport services and who potential customers might be. From its inception, Federal Express has been a market-driven company designed first and foremost to meet customers' needs and expectations.

Understanding the needs of the marketplace paid off, as satisfied customers fueled the company's meteoric growth. Within 10 years, FedEx was a $1 billion company, and only 16 years after it was founded, Federal Express became a $7 billion company serving 127 countries and 310 airports. To continue this upward trend, the company needed to establish even higher performance goals, make further technology investments, and, because of the complexity of its operation, emphasize running the business based of facts, data, and analysis.

Five-Point Strategy

The number-one objective of Federal Express is to improve the quality of service. To achieve this, Chairman, President, and CEO Smith has a five-point strategy, as shown in Figure 15.3.

Service Quality Indicators

FedEx's goal from the beginning has been 100 percent customer satisfaction, achieved through 100 percent on-time deliveries and 100 percent accurate information on every shipment. In a recent change to accelerate progress in meeting its goal, the company developed a Service Quality Indicator (SQI) system. SQI is a sophisticated measurement design that tracks performance tied to customer expectations. The method SQI replaced consisted of tracking the percent of on-time deliveries. The limitation of the percentage system was that as more shipments were carried, improving or staying at the same percent could still result in thousands of

FIGURE 15.3
Federal Express Five-Point Strategy

1. Use the Quality Improvement process to improve service levels to 100 percent and lower costs at the same time. [FedEx expresses this goal, in short, as $Q=P$ (Quality Equals Productivity).]
2. Use information and information systems as strategic weapons to achieve $Q=P$ goals.
3. Recognize that Federal Express must become a truly global company.
4. Get closer to customers.
5. Continue to emphasize a people-first philosophy by "investing" in employees.

Source: Federal Express Corporation

dissatisfied customers. A 99 percent success rate would translate to 2.5 million service failures a year.

To Federal Express, absolute success depends on absolute numbers. The SQI process measures service in absolute terms from daily reports. SQI is a 12-component weighted index that tracks customer satisfaction impacts. Key service factors are measured from the customer's viewpoint, and these factors are weighted based on the customer's level of concern. For example, a lost package would be weighted 10; a package one day late would be weighted five; a package five minutes late would be weighted one. The company designed the SQI system to enable it to quantify quality. With SQI, FedEx measures quality with real-time information using its COSMOS (Customer Operating Service Master Online System) tracking system. The SQI is the total of the daily failure point average of all 12 components. At the start of the SQI process in 1987, FedEx had approximately 150,000 SQI failure points. Despite a 20 percent increase in shipping volume, in 1989 the SQI was reduced to 133,000 points.

FedEx uses hand-held computers, Super Trackers, to scan package bar codes to track shipments. The performance data from these systems are gathered and analyzed, resulting in SQI reports that are transmitted daily to all company locations worldwide. Each day, management reviews the past day's results and trends.

The tracking system is so effective that the head of a multinational high-tech firm on a benchmarking trip to Federal Express observed that FedEx did a better job tracking an eight-by-eleven-inch package anytime, anywhere in the world than his company did keeping track of a product half the size of a school bus.

SQI data are used by Quality Action Teams to identify any problem's root cause and determine a remedy. Cross-functional teams (which include front-line employees, support personnel, managers, and a senior executive) have been established to work for improvements in each of the 12 SQI service components. Several corporate-wide teams network with over 1,000 employees. This methodology enables the loop to be closed on problems and allows the company to move to prevent problems from recurring. The SQI measurement tool is the key to identifying and reducing the number of absolute failures daily.

The Service Quality Indicator system is linked to corporate planning at Federal Express. Executives are evaluated based on SQIs, and executive bonuses depend on the entire corporation meeting performance improvement goals. Additionally, if the rating for management leadership (according to the annual employee survey) is not as high or higher than the previous year, there are no executive bonuses. In 1990, the goals were not met and no one received a bonus—not Fred Smith, not anyone.

People-Service-Profit

The Federal Express corporate philosophy is summed up in the phrase "People-Service-Profit." People are first. Customer satisfaction begins with employee satisfaction. "Quality is in the hands of our people. To understand the service side of quality, you must understand the human side of quality," says Chairman Smith. Smith believes that service companies such as Federal Express need an empowered work force even more than manufacturing companies, since service-sector workers form the front line of customer relations in what is often a widely dispersed enterprise.

At FedEx there are five layers of management between senior management and nonmanagement. As part of its drive to emphasize its cardinal goal of customer satisfaction, the company reversed the organizational hierarchy to place customer-contact people at the top. This inverted pyramid makes everyone in the organization the customer of the CEO and creates the environment of treating fellow-employees as customers.

Survey/Feedback/Action

People-Service-Profit has been the foundation for managing at FedEx. Valuable information is compiled through the use of the company's Survey/Feedback/Action (SFA) system. SFA has three components: an anonymous survey completed by all employees, feedback sessions for each employee work group to analyze and determine solutions for problems the survey identifies, and action plans that function as quality improvement plans. SFA information is aggregated and used in the continuous improvement of the company's leadership.

Continuous improvement is principally implemented by employees through the company's more than 3,000 Quality Action Teams (QATs). Employee morale is among the best of major American corporations, with innovative programs such as the company's no layoff philosophy and its guaranteed fair treatment procedure.

Recognition

Recognition is critical to service industries. Recognition of both team and individual contributions is central to the quality issue at Federal Express. The Bravo Zulu Award is named after the Navy signal for "well done." This recognition is widely used throughout the company. The Golden Falcon Award is the company's highest award. It is presented to nonmanagement employees who provide customer service above and beyond the call of duty. Exceptional contributions by management are recognized with the Five Star Award.

Quality Academy

The Quality Academy was developed to provide consistent quality training. Classes cover basic quality principles: the quality advantage, quality action teams, quality management skills, facilitation skills, leading teams, and Statistical Process Control (SPC). By 1990, 80 percent of the managers had been trained in the basic quality courses.

A worldwide training staff conducts needs assessments and designs responsive programs. Skill training is decentralized due to the number of Federal Express divisions and the unique skills needed by specific areas. An interactive video instruction (ITV) system supports training initiatives. The system merges audiovisual capabilities with computer technology, allowing interaction with the system. ITV has many uses, including new-hire orientation and recurrent training for customer service agents and couriers preparing for job knowledge tests.

The company has in place a corporatewide closed circuit television network called FXTV. It airs special programs on quality, and employees can call in and ask questions. Regularly scheduled broadcasts update daily SQI results.

Results

Since 1985, Federal Express's overall customer satisfaction ratings have averaged more than 95 percent on domestic service and 94 percent on international service. Federal Express scored above the competition in an air express industry survey, with 53 percent of respondents rating it perfect. (The company's nearest competitor received a 39 percent perfect rating.) With the goal of 100 percent customer satisfaction, the results to date show that 93 percent of FedEx customers are completely satisfied in the area of ease of doing business with the company, and 97 percent are completely satisfied with the couriers. Domestic market share in 1989 was 43 percent, with the nearest competitor at 26 percent.

When Federal Express was presented with the Baldrige Award on December 13, 1990, it became the first company in the service industry to be so recognized.

WALLACE COMPANY, INC.: BUILD QUALITY IN

I've learned that if change is going to take place in an organization, it has to be approached as if it were a revolution. True change doesn't come at a snail's pace. We have analyzed pretty well every one of our major processes and have changed about 80 percent of them significantly in the last three years.

John W. Wallace,
Chief Executive Officer,
Wallace Company, Inc.

Business Overview

Wallace Company, founded in 1942, is a family-owned industrial distributor of pipes, valves, fittings, and specialty products for the chemical and petrochemical industries. With corporate offices in Houston, Texas, Wallace has nine branch offices that distribute in the Gulf Coast region and internationally. The company has 280 employees. Sales in 1990 were $90 million.

During the boom years of the 1970s and early 1980s, Wallace enjoyed strong growth as a supplier of specialized industrial hardware for engineering and construction (E&C) projects. But by the mid-1980s, commercial industrial construction had ground to a halt, the result of a prolonged recession throughout the region. Wallace was left scrambling for new markets. The company chose to target the replacement market, building a new customer base from among existing plants that needed a steady stream of hardware for their maintenance and repair operations (MROs).

Survival Strategy

It was in 1985, in the midst of this change, that MRO customer Celanese Chemical gave Wallace the do-or-die Total Quality Management imperative: Embrace quality management or lose Celanese as a customer. Wallace officials, seeing an opportunity to take competitive advantage in quality, accepted the challenge.

Wallace's senior executive leadership formed the Quality Management Steering Committee to lead the company's quality improvement process.

The committee initiated a three-phase quality program to merge business and quality goals, build customer and supplier partnerships, and instill in all associates (employees) the aim of total customer satisfaction.

The Wallace Quality Business Plan is implemented by associates using a centralized, cooperative approach to quality improvement. Wallace seeks customer feedback for its planning by monitoring market analysis reports, customer complaint trends, and customer specification changes.

In the short term, the company hoped to achieve continuous quality improvement in its internal operations and show a measurable increase in customer satisfaction. In the long term, the company's goals included development of extended supplier partnerships, improvement of inventory management, and enhancement of human resource development.

Senior leaders wrote the quality mission statement, incorporating associate input into the document. The following is excerpted from the Wallace Mission Statement:

> Continuous Improvement means recognizing the need to improve all procedures on a regular, ongoing basis. We know that improving procedures in all areas requires a team effort; we combine the expertise of the people closest to the job with the knowledge of the people who design and review procedures. We utilize the basic tools of Statistical Process Control. In all company procedures, we "Build Quality In" and pledge company resources to help our people "Do it right the first time."

Driving Out Fear

Understanding the basic human aversion to change, senior management led the company's transformation by driving out fear and creating an environment that allowed employees to reach their full potential. Among other things, CEO John Wallace pledged that no one would lose his or her job as a result of the refocusing of Wallace's corporate culture.

Each of the five top leaders at Wallace participated in over 200 hours of training in continuous quality improvement. Senior management then took on the responsibility of spreading its knowledge through every level of the organization. In all of the company's quality activities, including associate training, there is at least one senior leader.

Wallace has two means of policy development. Teams are empowered to improve procedures and processes that do not meet objectives, and the Quality Management Steering Committee analyzes data on customer satisfaction, associate satisfaction, supplier performance, and sales and profit trends to develop policy.

Quality Strategic Objectives

The company developed 16 Quality Strategic Objectives to serve as a guide to making business decisions:

1. Leadership Development.
2. Quality Business Plan.
3. On-the-Job Training.
4. Information Analysis.
5. Statistical Process Control.
6. Quality Education.
7. Human Resource Development.
8. Quality Improvement Process (QIP) Team Involvement.
9. Customer Service /Satisfaction.
10. Employee Reinforcement/Incentive.
11. Quality Pathfinder.
12. Suggestion System.
13. Internal Audit.
14. Internal and External Benchmarking.
15. Vendor Quality Improvement Plan.
16. Community Outreach.

As the company built its quality process, it used a multidenominational approach, incorporating the concepts of various quality philosophies that would work best for Wallace. All that was missing was an overall structure. That was supplied by the Baldrige criteria, which the company used as a blueprint for its overall quality improvement plan.

To achieve its goal of becoming world-class, Wallace conducts comparative quality benchmarking of best practicing companies globally in areas such as on-time delivery, business operations, and service. Benchmarking is one of the company's Quality Strategic Objectives. According to C. S. Wallace, Jr., president, "We did a lot of benchmarking. We benchmarked every previous Baldrige winner. The way we went about it is we tried to look at the companies we were benchmarking and pick out the things they did more world-class than any others." Looking at past models gave Wallace a powerful tool to compare itself to top performers and internalize the lessons.

Human Resource Development

Early on, Wallace's top management recognized that human resources were central to the company's quality commitment. In fact, 9 of the 16 Quality Strategic Objectives specifically relate to human resources: On-the-Job-Training, Quality Education, Human Resource Development, Quality Improvement Process (QIP) Team Improvement, Employee Reinforcement/Incentive, Quality Pathfinder, Suggestion System, Internal and External Benchmarking, and Community Outreach.

As a result of the belief that it is the company's associates who power continuous quality improvement, $2 million was invested in training from 1987 to 1990. Wallace's major commitment to education has been fundamental to the company's survival. Courses available include: cycle-time reduction, benchmarking, sales training, leadership, vendor certification, Statistical Process Control (SPC), and SPC coordinator training. This training enables increased associate involvement in quality improvement. There has been a corresponding decrease in absenteeism, turnover, and work-related injuries.

Teams

Associate participation on cross-functional and multioffice teams has increased sixfold since the voluntary initiative began in 1985. There are three types of teams: Quality Strategic Objective (QSO) teams, job training teams, and project teams. The team process is aided by customer-focused data bases that associates can access. By 1990, there were 116 active teams.

Statistical Process Control (SPC) coordinators work with teams to help conduct problem analysis, chart trends, and assess progress. With 12 SPC coordinators, every district office has at least one expert available on-site. One day each week is spent reviewing and planning quality improvements. SPC coordinators are well prepared to take charge of quality improvement teams, having received at least 274 hours of SPC and team training.

Problem Solving

Wallace developed a handbook for quality improvement teams that addresses both the technical and the human side of quality. Teams use the eight-step process shown in Figure 15.4 to solve problems. Quality improvement teams are monitored by a QIP Team Coordinating Board that tracks with a team matrix all team activities and participants. Guidance Teams, composed of a district manager, an SPC coordinator, and a team leader, charter teams and authorize resources.

In 1987, the number of Occupational Safety and Health Administration (OSHA) recordable accidents at Wallace had put the company in a high-risk group. The business had major safety challenges: working with railroad spurs, overhead cranes, and 18-wheelers. The company used the quality process to work through the problem. A program called Safety First—Family First was developed by a Wallace team and implemented by associates as a continuous improvement cycle for reducing hazards. In the first year, injuries decreased dramatically, and the company was back on the standard program. Along with improved morale and worker safety, Wallace enjoyed a bottom-line impact of $500,000 annual savings in insurance premiums.

What Comes Around Goes Around

These days, it is Wallace who has informed its suppliers they must get on the quality bandwagon or risk losing a customer. In fact, Wallace was the first in its industry group to train suppliers in continuous quality improvement. Fifteen suppliers adapted the Wallace model to their businesses in 1990. Suppliers are required to provide shipment records that include statistical evidence of quality. The number of suppliers has been reduced from 2,000 in 1987 to 325 in 1990. Wallace implemented a vendor certification process whereby the company and its customers will continually assess supplier quality.

Providing customers with access to the Wallace data bases has benefited both Wallace customers and Wallace itself. Data are more accurate, errors are reduced, and inventory is better managed. Electronic ordering in 1990 accounted for 40 percent of sales, up from 5 percent 1988.

Results

In virtually every area, Wallace has seen dramatic quality improvements. On-time deliveries reached 92 percent in 1990, up from a low of 75 percent in 1987, and higher than the industry average of 86.3 percent.

From 1985 to 1990, inventory turns improved 175 percent, which

FIGURE 15.4
Wallace Company Eight-Step-Problem Solving Model

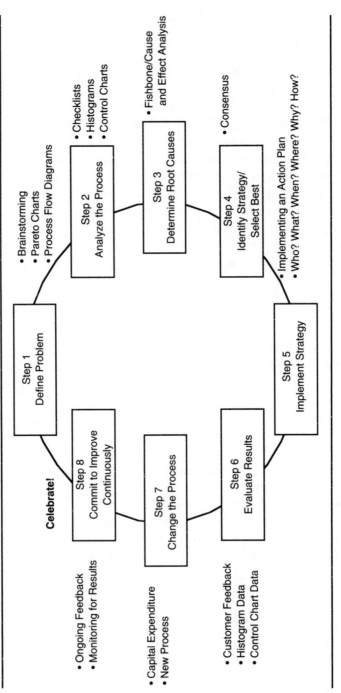

Source: Wallace Co., Inc.

was 27 percent better than industry averages. In 1981, Wallace's engineering and construction orders accounted for 80 percent of its business, but 10 years later maintenance and repair operations (MRO) accounts make up 70 percent of its business. Sales have increased from $52 million in 1987 to $90 million in 1990. The company's market share has increased from 10.4 percent in 1987 to more than 18 percent by 1990.

In 1990, Wallace Company won the Baldrige Award in the Small Business category. Wallace is only the second small business to be so honored.

CHAPTER 16

1991 AWARD WINNERS: ELECTRONICS QUALITY BLITZ

All three winners are leading-edge companies that clearly are succeeding in the most globally competitive industry sector—electronics—and are proof that U.S. firms don't have to be giants to be on top. They know that quality is the key to opening the doors of opportunity in this country and abroad.

Robert A. Mosbacher
October 29, 1991

SOLECTRON CORPORATION:
THIRD TIME'S THE CHARM

We would like to encourage all companies in the U.S. to apply for the Baldrige Award, especially the small and medium-sized companies which create new jobs. We believe that when hundreds or thousands of American companies apply for the Award and use it as the process for improvement, American industry can increase its competitiveness significantly.

Winston H. Chen, Ph.D.,
Chairman and Co-Chief Executive Officer,
Solectron Corporation

There are no shortcuts to gaining market share. It is very important that we gain market share to remain competitive. We must compete on a global basis to insure we have a positive balance of trade which will create meaningful employment to maintain and improve our standard of living in the United States.

Koichi Nishimura,
President and Co-Chief Executive Officer,
Solectron Corporation

Business Overview

Solectron assembles electronic equipment and systems for major manufacturers of personal computers, disk and tape drives, and personal computer peripherals. Since its incorporation in 1977, this Silicon Valley company has expanded from a small job shop to one of the United States' largest surface mount facilities. As an independent provider of custom, integrated manufacturing services, Solectron employs more than 3,300 people in nine facilities throughout San Jose and Milpitas, California, and Penang, Malaysia. Solectron supplies major original equipment manufacturers (OEMs) such as Apple Computer, Hewlett-Packard, Honeywell, IBM, and Sun Microsystems. Approximately 80 percent of the company's business is printed circuit board assembly. The rest includes other assembly operations for electronic systems and subsystems, disk duplication, software packaging, and remanufacturing of customer products. Solectron typically manufactures products based on customers' designs, but it also provides original equipment design and testing services. Fiscal 1991 sales were approximately $265 million, with profits of $9 million.

Quick Quality Turnaround

In 1978, shortly after it was founded, Solectron almost went down for the count. Enter Winston Chen to the rescue. A Taiwanese immigrant, Harvard Ph.D., and IBM alumnus, Chen used $100,000 of his savings to buy half the gasping company and began resuscitation with a healthy dose of quality. Dr. Chen's prescription ultimately resulted in Solectron's spectacular comeback.

Pressure for the quality change came from important Solectron OEM customers who demanded higher quality levels. IBM, for instance, required disk drives with one defect or fewer per 2,000 parts. Change was further stimulated when Chen and other Solectron managers took three benchmarking trips to Japan. The lessons learned drove home the message that to succeed in the world market, Solectron had to at least equal or, even better, exceed competitors' quality levels.

At the onset of its quality journey, Solectron's original crew of 15 people worked at building products to customer standards and achieved standard quality levels using inspection methods. Then in the early 1980s, the company instituted Quality Control circles to involve workers directly in quality improvement. Statistical process control implemented in 1984 initially resulted in one division attaining, and ever since maintaining, an impressive zero defects record. Further strides came from adapting Kaizen systems (continuous improvement) in 1986. In 1987, quality through prevention was launched along with Quality and Productivity Improvement (QIP) teams. (Fig. 16.1 maps Soletron's quality evolution.)

In 1989, quality progress jumped to warp speed when Solectron set two astronomical goals. The company's senior team targeted to reach Six Sigma (3.4 errors per million) by 1994. Even more of a stretch, Solectron set a uniquely aggressive strategy designed to dramatically accelerate the company's quality progress. It adopted the Malcolm Baldrige National Quality Award (MBNQA) as its continuous improvement roadmap and decided to apply for Baldrige every year until it won the Award. The company first applied for the MBNQA in 1989. Momentum grew with reapplication in 1990 and then 1991. It was this third attempt that brought with it the Baldrige thrill of victory.

Solectron's focus is to exceed customer expectations. That is basically

FIGURE 16.1
Solectron's Quality Evolution

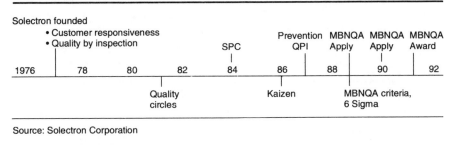

Source: Solectron Corporation

how it defines quality. By emphasizing value-added products that require high levels of quality, reliability, and quick turnarounds, the company has captured new business. Solectron's competitive edge results from its ability to produce materials not only faster, but cheaper and better (i.e. higher quality) than its customers could do the work themselves.

Total Leadership Dedication

It requires nothing less than total dedication from Solectron's leadership to reach the company's stratospheric quality targets. This dedication begins at the top with Chairman Winston Chen. He leads the executive team in three weekly top management quality-related reviews that begin at 7:30 a.m. Tuesday sessions examine Training and Profit and Loss; Wednesday's assess Quality Assurance; and Thursday's probe the Customer Satisfaction Index and Program Management. Eighty to a hundred managers attend and contribute to the constant thrust to create a shared vision, set examples, empower and enable people, nurture an environment for success, and provide positive reinforcement.

Work Force Involvement

Solectron's human resource system begins with the company's values: customer first, respect for the individual, quality, supplier partnerships, business ethics, shareholder value, and social responsibility.

Absolutely unique to Solectron is that worldwide immigrants make up at least half the company's world-class work force. Many of these workers have come from Asia with others from the Middle East and Latin America. Employees speak more than 12 languages and 20 dialects. To manage this multicultural, multilingual environment, it is essential to have a unified focus on mentoring, teamwork, and training.

Solectron practically wallpapers its factories and offices with company charts and posters that clearly show daily, monthly, and weekly performance. These always appear in four languages: English, Chinese, Vietnamese, and Spanish.

Solectron University

The bottom line for empowerment rests on the knowledge base of each individual employee. To truly empower employees, the company created its own education enterprise that acts as a corporate umbrella for all employee training. Classes at Solectron University started in July 1990. The University is regarded as a key element in Solectron's cultural transformation and its broad-based curriculum delivers courses ranging from basic electrical assembly to American culture. Corporate-wide quality training has been provided. Given Solectron's diversity, there are classes in English as a second language to promote common communication skills. Emphasis is given to management development, supervisory skills, and technical training, which includes statistical process control. The University's goal is to strengthen employees' growth through life-time learning. In 1991, Solectron University provided more than 85 hours of training for each worker. That number grew to 95 hours in 1992. The near-term goal for 1995 is 150 hours of training for each employee annually.

Training and education truly are the keys to employee empowerment and teamwork. For example, line workers understand process control and know how to use trend charts to judge if and when they need to stop the production line. Customer-contact employees alert to customer needs provide ready responses through well-orchestrated internal coordination.

Teams, Recognition, and Reward

Quality objectives receive added support through deployment of a network of teams. Every customer and project has a Project Management Team (PMT) that ensures customer needs are supported. Total Quality Control (TQC) Teams ride herd on manufacturing process developments. Cross-functional Quality Improvement Process (QPI) Teams tackle coorective actions, customer complaint resolution, benchmarking, and cycle-time improvements. In addition to the PMTs, TQCs, and QPIs, virtually every department has its own active quality circle. This systemwide team process enables employees to tangibly contribute to Solectron's customer satisfaction goals.

This high level of employee involvement, empowerment, and teamwork fuels the need for continual recognition and innovative reward systems. While there are a variety of awards, including individual ones, the company's primary emphasis is on its teams and therefore it stresses team recognition. Through the company's decentralization, most recognition is done directly in the operating divisions at the discretion of division managers. Additionally, Solectron's compensation system is performance based and more that 90 percent of the work force can participate in the bonus plan.

Customer Satisfaction Index

The company's marketplace competitive edge is a result of carefully honing its quality, service, and cost tools. Its lead device to gain customer feedback is dubbed the Customer Satisfaction Index (CSI). Each week, Solectron calls every one of its 60 customers to check on satisfaction levels for key items: quality, on-time delivery, communication, service, and performance. This information is relentlessly tracked, consolidated by customer segment and division, then pooled into an overall customer satisfaction level. CSI results are reviewed by top executives in the weekly Thursday morning meeting.

The process emphasizes understanding if and where any dissatisfaction may be lurking. Ko Nishimura says CSI is a mechanism to find out what customer expectations are, "Now they will give us grades on these: 100 is an A, 80 is B. You get zero for C work. We don't accept average work. It's worth nothing. What's important about this is, if you do get a grade of something less than an A, it's a communication vehicle." This is because CSI is an efficient closed-loop process—quality lingo meaning problems are identified, the root cause is determined and remedied, and recurrence prevented. This process constantly and continuously improves customer satisfaction levels.

Technology Investments

Solectron was quick to recognize the potential of Surface Mount Technology methods (SMT) when they became available. This technological advancement enables components to be mounted on both sides of a circuit board. The company currently has 19 surface mount assembly lines and is developing new SMT techniques. One of the significant ways Solectron stays ahead of its competition is by making wise investments in technology.

Persistence Pays

Solectron used its three attempts at Baldrige as a key improvement strategy. During those three years, both sales and profits shot up nearly 300 percent.

Ko Nishimura believes that if you *want* to be the best, you need to set up a process to *enable* you to be the best. Solectron used Baldrige feedback to do just that. For example, the 1989 Award feedback highlighted strengths in Solectron's Customer Satisfaction Index, use of Statistical Process Control, and top executives drive. Areas for improvement included human resource utilization and benchmarking. Solectron concluded the feedback was on target, and with the company's characteristic dogged determination, rolled up its sleeves to implement needed improvements. These included Solectron University, the President's Award for team accomplishments, and bolstering of its benchmarking.

Among the 1990 Baldrige feedback strengths were the company's executive round tables, investment in manufacturing capability, and employee surveys. Compared to 1989 feedback, though the number of areas for improvement were reduced, the company still needed additional improvements to systems and public involvement. To fill in the holes, Solectron beefed up its structured process tools, cycle-time reduction, and customer complaint resolution, as well as placing renewed focus on community involvement.

Baldrige feedback in 1991 cited Solectron's strengths, which included employee empowerment and quality results. Not resting on its Award-winning laurels, the company continues its improvement efforts and uses the feedback to focus on future information management systems and to augment supplier partnerships.

In the edition of Solectron's quarterly newsletter published just after the company won the Baldrige Award, Walt Wilson, Senior Vice President of Operations, commented, "We always knew we were good. But now we know we're the best. Now we have to live up to the best. A lot of work remains to be done on the road to excellence."

This quest for excellence requires the constant challenge to keep improving. Solectron knows that the key to long-term success is continuing its commitment to customer satisfaction.

Results

Solectron has emerged as a premier company. It has won 41 superior performance awards. One customer singled out Solectron as the best contact manufacturer in the United States.

From 1987 to 1992, defects have been reduced from several hundred parts per million to five or six. In early 1992, the defect rate at the finished product level was between 2,000 and 1,000 parts per million (ppm). The goal is to reach Six Sigma 3.4 by 1994.

Solectron's growth has been spectacular. The company's compounded annual growth rate over the past 14 years has been 59 percent per year. In the last three years it has been 42 percent. And an average return on equity of 26 percent—twice the industry average—has attracted an eager troop of new investors. Solectron went public in 1990 with stock at six dollars a share; two years later it had soared to 42 dollars.

During the recent recession, Solectron sharpened its pencil, lowered prices, and amazingly profits increased. Attributing this as yet another demonstration of how quality pays, Winston Chen commented, "It's not only that quality is free, as people like to say. We find quality is very profitable."

Solectron's ongoing mission is to contribute to the renaissance of America's manufacturing competitiveness. The company's crusade is to revitalize American business through better quality. And with all its accomplishments Solectron, as a new symbol of American competitiveness, is qualified to lead the charge. It demonstrates that high quality and productivity yield competitive costs and high profits.

ZYTEC CORPORATION: TWICE IN ONE YEAR

We have been driving the issue of quality since the middle of our first year in 1984 and we went through some very, very difficult times. I believe the only reason we survived was our focus on quality.

Ronald D. Schmidt,
Chairman, President and Chief Executive Officer,
Zytec Corporation

Business Overview

Zytec designs and makes electronic power supplies for original equipment manufacturers (OEMs) and other manufacturers. It also repairs cathode-ray tube (CRT) monitors and power supplies. In 1984, Zytec began independent operation after a leveraged buy out from the Power Supply Operation of Control Data Corporation. Headquartered in Eden Prairie, Minnesota, with manufacturing and repair facilities in Redwood Falls, Minnesota, Zytec is an employee-owned company with a work force of approximately 800 people. Zytec is North America's largest power supply repair company, the United States' fastest growing electronic power supply, and the nation's fifth largest multiple output switching power supply company. Most of Zytec's customers are major multinational companies, which results in Zytec's products being shipped not only to 400 U.S. corporations, but also to many companies in Europe and the Far East. Ninety percent of its revenues come from the sales of customized power supplies, with the remainder coming from its repair business. Revenues in 1991 were $72.7 million.

Quality from the Start

Since Zytec commenced independent operation in 1984 it has focused on three imperatives: quality, service, and value. In 1983, when the company's three founders drafted the original business plan to establish Zytec, they chose quality as the key strategy to differentiate the company from the competition. Ron Schmidt, one of the founders, had seen the NBC documentary, "If Japan Can Why Can't We?" which urged America to reexamine how it ran its companies. Another founder, John Steel, had attended a Dr. W. Edwards Deming seminar. Spurred by new insights that there must be a better way to manage business, Zytec's original crew took what no doubt appeared to be a bold direction in the early eighties and set a course using quality as the guide to move the business forward.

Zytec's senior team led the charge to instill quality values throughout the new enterprise. They developed the mission statement (Fig. 16.2) focusing on quality, service, and value and the words were placed on every employee's badge.

In the throes of commencing operations in early 1984, ramping up to production brought with it some major problems. The tough job of bringing the lofty ideals of Zytec's mission to life required a real-world quality strategy. Halfway into the year, the company sat down for its first long-range planning session. The agenda included review of Dr. Deming's 14 points (Fig. 16.3). Although the group struggled with exactly how to buy into the total philosophy, many of the points made sense—enough so that the group took what Ron Schmidt describes as a "leap of faith" and decided to use the 14 points as their guide to move the business forward. A Deming Steering Committee, consisting of Schmidt and the senior staff, was established and began organizing around its new quality initiative.

Over the next six months, with some outside help, this steering committee labored to clarify exactly what the 14 points meant to Zytec and how they could actually be used to run the business. Cross-functional implementation teams were established to sort, study, and summarize precisely how the philosophy could be made operational and used to change Zytec. The result was a process that cascaded quality information throughout the company.

This effort wrapped up in 1985. One of the deliverables was an eight-hour statistical process control (SPC) course that was taught to all non-exempt employees. Then a 40-hour intermediate quality course was de-

FIGURE 16.2
Zytec Corporation's Mission Statement

- Zytec is a company that competes on value, it provides technical excellence in its products and believes in the importance of education.
- We believe in a simple form and a lean staff, the importance of people as individuals, and the development of productive employees through training and capital investment.
- We focus on what we know best, thereby making a fair profit on current operations to meet our obligations and perpetuate our continued growth.

Source: Zytec Corporation

FIGURE 16.3
Dr. Deming's 14 Points Condensed

1. Create a constancy of purpose
2. Adopt a new philosophy
3. Cease dependence on inspection
4. Move toward supplier relationships
5. Improve constantly
6. Institute training
7. Institute leadership
8. Drive out fear
9. Break down departmental barriers
10. Eliminate slogans
11. Eliminate work quotas and management by objective
12. Remove barriers to workers' pride
13. Institute education
14. Make everyone's job the transformation

veloped and subsequently delivered to the entire company, including Schmidt.

Amazingly, the first results of the quality effort came from accounting and not manufacturing. The company's controller embraced the new quality way of thinking and succeeded in making great process improvement strides. Zytec's warehouse was the scene of the second success story. Good news stories such as these were publicized in a major campaign to spread the word that this new quality stuff really did work and could help others in the company.

In 1985, the outgrowth of all this was named the Total Quality Commitment (TQC). Note that the word is Commitment, not Control. This is important, for it signifies that a company can do it all if it *commits* to creating a utopian TQC environment. Zytec's TQC embodies four major principles:

- *Everyone has a customer for his or her work*
- *Everyone needs to completely understand their customer requirements*
- *Individuals accept complete responsibility for the quality of their output/product*
- *For every output/product, a process is in place to control and constantly improve it*

Considerable progress ensued, including the following highlights: In

1985, stock options were provided for all employees and SPC training courses were developed and delivered. In 1986, JIT was implemented throughout Zytec and the company installed its first auto insertion equipment. In 1987, Zytec's values statement was expanded to a book: *Guidelines to Zytec Values*. In 1988, the company introduced the engineering partnership concept to its customers, initiated self-managed work groups, Electronic Data Interchange (EDI) came on line with its first customer.

By 1989, Zytec concluded that it wanted to establish a finite goal. The company committed to winning the Baldrige Award by 1995 and pledged to use the process as a way to realign its continuous improvement culture. A Baldrige Steering Committee was formed consisting of the senior staff.

Trusting Employees

Zytec has a focus on trust and believes it is one of the most important things a company can do for its people. It sends that message to all its managers and employees. This is demonstrated in a number of ways. For instance, when Zytec was formed, it was decided that sick time and vacation time would not be tracked in traditional corporate ways. Instead, the days off are lumped together and employees manage their time off. Another example of trust was the elimination of time cards. Any full-time employee is automatically paid for forty hours a week. It is up to the employees to report if they worked more and earned overtime, or if they worked less and thereby earned less. Early on in the company, the decision was made to eliminate inspectors in manufacturing areas as the way to ensure quality standards were meet. The result was amazing. Quality levels improved! Workers rallied to being responsible for their own work.

Zytec is an employee-owned company and after one year of service, every full-time employee is given a stock option for a minimum of one thousand shares.

Training, Empowerment, and Recognition

To reach Zytec's goals, everybody works on quality transformation, and training is one of the key ways of providing employee growth and development. Courses cover total quality material, as well as personal development. Training includes the seven basic quality tools: check sheets, flow charts, scatter diagrams, histograms, control charts, Pareto charts, and fishbone diagrams, as well as Design of Experiments (DOE). Most employees have had 72 hours of quality coursework.

On the issue of employee empowerment, Zytec clearly puts its money where its mouth is. Every employee, without any prior approval, has the authority to spend up to $1,000 to delight a customer by resolving her or his complaint with Zytec's products or services. John Steel, Vice President of Sales and Marketing, says that while this sytem drives the controller crazy, it gives the employees the feeling that they do in fact have some power. Another empowerment example is that process changes can be made by hourly workers simply and quickly with the agreement of one other employee. Additionally, to foster customer service, Zytec sales personnel can authorize travel whenever they feel it is needed.

Zytec has a unique recognition program titled "Implemented Improvement Systems." It works this way: Employees that contribute to the company's suggestion program receive a dollar for their improvement idea. They then are asked to implement the suggestion after making sure it has their supervisor's approval. With that accomplished, their names go into a hopper, and if an employee's card is pulled out he or she can choose anyone in the company—another employee or any one of the executive team—to work in her or his place for a day. This is an earned day off with pay. As might be expected, the program has been a big hit with multiple payoffs— the employee is recognized with a paid day off, the company gains from the improvement, and the "stand-in" employee learns what is involved in the other's work. It gives new meaning, and sometimes more than a little humor, to the term cross-training.

Results

Zytec's product reliability, as demonstrated by field performance, has rocketed from less than 200,000 hours in 1985 to more than 4,600,000 hours in 1991. Product quality, as measured by customers, is up from 99 percent in 1988 to 99.9 percent in 1991. On-time delivery has improved from 75 percent in 1989 to 98 percent in 1991. Cycle time for new product design has been reduced 50 percent since 1988. Inventory turns have gone from 3.6 times in 1985 to 7.3 in 1990. With industry average sales per employee of $80,000, Zytec tops that at nearly $100,000. Since 1988, manufacturing yields are up 50 percent, cycle time is down 26 percent, and product costs have decreased 30 to 40 percent. Over the last three years, annual growth has been in the double digits. According to customer data, quality has come up to a four sigma range and Zytec is on course to reach its Six Sigma target by 1995. Additionally, Zytec's customers have recognized the company with nine supplier excellence awards.

The Minnesota Marvel—A New Benchmark

Zytec deserves a close examination by companies eager to apply for the Baldrige, but with limited resources. Consider what Zytec accomplished. Applying first in 1990 with an investment of 767 hours and $9,000 out-of-pocket expenses to cover site visits to Motorola and Xerox and the application fees, it made stage two in the evaluation process. Using the valuable feedback from its first year, the company improved and submitted again in 1991. Again costs were minimal: the application fee and the site visit of $11,000. Then in 1991, ahead of schedule (the target date to win was 1995) and on a modest budget, Zytec emerged victorious, both with the Baldrige Award at the national level and the Minnesota Quality Award, the state's quality prize. In a two-for-one sweep, Zytec deserves the title Minnesota Marvel. With costs at a minimum and payoff at a maximum, Zytec is a benchmark for others to emulate, not only in what it accomplished but in the manner in which it was done.

Zytec cofounder, John Steel, referring to his employees and the Baldrige win, said: "These are hard-working, quality-committed Americans, very excited about what the Malcolm Baldrige National Quality Award has done for us with respect to showing us precisely where we can take quality. It has armed us with a passion for quality and service excellence that has us excited about the decade of the '90s, and totally prepared to compete with anybody, anywhere, on quality and service excellence."

MARLOW INDUSTRIES, INC.:
TAKING THE QUALITY PLEDGE

> *When I first started Marlow Industries, I thought it was a quality company—being a high-tech, speciality oriented government supplier. But that was just the start. After much research and reflection, we decided quality to us meant meeting customer requirements. You may define it differently: meeting the customers' need or expectations or desires. The important thing is that all your employees know what quality means relative to your company.*

Raymond Marlow,
President,
Marlow Industries, Inc.

Business Overview

Marlow Industries, Inc., founded by Raymond Marlow in 1973 with five employees, has grown to become the world's leading manufacturer in thermoelectric coolers—solid state devices that control the temperature of electronic equipment. Headquarter in Dallas, Texas, Marlow is a privately held company employing 160 people. Facilities and equipment provide a fully vertically integrated operation. Manufacturing is organized into operations called minifactories, with three materials and five assembly minifactories. Customers include Fortune 500 corporations and international companies, as well as university and research facilities. Marlow's customer list includes such familiar names as Texas Instruments, telecommunications companies such as AT&T, and defense contractors, such as Hughes Aircraft, and the Loral Corporation. Commercial applications of Marlow's products include medical instrumentation and laser diodes. Defense- and space-related applications include inertial navigation systems, heat-seeking missiles, and satellites. Annual sales are approximately $13 million, with 15 percent coming from exports. Marlow provides both standard and custom-designed products in a highly specialized market. Since its founding, the company has grown to capture over half the thermoelectric cooler world market.

Launching the Quality Voyage

In 1986, Marlow launced its "quality voyage" with the goal to improve both manufacturing and service operations. The impetus for this voyage was not the usual story of market share losses, plummeting profits, or competitive pressure. Rather, it was Ray Marlow's concern with mounting problems that could potentially undermine the operation: a shortage of sound leadership, deteriorating employee morale, and poor communication between management and manufacturing. Frustrated customers were rejecting defective products. Employee turnover—already high—was getting higher.

Marlow's response was to begin what turned out to be a quality transformation. After some soul searching and putting to use his engineering background (he has previously worked at Texas Instruments), Ray Marlow began to establish a new system he and his employees could work on together. First, they discussed, deliberated, and finally agreed on some new language. Key terms became: culture, prevention, customers (both those inside the company as well as outside clients), world class, and, of course, quality, which they defined as meeting customer requirements. This common language base laid the foundation for Marlow's Total Quality Management system. The cornerstone of the system, shown in Figure 6.4, became the quality policy.

With a goal of becoming a world-class company, it was natural that Marlow's TQM system theme became: "The Voyage to World-Class and Beyond." Along with the goal came the awareness that winning the Baldrige Award meant a company was regarded as world class. With that, the destination for Marlow's quality voyage became to win the Award.

A Total Quality Management Council was formed to provide structure and focus for the emerging TQM system. Chaired by Ray Marlow, the TQM Council oversees the company's quality system, reviews quality processes, and identifies improvement areas. Work ranges from creating the strategic plan, assigning specific problems to department action teams, and handling the Baldrige Award application. The Council's weekly meetings

FIGURE 16.4
Marlow Industries Quality Policy

For every product or service we provide,
we will meet or exceed the customers'
requirements, without exception.
Our standard of performance is:
Do it Right Today, Better Tomorrow.

Source: Marlow Industries, Inc.

are attended by the six senior teams members and seven worker representatives who rotate participation annually.

Worth noting is a false start that occurred early in Marlow's quality push. In Ray Marlow's eagerness to implement quality, he began to convert the troops, going directly to the hourly employees and describing to them this quality thing. He set up weekly meetings where he would answer any quality questions they had. About six weeks into this program, not only were the questions pilling up faster than he could handle, they were getting more complex, and the whole process was becoming incredibly time consuming. By the end of the third month, Marlow concluded his quality system had become a disaster. Hourly people were mad because he was not answering all their questions; management was angry because they were not involved. He laments, "I had no friends within the company." A determined and wiser Ray Marlow regrouped to come back with a top-to-bottom plan that worked: first, get the senior team on board, then have them teach their people through a structured training and education system. Ray Marlow, with typical candor, shares this story that can serve as a lesson learned and provide some insight to help other organizations about to take the quality plunge.

Employees, Empowerment, and Cultural Change

Marlow believes that customer satisfaction comes from people, not companies. Customer satisfaction is really people dealing with people. Only through a commitment to total employee satisfaction can a company achieve total customer satisfaction. In benchmarking human resources, Marlow found all successful companies have one factor in common—a deep respect for people. At Marlow, people are regarded as partners, not tools. Marlow has worked to create a quality culture. The eight cultural changes that Marlow worked to achieve with each employee are as follows:

Marlow's Eight Cultural Changes

1. Quality Paramount
2. Market Segment Focus
3. External & Internal Customers
4. Prevention
5. Process Versus Product
6. Cross-Functional Involvement

7. Team-Based Activities

8. Empowerment & Involvement

Employee empowerment is one of Marlow's most important values. The company's flat organizational structure encourages worker involvement and empowerment. In order for employees to make decisions, training is absolutely critical.

Two of the company's most significant training approaches are the Professional Qualification System (PQS) Certification and Marlow Employee Effectiveness Teams (MEETs). The PQS certification is skills training for all job categories. The system requires that managers and supervisors be certified as well as workers. It includes an annual recertification, accompanied by a recognition. MEETs develop problem-solving and team-building skills. These voluntary teams select and resolve problems in their work area. Each team receives an 11-week initial training and is mentored by a TQM Council member. Solutions are presented to the TQM Council and each team is recognized with a plaque presented to all of the team members.

In 1988, 44 percent of all personnel participated on teams. That number jumped to 88 percent by 1990. About one percent of the company's revenues are invested in quality-related training. In 1991, that amounted to $120,000 for employees and $20,000 for suppliers.

The Quality Pledge

Marlow Industries has an individual, voluntary commitment to the company's performance standard, shown in Figure 16.5.

No pressure is applied to workers to sign the pledge. In fact, the company recommends that for the first 90 days of employment, a new employee not sign the pledge in order to have time to become oriented into the system. To date, all have signed up for quality—from the president to the hourly workers.

FIGURE 16.5
Marlow Industries Quality Pledge

I pledge to make a constant, conscious effort to do my
job right today, better tomorrow, recognizing that my individual
contribution is CRITICAL to the success of Marlow Industries.

Source: Marlow Industries, Inc.

First and foremost, it is essential that all employees believe and act on the company's value that quality is paramount. Focus on market segments enables workers to get close to the customer. Understanding both external and internal customer needs ensures smooth processes. Prevention, as opposed to product inspection, is the heart of systematic quality. Integration can be achieved by involving employees in cross-functional ways. Activities based on worker teams are the key mechanism for empowerment and involvement.

The cultural change has succeeded, as judged by the annual employee survey, where employees rated all the following key indicators 97 to 99 percent: They enjoy their jobs, believe in the company's Quality Policy, regard both the president and their supervisors as active quality supporters, and state they are able to meet internal customer requirements.

Customers

Customer Satisfaction has become the catalyst for Marlow's quality effort. The company attributes its impressive results directly to its customer-driven business philosophy, which includes keen, clear emphasis on market segmentation. Each segment with its own unique product and service requirements is supported by a market segment manager, an engineering design group, a customer service representative, and a manufacturing minifactory. This system enables a fast response to each customer, because employees know the customer who buys the product, the customer's requirements, and the product's model number. This translates into a well-honed system that does not build products for inventory, but products for customers.

As an authentic world-class company, Marlow firmly believes that its most important product is not thermoelectric coolers, but customer satisfaction. This is demonstrated in the quality policy, which appears on business cards, company literature, and packaging materials. Marlow accepts its customers' terms and conditions unconditionally. The company's product warranty is four times the industry norm. Its implied warranty includes product replacement beyond the usual warranty period, if the customer requires. Marlow stands alone in its industry as the only company to provide product reliability data to its customers.

Results

Over the past three years, Marlow's prices have stayed stable or been reduced. By taking this action, Marlow is able to make its customers more competitive. It also demonstrates that the company's quality system has lowered product costs and increased competitiveness.

Since 1987, worker productivity has soared at an average annual rate of 10 percent. During that same period, sales per employee is up about 50 percent, and engineering design cycle time has been cut 66 percent since 1988. Cost of nonconformance (poor quality) has been reduced approximately 50 percent since 1989—that is, scrap has been cut, rework reduced, warranty costs are down, and all the time it would have taken to redo all those things gone wrong has been saved.

Marlow's devotion to total customer satisfaction has paid major dividends. In the past 10 years the company has not lost a single major customer. In the past five years sales have grown at the rate of 15 percent per year. Market share has jumped more than 80 percent in the past three years, and new customers have increased from 780 to 1,200. In 1990, Marlow's top 10 customers rated the company's thermoelectric coolers at 100 percent—perfection! Since 1988, six major customers bestowed quality awards on Marlow.

The Quality Ship Sails On

Knowing well the need to continually improve to stay competitive, Marlow, in a pattern characteristic of Baldrige winners, is using its itemized Baldrige feedback to set its course for the next two to three years. Ray Marlow stated, "Our quest for world-class status resulted from the realization that total quality was not an option we could accomplish in our spare time; it was a matter of survival." Marlow added, "Total quality management took us from mere survival to national recognition. Our hope is that by sharing our story of success, you will take your insight back with you and put it to work in your organization and inspire the same creativity in others. Encouraging a generous flow of knowledge in an expanding and supportive network is an excellent start to securing the economic future of our country."

CHAPTER 17

BALDRIGE AND TQM
IMPACTS: U.S. AND GLOBAL

The success of the Malcolm Baldrige National Quality Award has demonstrated that government and industry, working together, can foster excellence.

Robert Mosbacher, Secretary of Commerce

As evidence mounted that Total Quality Management could invigorate even the most moribund coporation, it was inevitable that someone would wonder if quality management might not be a useful tool in other sorts of organizations and institutions.

If one thinks of information as a sort of virus, one can say that the quality virus began in this country but first reached epidemic proportions in Japan, where there was more sharing of knowledge between businesses in the post–World War II environment.

The quality virus reentered the American business population via manufacturing companies that visited Japan to see its effect firsthand, became infected, and then brought the virus home with them. Since then, these "Typhoid Marys" of quality have helped create an American epidemic of quality that first spread slowly, then more quickly, through the manufacturing and high-tech sectors and then into the general business population.

Twenty years after the quality virus returned to our shores, it has begun to spread into populations other than business. State and local government leaders, often smarting from declining tax revenues and increased demand for services, are looking to quality as a way to bring productivity, efficiency, and responsiveness back to government. Federal departments and agencies, smarting from budget cutbacks, are looking to quality as a way to streamline and invigorate their operations. (The Department of Defense, for instance, has discovered that sole sourcing, combined with quality education, is a very good way to get more "bang" for its bucks.)

Nonprofit institutions, which for a decade or more have seen the wisdom of emulating good business practices, are discovering quality as a means of survival in a lean economy. As with business, those institutions feeling the greatest threat are among the most eager students of quality. Quality seems tailor-made for the health care industry, where providers struggle with the dual mandate of providing the best possible quality care at the lowest possible cost. Likewise, educators are showing greater interest in quality management both as an administrative tool and as a discipline to be taught.

It would be wrong to paint a picture of a quality epidemic that is inevitable or unstoppable. In many institutions (not to mention tens of thousands of businesses), awareness is still very low, skepticism is still very high, or both. But the evidence is growing that quality can be applied to any organization's processes with positive effect. Only time will tell which institutions in this country will seize the opportunity to improve and which will fall by the wayside.

FEDERAL, STATE, AND LOCAL GOVERNMENTS DISCOVER TQM

Federal Government

Total Quality Management is being put to use in a variety of federal government departments and agencies. As the Baldrige Award administrator, the National Institute of Standards and Technology (NIST) has shared information and cooperated in activities with, among others, the Defense, Education, Labor, and Health and Human Services departments, and with the Federal Quality Institute, the General Accounting Office, and the Office of Management and Budget. Within various branches and agencies of the federal government, more than 20,000 Baldrige Award guidelines have been distributed.

Federal Quality Institute

In June 1988, the Federal Quality Institute was established by an executive order.

The mission of the Federal Quality Institute (FQI) is to promote and facilitate the implementation of Total Quality Management (TQM) throughout the federal government in order to improve the quality, timeliness, and efficiency of federal services to the American people.

To accomplish its mission, the Federal Quality Institute will serve as the catalyst for TQM in government in five major areas: coordination; training; technical assistance; information, resources and referrals; and model projects. In carrying out this role, FQI will collaborate with the Office of Management and Budget, the Office of Personnel Management, and the President's Council on Management Improvement toward the common goal of establishing TQM in federal agencies.

With 3.8 million government employees, this could be a somewhat daunting job for the FQI staff of 34. The game plan they have developed is to prudently use their resources and to initiate TQM awareness in government agencies.

Working with the agencies, FQI initially presents a TQM awareness overview, materials, and quality case histories of government agencies. FQI also provides agencies with start-up services, including top management briefings, readiness assessments, a quality council launching, and implementation planning. FQI has selected six federal agencies to participate in its Total Quality Model Partnership Program:

1. The Federal Communications Commission.
2. The Department of Energy, Richland, Washington, Regional Office.
3. The Department of Transportation, National Direct Program.
4. The Veteran's Administration.
5. The Department of Air Force, Office of the Secretary.
6. The Defense Logistics Agency.

For these agencies, the FQI game plan is getting results.

FCC's Sikes: Quality Role Model

The Federal Communications Commission (FCC) in 1990 launched a Total Quality Management process with the help of FQI. The FCC has established a quality council, been trained in Total Quality Management, and set up quality improvement teams.

FCC chairman Alfred C. Sikes ran the National Telecommunications and Information Administration at the Department of Commerce when Malcolm Baldrige served as secretary. In 1989, President Bush tapped Sikes for the FCC position. As chairman, Sikes speaks out on the critical need for service excellence in the communications industry. His quality orientation is evidenced in the statement, "I want to make sure we align our regulations to the new competitive realities of the marketplace."

When Congress established the Baldrige Award, Sikes was at the Department of Commerce and became steeped in the Award. His current agenda includes promotion and advancement of service excellence. Under Sikes's leadership, the FCC goals have decided TQM underpinnings. One states: "Provide excellent service to the public in the most efficient, uncomplicated, timely, and courteous manner possible." Another goal is: "Promote the vital interests of the American people in international communications and competitiveness."

Sikes chairs the FCC's nine-member quality council and hopes to provide a role model for the entire communications industry. Given his prior association with Malcolm Baldrige, Sikes is especially proud to be involved in the application of Baldrige Award Total Quality Management principles to the federal government. Lessons learned from the FCC and the other five participants in the FQI's model program will be used as case studies to advance other federal agencies in their TQM pursuits.

President's Award

The FQI also administers the President's Award for Quality and Productivity Improvement. This award was initiated in 1988 by President Ronald Reagan to recognize Total Quality Management excellence in the federal government. This presidential award is closely modeled after the Malcolm Baldrige National Quality Award process. Eligible agencies document their accomplishments in the award's criteria, as shown in Figure 17.1.

Applications are evaluated by a panel of private- and public-sector quality management experts, and site visits are conducted with the finalists. There can be up to two winners selected each year. Eligibility for the President's Award is secured by an organization's receipt of one or more Quality Improvement Prototype (QIP) Awards.

QIP Awards

In the QIP program, applicants prepare written reports of their performance according to TQM criteria. An examiner panel recommends finalists to

FIGURE 17.1
President's Award for Quality and Productivity Improvement, 1991

- Top Management Leadership and Support.
- Strategic Planning.
- Focus on the Customer.
- Employee Training and Recognition.
- Employee Empowerment and Teamwork.
- Measurement and Analysis.
- Quality Assurance.
- Quality and Productivity Improvement Results.

Source: Federal Quality Institute

receive site visits. After review, a panel of judges selects up to six winners. Quality Improvement Prototype winners are then responsible for preparing case studies detailing their Total Quality Management successes, which they share at workshops. In this way, lessons learned from the exceptional federal organizations can be emulated by others.

The Internal Revenue Service Federal Tax Deposit System (FTD) won a 1988 Quality Improvement Prototype Award. The FTD affects over five million business taxpayers, who make 70 million deposits annually totalling over $700 billion in revenue. By using Total Quality Management methods, including statistical techniques, in one year the IRS reduced errors of items not posted to accounts from 35,000 to less than 4,000 per week. By improved work processes, better tracking, and employee training, the error rate continues to decline.

In 1990, the Defense Industrial Supply Center (DISC) received a Quality Improvement Prototype Award. DISC is part of the Defense Logistics Agency of the Department of Defense. The center buys and manages hardware in support of U.S. and allied military services. Since introducing TQM in 1986, the center has seen impressive results. In the area of materials testing and evaluating, DISC established a nationwide laboratory network to reduce test turnaround time from 120 days to three weeks. In another area, supply availability reached 89 percent, the highest level in five years.

The Naval Aviation Depot in Cherry Point, North Carolina, is one of seven NAVAIR depots. This government installation has dramatically reduced repair costs for components, engines, and aircraft. From 1985 to 1987, the average cost of repairing an engine component dropped $7,000 per unit. From January 1986 to September 1989, standard repair and maintenance on one type of aircraft decreased by as much as $55,000. Productivity gainsharing reinforces workers' quality involvement efforts. In February 1988, a 10 percent productivity increase earned each employee a first quarterly payout of $265. In 1988, Cherry Point was recognized with a Quality Improvement Prototype Award for substantial quality improvement results.

The Naval Air Systems Command (NAVAIR) was presented with the first Presidential Award for Quality and Productivity Improvement on June 2, 1989, at the Second Annual Conference on Federal Quality and Productivity Improvement. NAVAIR has 28 U.S. sites and employs 48,000 people. It is responsible for acquisition, testing, support, and maintenance of naval aircraft and aviation weapon systems. Since 1984, NAVAIR has used Total Quality Management to drive its operations.

The Navy's TQM achievements reflect the guidance of Secretary of the Navy H. Lawrence Garrett III and the commanding admirals. Commitment to training over 300 top officers has given TQM a solid foundation, and the tight budget constraints have propelled implementation.

Department of Defense

The Defense Department's TQM thrust is like a corporate quality program writ large. Consider that the Department of Defense (DOD) employs 4.3 million people and produces 11 percent of our country's manufactured output. The drivers of DOD's quality push are similar to those of industry's: costs in the form of budget constraints, foreign competition (notably in the aerospace industry), and a growing commitment to improvement. The quality strategies are similar as well: involve leadership, educate employees, and implement continuous improvement.

Secretary of Defense Dick Cheney is a total quality advocate. Under the Pentagon's coordination, each of the armed services is tailoring its own quality process. To quicken the pace of quality improvement, the Pentagon has benchmarked various industries' quality initiatives with visits to world-class companies. Pentagon briefings have featured quality leaders such as Bob Galvin of Motorola. Quality gurus W. Edwards Deming and Joseph M. Juran both have made presentations to DOD. All signs indicate the Defense Department is on an all-out, sustained campaign to secure quality. In 1991, another victory was scored when the Air Force Logistics Command captured the second Presidential Award for Quality and Productivity Improvement.

State Governments

The impact of TQM has extended beyond the federal level out into the states. Regions hit by economic erosion and competitive challenge have increasingly turned to quality. Throughout the country, networks have sprung up to use quality as a primary tool for economic development. Among such organizations are the Arkansas Industrial Development Commission's Quality Productivity Task Force, the Iowa Quality Coalition, the Minnesota Council for Quality, and the Ohio Quality and Productivity Forum. Workshops and training are being offered; quality councils are being formed; improvements are underway. The Baldrige criteria and its Total Quality Management blueprint are being used by many of these groups to advance their efforts.

Just as the impetus for the MBNQA was to improve competitiveness and economic viability on a national level, so it goes for the states. A number of states have established quality awards based upon the Baldrige criteria, including Minnesota, New York, Wyoming and at least 30 others, are planning an award or are involved in some other program to push quality. Much of this work is still in the formation stages. Information from many groups is just beginning to come together.

The framework of the state awards replicates most, if not all, of the Baldrige process. The National Quality Award (NQA) director, Curt Reimann, has been supportive of state award initiatives, viewing them as a way to further the national interest.

New York

New York State has created the Governor's Excelsior Award, modeled after the Baldrige Award. Unique to New York's effort is the strong labor-management partnership that supported its development. Manufacturing and service businesses, state or local government entities, and educational institutions are eligible for the Excelsior Award. Application criteria have been tailored for the three award categories: private sector, public sector, and education. The first awards will be given in 1992. Governor Mario M. Cuomo has stated, "To win the Award, businesses, government organizations, and educational institutions must demonstrate commitment to quality products and services, a quality work force, and cooperative labor-management relations."

Wyoming

Governor Mike Sullivan presented Wyoming's first quality award in May 1988. The Wyoming award, based on the Baldrige criteria, recognized Unilink, a computer software company, for its outstanding commitment to quality improvement. The state's International Trade Office was a strong sponsor of this recognition, out of the conviction that quality-committed companies are best suited for export development.

Minnesota

The Minnesota Quality Award also follows the NQA framework. It utilizes the same three categories—manufacturing, service, and small business—with up to two awards in each category. Volunteer examiners attend a Baldrige-like training program. The Minnesota Council for Quality sponsors the award. Many organizations are already conducting internal Baldrige self-assessments to upgrade their quality, and the state award furnishes an invaluable third-party review. This process not only yields a second level of evaluation, it also helps companies prepare for a third level—actually competing nationally for the Baldrige Award. Minesota presented its first award in October 1991 to Zytec Corporation of Eden Prairie. That same month, Zytec became one of three 1991 Baldrige Award winners.

Colorado

The Colorado Quality Award being developed is based on Baldrige. But unlike the National Quality Award, it will not limit the number of winners in each of its categories, which—in addition to manufacturing, service, and small business—will include educational institutions, nonprofit organizations, and government entities. This means that public and private schools, health care and charitable organizations, and state and local governments will be eligible.

As a part of Colorado's growing support of Total Quality Management, Governor Roy Romer and his staff in 1990 participated in two days of quality training presented by quality practitioners from Colorado companies and a state university with its own quality program.

Baldrige-winning companies are in a key position to provide considerable support to the states in which they reside. They can explain Total Quality Management and illustrate the vital importance of TQM in helping the organizations within the state be stronger and more competitive.

Local Governments

The quality revolution is having a ripple effect in cities across the country as local areas become involved in Total Quality Management. People who have seen quality improvement in the workplace want to use those same techniques to strengthen their municipalities. Communities in California, Colorado, Indiana, Minnesota, Ohio, Pennsylvania, Tennessee, Washington, Wisconsin, and elsewhere have both private and public groups putting together TQM resources.

Madison, Wisconsin

Madison, Wisconsin, is one of the pioneers in community quality improvement. Until 1980, Madison's economy was stable, with a historically secure service-sector base. The city is the county seat, state capital, and home of the state university. Several large manufacturing firms also are based in Madison. However, two linked events in the early 1980s began to change relative security to uncertainty. First, as Madison's demographics changed, so did its economy. The waning baby boom spelled declining university enrollments and fewer consumers. Second, state government spending was restrained.

When things get tough, people begin to consider alternatives. In 1983, quality practitioners from government and the private sector began to coalesce around the idea of involving the city in quality management. With the support of industry, education, and government, the mayor got behind this venture. By 1985, this effort had evolved into the Madison Area Quality Improvement Network, or MAQIN.

MAQIN supplies the leadership support for local quality improvement. The group sponsors annual national conferences, furnishes quality resources, and sponsors improvement projects. In 1984, a quality project was launched in the municipal motor vehicle repair center. Complaints were growing that city vehicles broke down too often and took too long to repair. Low morale and labor-management contentiousness added to the frustration. A team trained in quality techniques, including statistics and group skills, was launched. The first project tackled was improving repair time and customer relations. Problem-solving produced multiple results: Repair turnaround time was cut to two and a half days from more than nine, workers' sense of pride in their work increased, and the local union president became a supporter of quality improvement. The success of this teamwork inspired other achievements and moved Madison down the road on its quality journey.

HIGHER EDUCATION ENROLLS IN QUALITY

At present, relatively few universities offer formal courses in TQM. This lack of quality education is a major stumbling block to the United States improving its competitive position.

Corporations that have led the way in quality knowledge are providing a remedy to this problem. Many Baldridge-winning companies, including Motorola and Xerox, have developed their own comprehensive quality curricula, ranging from new employee quality orientation to design for manufacturability. There are even advanced courses in statistics and cycle-time reductions. But it has been clear from the beginning that the need for quality education far outstripped the ability of even the largest and most commited companies. Now these companies have begun to work with colleges and universities to remedy this problem.

In 1989, when David Kearns, chairman of Xerox Corporation, served as chair of the 1989 National Quality Month campaign, he sponsored a Quality Forum in Leesburg, Virginia. The forum brought together leaders from industry, government, and business schools in an effort to generate interest and support from the higher education community for reinforcing quality as a part of the curriculum. It was hoped that an industry-academic partnership would develop strategies for working together to improve competitiveness.

Representatives attended from 21 academic institutions, including Carnegie Mellon University; the University of Chicago; Columbia University; Duke University; the European Institute of Business Administration; Harvard University; the University of Hull, England; Massachusetts Institute of Technology (MIT); the University of Michigan; the University of Tennessee; and the University of Tokyo. Among the corporations participating were Alcoa, AT&T, General Motors, Milliken, and Motorola. Government agencies present were the Department of Commerce and the Department of Education.

"To be competitive as a nation, we must do two things: improve quality and improve education," asserted David Kearns to business school participants. "U.S. business, collectively or singly, cannot survive in world competition by itself. We need your help." Kearns cited the country's business schools as a critical resource and called on them to:

- Understand the needs of industry.
- Graduate a generation of managers who understand quality.
- Imbed statistics, total quality, and participative management into their curricula.
- Intensify the study of culture change.
- Form a partnership with industry to recapture worldwide competitive advantage.

Crucial to the United States having a competitive edge is the knowledge base the business schools can provide. The forum's major outcome was agreement about the need for industry, business schools, and government to work in partnership for Total Quality Management.

The momentum of the first Xerox Quality Forum led to a second, held in July and August of 1990 and again hosted by Kearns. Its purpose was to continue to look at ways business schools can be involved in improving U.S. competitiveness.

At this meeting, Lester Thurow, dean of the MIT Sloan School of Management, described disturbing changes in factors that once ensured U.S. economic success: The United States long dominated the global economy, thanks to its abundant natural resources, capital, and technology, and to an educated work force. But in the new global environment, natural resources, capital, and technology no longer guarantee competitive advantage. According to Thurow, "The education and skills of the work force will be the key competitive weapon in the 21st century."

New technologies require that the average worker possess state-of-the-art skills and adapt to the rapid pace of change. American companies traditionally invest less to educate the average employee than their Japanese or German counterparts . The bulk of our monies are invested in training the professional manager. To survive, the United States needs not only to increase its overall investment in education, but also to significantly increase the proportion invested in educating nonprofessional (skilled and nonskilled) workers.

Don Ritter, the Pennsylvania congressman who authored legislation designating October as National Quality Month, thinks that universities, colleges, and business and engineering schools need to take a larger role in solving education problems facing the United States. He believes businesses should become the linchpin in the quality revolution instead of the missing link.

Several academic institutions reported significant steps toward integrating Total Quality Management into their curricula. The first undergraduate degree in quality was offered at Marian College in Fond du Lac, Wisconsin. This school took a customer-driven approach and worked with the business community in designing a program whose curriculum includes both conceptual quality fundamentals and practical methods for improvement for manufacturing and service industries.

Bob Galvin, chairman of the Motorola Executive Committee, offered a partnership to the Kellogg Graduate School of Management at Northwestern University whereby Motorola provided the quality teaching resources and Kellogg agreed to incorporate quality into its MBA program as an elective operations management course. While electives typically draw approximately 20 students, this particular course was such a hit that a second session had to be opened.

The Xerox Quality Forum panel concluded that universities need to link quality to their institutional missions and not only teach the quality process but also use it to improve from within. There was also agreement that business needs to intensify education requirements with a strong message that TQM is an employment essential. Partnerships such as the Motorola-Kellogg collaboration should be models others emulate.

Some business schools have responded to the quality call and introduced quality into their programs. Classes in quality management theory and practice are now either offered as electives or required at Columbia University, the Rochester Institute of Technology, the University of Chicago, the University of Colorado at Denver, the University of Denver, the University of New Mexico, New York University, the University of Pennsylvania, the University of Pittsburgh, the University of Tennessee, the University of Virginia, and George Washington University.

FUTURE TRENDS: THE RACE GOES ON

Global competitiveness continually escalates the race for quality. The Pacific Rim relentlessly pushes its quality initiatives. As the European Community (EC) evolves, so does support for common quality standards. The EC plans to become a single market by December 31, 1992. This will represent a united body of 12 member states and over 350 million people. The advent of EC 1992 intensifies the need for a common European quality standard. The challenge has been to develop "Euronorms" to provide uniform standards from the existing conglomeration of quality certification and specification systems.

The International Organization for Standardization in 1987 published the ISO-9000 series of quality systems standards. These have gained wide acceptance in Europe. The ISO series of standards—ISO-9000, -9001, -9002, -9003, and -9004—are guidelines for the design and development, production, final inspection and testing, installation, and servicing of products, processes, or services. ISO standards require a company to have documentation of its quality systems and go through a registration process that consists of an extensive third-party audit.

While to date a limited number of U.S. companies have registered for ISO-9000, factors are converging that could change this. These factors include 1) growing worldwide acceptance of ISO-9000 as quality systems standards and 2) belief that ISO-9000 registration will be required for doing business in Europe and elsewhere, and by regulatory agencies for product certification.

ISO-9000 is part of the worldwide movement toward systematic quality. Undergoing the ISO-9000 audit process is valuable to companies with no established quality system, since it addresses some of the essential elements for a quality management system. Elements not addressed by ISO-9000, but embodied in MBNQA, include emphasis on Total Quality Management, continuous improvement, and customer satisfaction.

A considerable number of companies doing international business have discovered that the Malcolm Baldrige National Quality Award and ISO-9000 work well together. The ISO-9000 process is being used by many companies as a stepping-stone to the Baldrige Award. It is significant to note that all Baldrige Award winners to date have been international competitors, and a number of them are involved in using ISO standards.

European professional societies have made various attempts to establish a national quality award similar in scope and impact to the Baldrige Award. Approximately 25 nations have asked for and received information about the U. S. Award. The European Foundation for Quality Management (EFQM), established in 1988, has studied the Malcolm Baldrige National Quality Award. A pan-European quality management award will be presented for the first time by the EFQM in 1992. The European Quality Award will recognize exceptional Total Quality Management assessed according to the criteria shown in Figure 17.2.

FIGURE 17.2
The European Quality Award

- **Customer Satisfaction**—The perceptions of external customers, direct and indirect, of the company and of its products and services.   20%
- **People**—The management of the company's people and the peoples' feelings about the company.   18%
- **Business Results**—The company's achievement in relation to its planned business performance.   15%
- **Processes**—The management of all the value-adding activities within the company.   14%
- **Leadership**—The behavior of all managers in transforming the company towards Total Quality.   10%
- **Resources**—The management, utilization and preservation of financial resources, information resources, and technological resources.   9%
- **Policy and Strategy**—The company's vision, values, and direction, and the ways in which it achieves them.   8%
- **Impact on Society**—The perceptions of the community at large of the company. Views on the company's approach to quality of life, to the environment, and to the need for preservation of global resources are included.   6%

Source: European Foundation for Quality Management

It's Just the Beginning

The United States has been a dominant world economic force for the past 100 years. Dramatic global changes now threaten our competitive position. The Japanese and other Pacific Rim countries continue to deliver their unrelenting competitive blows. With the advent of EC 1992, the U.S. economy may be further impacted.

In Akio Morita and Shintaro Ishihara's book *The Japan that Can Say No: The New U.S.–Japan Relations Card,* Morita, chairman of Sony Corporation, states that in the 21st century Japan will emerge as the victor in the superpower economic wars. German Chancellor Helmut Kohl has said the decade of the 1990s belongs to Europe. Both of these opinions reflect a growing perception that economic leadership will come down to a battle between Europe and Japan. In each case, the United States is not mentioned as a contender.

To be competitive, in fact to survive, the United States must embrace Total Quality Management. The Baldrige Award is, indeed, a blueprint that can guide us to a economic renaissance. The National Quality Award helps us look farther ahead than the next quarter. It gives us the means to integrate and strengthen our organizations.

Baldrige winners are proof that it is possible for U.S. companies to be competitive and to win in the tough global marketplace. They demonstrate—through their customer focus, committed leadership, management by fact, human resources investments, and quality systems that produce competitive results—that it is possible to succeed through constant and continual improvements. The issue is no longer what we need to do to improve quality. Much of that issue is addressed by the requirements of the Baldrige Award. The issue now is the rate of change that companies must meet to stay competitive. To survive, the pace of quality improvement must be revolutionary, not evolutionary. The times call for nothing less, and Baldrige can help us get there by the shortest route possible.

APPENDIX A

MALCOLM BALDRIGE NATIONAL QUALITY AWARD EXAMINATION CATEGORIES AND ITEMS, 1988–1992

Malcolm Baldrige National Quality Award Evolution

1992 Examination Categories

Categories/Items		Maximum Points	Percent of Total
1.0 Leadership		90	9
1.1 Senior Executive Leadership	45		
1.2 Management for Quality	25		
1.3 Public Responsibility	20		
2.0 Information and Analysis		80	8
2.1 Scope and Management of Quality and Performance Data and Information	15		
2.2 Competitive Comparisons and Benchmarks	25		
2.3 Analysis and Uses of Company-Level Data	40		
3.0 Strategic Quality Planning		60	6
3.1 Strategic Quality and Compnay Performance Planning Process	35		
3.2 Quality and Performance Plans	25		
4.0 Human Resource Development and Management		150	15
4.1 Human Resource Management	20		
4.2 Employee Involvement	40		
4.3 Employee Education and Training	40		
4.4 Employee Performance and Recognition	25		
4.5 Employee Well-Being and Morale	25		
5.0 Management of Process Quality		140	14
5.1 Design and Introduction of Quality Products and Services	40		
5.2 Process Management—Product and Service Production and Delivery Processes	35		
5.3 Process Management—Business Processes and Support Services	20		
5.4 Supplier Quality	20		
5.5 Quality Assessment	15		
6.0 Quality and Operational Results		180	18
6.1 Product and Service Quality Results	75		
6.2 Company Operational Results	45		
6.3 Business Process and Support Service Results	25		
6.4 Supplier Quality Results	35		
7.0 Customer Focus and Satisfaction		300	30
7.1 Customer Relationship Management	65		
7.2 Commitment to Customers	15		
7.3 Customer Satisfaction Determination	35		
7.4 Customer Satisfaction Results	75		
7.5 Customer Satisfaction Comparison	75		
7.6 Future Requirements and Expectations of Customers	35		
TOTAL POINTS		1000	

Malcolm Baldrige National Quality Award Evolution

1991 Examination Categories

Categories/Items		Maximum Points	Percent of Total
1.0 Leadership		100	10
1.1	Senior Executive Leadership	40	
1.2	Quality Values	15	
1.3	Management for Quality	25	
1.4	Public Responsibility	20	
2.0 Information and Analysis		70	7
2.1	Scope and Management of Quality Data and Information	20	
2.2	Competitive Comparisons and Benchmarks	30	
2.3	Analysis of Quality Data and Information	20	
3.0 Strategic Quality Planning		60	6
3.1	Strategic Quality Planning Process	35	
3.2	Quality Goals and Plans	25	
4.0 Human Resource Utilization		150	15
4.1	Human Resource Management	20	
4.2	Employee Involvement	40	
4.3	Quality Education and Training	40	
4.4	Employee Recognition and Performance Measurement	25	
4.5	Employee Well-Being and Morale	25	
5.0 Quality Assurance of Products and Services		140	14
5.1	Design and Introduction of Quality Products and Services	35	
5.2	Process Quality Control	20	
5.3	Continuous Improvement of Processes	20	
5.4	Quality Assessment	15	
5.5	Documentation	10	
5.6	Business Process and Support Service Quality	20	
5.7	Supplier Quality	20	
6.0 Quality Results		180	18
6.1	Product and Service Quality Results	90	
6.2	Business Process, Operational, and Support Service Quality Results	50	
6.3	Supplier Quality Results	40	
7.0 Customer Satisfaction		300	30
7.1	Determining Customer Requirements and Expectations	30	
7.2	Customer Relationship Management	50	
7.3	Customer Service Standards	20	
7.4	Commitment to Customers	15	
7.5	Complaint Resolution for Quality Improvement	25	
7.6	Determining Customer Satisfaction	20	
7.7	Customer Satisfaction Results	70	
7.8	Customer Satisfaction Comparison	70	
TOTAL POINTS		1000	

1990 Examination Categories

Categories/Items		Maximum Points	Percent of Total
1.0 Leadership		100	10
1.1	Senior Executive Leadership	30	
1.2	Quality Values	20	
1.3	Management for Quality	30	
1.4	Public Responsibility	20	
2.0 Information and Analysis		60	6
2.1	Scope and Management of Quality Data and Information	35	
2.2	Analysis of Quality Data and Information	25	
3.0 Strategic Quality Planning		90	9
3.1	Strategic Quality Planning Process	40	
3.2	Quality Leadership Indicators in Planning	25	
3.3	Quality Priorities	25	
4.0 Human Resource Utilization		150	15
4.1	Human Resource Management	30	
4.2	Employee Involvement	40	
4.3	Quality Education and Training	40	
4.4	Employee Recognition and Performance Measurement	20	
4.5	Employee Well-Being and Morale	20	
5.0 Quality Assurance of Products and Services		150	15
5.1	Design and Introduction of Quality Products and Services	30	
5.2	Process and Quality Control	25	
5.3	Continuous Improvement of Processes, Products and Services	25	
5.4	Quality Assessment	15	
5.5	Documentation	10	
5.6	Quality Assurance, Quality Assessment and Quality Improvement of Support Services and Business Processes	25	
5.7	Quality Assurance, Quality Assessment and Quality Improvement of Suppliers	20	
6.0 Quality Results		150	15
6.1	Quality of Products and Services	50	
6.2	Comparison of Quality Results	35	
6.3	Business Process, Operational and Support Service Quality Improvement	35	
6.4	Supplier Quality Improvement	30	
7.0 Customer Satisfaction		300	30
7.1	Knowledge of Customer Requirements and Expectations	50	
7.2	Customer Relationship Management	30	
7.3	Customer Service Standards	20	
7.4	Commitment to Customers	20	
7.5	Complaint Resolution for Quality Improvement	30	
7.6	Customer Satisfaction Determination	50	
7.7	Customer Satisfaction Results	50	
7.8	Customer Satisfaction Comparison	50	
TOTAL POINTS		1000	

1989 Examination Categories

Categories/Items	Maximum Points	Percent of Total
1.0 Leadership	120	12
1.1 Senior Management	30	
1.2 Quality Values	20	
1.3 Management System	50	
1.4 Public Responsibility	20	
2.0 Information and Analysis	60	6
2.1 Scope of Data and Information for "Management by Fact"	25	
2.2 Data Management	15	
2.3 Analysis and Use of Data for Decision Making	20	
3.0 Strategic Quality Planning	80	8
3.1 Planning Process	30	
3.2 Plans for Quality Leadership	50	
4.0 Human Resource Utilization	150	15
4.1 Management	25	
4.2 Employee Involvement	40	
4.3 Quality Education and Training	30	
4.4 Employee Recognition	20	
4.5 Quality of Work Life	35	
5.0 Quality Assurance of Products and Services	140	14
5.1 Design and Introduction of New or Improved Products and Services	25	
5.2 Operation of Processes Which Produce the Company's Products and Service	20	
5.3 Measurements and Standards for Products, Processes and Services	15	
5.4 Audit	20	
5.5 Documentation	10	
5.6 Quality Assurance of Operations and Business Processes	25	
5.7 Quality Assurance of External Providers of Goods and Services	25	
6.0 Quality Results	150	15
6.1 Quality of Products and Services	70	
6.2 Operational and Business Process Quality Improvement	60	
6.3 Quality Improvement Applications	20	
7.0 Customer Satisfaction	300	30
7.1 Knowledge of Customer Requirements and Expectations	40	
7.2 Customer Relationship Management	125	
7.3 Customer Satisfaction Methods of Measurements and Results	135	
TOTAL POINTS	1000	

1988 Examination Categories

Categories/Items		Maximum Points	Percent of Total
1.0 Leadership		150	15
1.1	Senior Corporate Leadership	50	
1.2	Policy	30	
1.3	Management System and Quality Improvement Processes	30	
1.4	Resource Allocation and Utilization	20	
1.5	Public Responsibility	10	
1.6	Unique and Innovative Leadership Techniques	10	
2.0 Information and Analysis		75	7.5
2.1	Use of Analytical Techniques or Systems	15	
2.2	Use of Product or Service Quality Data	10	
2.3	Customer Data and Analysis	20	
2.4	Supplier Quality and Data Analysis	10	
2.5	Distributor and/or Dealer Quality and Data Analysis	10	
2.6	Employee Related Data and Analysis	5	
2.7	Unique and Innovative Information/Analysis	5	
3.0 Strategic Quality Planning		75	7.5
3.1	Operational and Strategic Goals	20	
3.2	Planning Function	20	
3.3	Planning for Quality Improvement	30	
3.4	Unique and Innovative Planning	5	
4.0 Human Resource Utilization		150	15
4.1	Management and Operations	30	
4.2	Employee Quality Awareness and Involvement	50	
4.3	Quality Training and Education	30	
4.4	Evaluation, Incentive, and Recognition Systems	30	
4.5	Unique and Innovative Approaches	10	
5.0 Quality Assurance of Products and Services		150	15
5.1	Customer Input to Products and Services	20	
5.2	Planning for New or Improved Products or Services	20	
5.3	Design of New or Improved Products and Services	30	
5.4	Measurements, Standards, and Data System	10	
5.5	Technology	10	
5.6	Audit	15	
5.7	Documentation	10	
5.8	Safety, Health and Environment	10	
5.9	Assurance/Validation	15	
5.10	Unique and Innovative Approaches	10	
6.0 Results from Quality Assurance of Products and Services		100	10
6.1	Reliability and Performance of Products or Services	25	
6.2	Reductions in Scrap, Rework and Rejected Products or Services	20	
6.3	Reductions in Claims, Litigation and Complaints Related to Quality	25	
6.4	Reductions in Warranty or Field Support Work	20	
6.5	Unique or Innovative Indicators of Quality Improvements or Economic Gains	10	

7.0	Customer Satisfaction		300	30
	7.1 Customer Views of Quality of Products or Services	100		
	7.2 Competitive Comparison of Products or Services	50		
	7.3 Customer Service and Complaint Handling	75		
	7.4 Customer Views of Guaranties/Warranties	50		
	7.5 Unique or Innovative Approaches to Assessing Customer Satisfaction	25		
	TOTAL POINTS		1000	

BIBLIOGRAPHY

Abrahamson, Peggy. "Malcolm Baldrige Award Encourages U.S. Industry's Quest for Quality." *Business America*, May 22, 1989, pp. 8–9.

Application Guidelines 1988, 1989, 1990, 1991: Malcolm Baldrige National Quality Award. Gaithersburg, Md: National Institute of Standards and Technology, United States Department of Commerce.

Bemowski, Karen. "Big Q at Big Blue." *Quality Progress*, May 1991, pp. 17–21.

Bennett, Amanda, and Jolie Solomon. "Is Quality Award Becoming Job 1 for U.S. Companies?" *The Wall Street Journal*," November 3, 1989.

Bhote, Keki R. "Motorola's Long March to the Malcolm Baldrige National Quality Award," *National Productivity Review* vol. 8, no. 4, (Autumn 1989), pp. 365–76.

Braun, Carl, John Foley, Eileen Sweeny and Glegg Watson, edited by Ken Breen, Eileen Sweeny and Hal Tragash. *The Xerox Corporation 1989 Xerox Quality Forum Report*. Stamford, Connecticut: Xerox Corporation, 1989.

Buzzell, R. D. and B. T. Gale. *The PIMS Principles*. New York: Free Press, 1987.

Caldwell, Bruce, Paul Schindler; and J. B. Miles. "Making It Like They Used To." *Information Week*, January 7, 1991, pp. 36–39.

Castro, Janice. "Making It Better." *Time*, November 13, 1989, pp. 78–81.

DeCarlo, Neil J., and W. Kent Sterett. "History of the Malcolm Baldrige National Quality Award." *Quality Progress*, March 1990, pp. 21–27.

Deming, Edwards W. *Out of the Crisis*. Cambridge: Massachusetts Institute of Technology, Center for Advanced Engineering Study, 1982.

———. *Quality, Productivity, and Competitive Position* Cambridge: Massachusetts Institute of Technology, Center for Advanced Engineering Study, 1982.

Dobyns, Lloyd. "Ed Deming Wants Big Changes, and He Wants Them Fast." *Smithsonian*, August 1990, pp. 74–82.

Dreyfuss, Joel. "Victories in the Quality Crusade." *Fortune*, October 10, 1988, pp. 80–88.

Drucker, Peter E. "The Emerging Theory of Manufacturing." *Harvard Business Review*, May–June 1990, pp. 94–102.

Electronic Business. Special Issue, "Commitment to Quality." October 1990.

————. Special Issue, "Quest for Quality." October 1989.

Feigenbaum, Armand V. "Time to Get Up Front on Quality." *The Quality Review*. Spring 1988, p. 15.

Flint, Jerry. "A Year for Living Dangerously." *Forbes*, March 4, 1991, pp. 84–85.

Fortune. Special Issue, "The New American Century." Spring/Summer 1991.

Foster, Geoffrey. "The Juran Quality Cure." *Management Today*, November 1987, pp. 80–81.

Fuchsberg, Gilbert. "Nonprofits May Get Own Baldrige Prizes." *The Wall Street Journal*, March 14, 1991.

Gallagan, Patricia A. "How Wallace Chaged Its Mind." *Training & Development*, June 1991, pp. 23–28.

Garvin, David A. "Competing on the Eight Dimensions of Quality." *Harvard Business Review*, November–December 1987, pp. 101–109.

Gilbert, Gaye E. "Be Bold and Be Right: The Wallace Co., Inc., Wins 1990 Baldrige Award." American Productivity & Quality Center, February 1991, pp. 1–8.

Glover, M. Katherine. "Malcolm Baldrige National Quality Award: The Quest for Excellence." *Business America*, December 5, 1988, pp. 2–11.

Gustke, Constance A. "Making Big Gains from Small Steps." *Fortune*, April 23, 1990, pp. 119–122.

Halberstam, David. *The Reckoning*. New York: William Morrow & Co., Inc. 1986.

Harris, Lana J., editor. A *Report of the Proceedings from the Xerox Quality Forum II*. Stamford, Connecticut: Xerox Corporation, 1990.

Henkoff, Ronald. "Make Your Office More Productive." *Fortune*. February 15, 1991, pp. 72–84.

Holusha, John. "The Baldrige Badge of Courage—and Quality." *The New York Times*, October 21, 1990.

————. "Stress on Quality Lifts Xerox's Market Share." *The New York Times*, November 9, 1989.

Horton, Marion. "Wallace Goes for the Baldrige." *Supply House Times*, October 1990, pp. 143–249.

Howard, Robert. "Can Small Business Help Countries Compete?" *Harvard Business Review*, November–December 1990, pp. 88–103.

Inglesby, Tom. "How They Brought Home the Prize." *Manufacturing Systems*, April, 1989, pp. 26–32.

Irving, Robert R. "What One Expert Says about Our Product Quality." *Iron Age*, July 15, 1981, pp. 49–50.

Ishikawa, Kaoru. *What Is Total Quality Control?: The Japanese Way.* Englewood Cliffs, N.J.; Prentice-Hall, 1985.

Johansson, Hank and Dan McArthur. "Rediscovering the Fundamentals." *Management Review*, January 1988, pp. 34–37.

Juran, J.M. *Juran on Leadership for Quality.* New York: Free Press, 1989.

————. *Juran on Planning for Quality.* New York: Free Press, 1988.

————. "Strategies for World-Class Quality." *Quality Progress*, March 1991, pp. 81–85.

Kalinsoky, Ian S. "The Total Quality System—Going Beyond ISO 9000." *Quality Progress*, June 1990, pp. 50–54.

Kanter, Rosabeth Moss. *The Change Masters: Innovation for Productivity in the American Corporation.* New York: Simon and Schuster, 1983.

Karabatsos, Nancy A. "The State of Quality: What the Numbers Say." *Training*, *Quality* Supplement, March 1991, pp. 27–34.

Kearns, David T. "Chasing a Moving Target." *Quality Progress*, October 1989, pp. 29–31.

Kuhn, Susan E. "Eager to Take On the World's Best." *Fortune*, April 23, 1990, pp. 71–74.

Kupfer, Andrew. "Success Secrets of Tomorrow's Stars." *Fortune*, April 23, 1990, pp. 77–84.

Leach, Kenneth E. *The Development of the Globe Metallurgical Quality System.* Cleveland: Globe Metallurgical Incorporated, 1989. [Case Study]

————. "Quality Audits Pay Off for Baldrige Award Winner." *Modern Casting*, May 1989, pp. 46–47.

Lofgren, George Q. "Quality System Registration." *Quality Progress*, May 1991, pp. 35–37.

Main, Jeremy. "How to Win the Baldrige Award." *Fortune*, April 23, 1990, pp. 101–116.

————. "Is the Baldrige Overblown?" *Fortune*, July 1, 1991, pp. 62–65.

Management Practices—U.S. Companies Improve Performance through Quality Efforts (GAO/NSIAD-91-190). Washington, D.C.: United States General Accounting Office, May 1991.

Mann, Nancy R. *The Keys to Excellence: The Story of the Deming Philosophy.* Los Angeles: Prestwick Books, 1985.

Markhoff, John. "Xerox Is Trying a Comeback." *New York Times*, July 10, 1989.

Marquardt, Donald; Jacques Chove; K. E. Jensen; Klaus Petrick; James Pyle; Donald Strahle. "Vision 2000: The Strategy for the ISO 9000 Series Standards in the 90s." *Quality Progress*, May 1991, pp. 25-31.

Murray, Thomas J. "Bob Galvin's Grand Vision." *Business Month*, July 1989, pp. 28-31.

Peach, Robert W. "State of Quality System Certification in the United States." ASQC *Quality Congress Transactons—May 1991*, pp. 708-711. Milwaukee, Wis.: American Society for Quality Control, 1991.

Pennar, Karen. "Americans Quest Can't Be Half-Hearted." *Business Week*, June 8, 1987, p. 136.

Penzer, Erika. "Making the Quality Commitment." *Incentive*, September 1989, pp. 88-94.

Petre, Peter. "Lifting American Competitiveness." *Fortune*, April 23, 1990, pp. 56-66.

Performance Leadership Through Total Quality: A Case Study in Quality Improvement. Pittsburgh: Westinghouse Electric Corporation, 1989. [Case Study]

Phillips, Stephen, Amy Dunkin, James B. Treece, and Keith H. Hammonds. "King Customer: At Companies that Listen Hard and Respond Fast, Bottom Lines Thrive." *Business Week*, March 12, 1990, pp. 88-94.

Pierson, John. "Is the Sky Falling on American Competitiveness?" *The Quality Review*, Summer 1987, pp.2-6.

Pitta, Julie. "Bean Counters Invade the Ivory Tower." *Forbes*, September 18, 1989, pp. 198-199.

Pollan, Stephan M. and Mark Levine. "The Secrets to Surviving the 90s and Flourishing in the 21st Century." US. *News and World Report*, October 29, 1990, Special Advertising Supplement.

Port, Otis. "The Push For Quality." *Business Week*, June 8, 1987, pp. 130-135.

Rehfeld, John E. "What Working for a Japanese Company Taught Me." *Harvard Business Review*, November–December 1990, pp. 167-176.

Reich, Robert B. "Who Is Us?" *Harvard Business Review*, January–February 1990, pp. 53-64.

Reichheld, Frederick E. and W. Earl Sasser, Jr. "Zero Defections: Quality Comes to Services." *Harvard Business Review*, September–October 1990, pp. 105-111.

Reimann, Curt W. "National Quality Award Brings Opportunities for Industry" *Business America*, May 9, 1988, pp. 5-7.

———. "The Baldrige Award: Leading the Way in Quality Initiatives." *Quality Progress*, July 1989, pp. 35-39.

———. "Winning Strategies for Quality Improvement." *Business America*, March 25, 1991, pp. 8-11.

Rohan, Thomas M. "Sermons Fall on Deaf Ears." *Industry Week*, November 20, 1989, pp. 35–36.

Roman, Monica, edited by Robert Mims. "That Sinking Feeling Hits Business Again." *Business Week*, March 18, 1991, pp. 52–54.

Ryan, John. "Quality: A Job with Many Vacancies." *Quality Progress*, November 1990, pp. 23–26.

Sawin, Stephen D.; Spencer Hutchens, Jr. "ISO-9000 In Operation." *ASQC Quality Congress Transactions—May 1991*, pp. 914–920. Milwaukee, Wis.: American Society for Quality Control, 1991.

Scholtes, Peter R. and Heero Hacquebord. "Six Strategies for Beginning the Quality Transformation." Parts 1, 2. *Quality Progress*, July, August 1988. pp. 28–33, 44–48.

Smith, Bill. *The Motorola Story*. Schaumburg: Motorola, Inc., 1989. [Case Study]

Smith, Frederick W. "Our Human Side of Quality." *Quality Progress*, October 1990, pp. 19–21.

Stewart, Thomas A. "Lessons from U.S. Business Blunders." *Fortune*, April 23, 1990, pp. 128–137.

Stratton, Brad. "A Different Look at the Baldrige Award." *Quality Progress*, February 1991, pp. 17–20.

————. "A Forum for the Power of Quality." *Quality Progress*, February 1990, pp. 19–24.

————. "Federal Quality Missionaries." *Quality Progress*, May 1991, pp. 67–69.

————. "Four to Receive 1990 Baldrige Awards." *Quality Progress*, December 1990, pp. 19–21.

————. "Payment in Kind." *Quality Progress*, April 1989, pp. 16–20.

————. "The Value of Implementing Quality." *Quality Progress*, July 1991, pp. 70–71.

————. "Xerox and Milliken Receive Malcolm Baldrige National Quality Awards." *Quality Progress*, December 1989. pp. 17–20.

Therrien, Lois. "The Rival Japan Respects." *Business Week*, November 13, 1989, pp. 108–118.

U.S. Congress. Public Law 100–107, August 20, 1987.

U.S. Department of Commerce. National Institute of Standards and Technology. *Alpha Telco*, Malcolm Baldrige National Quality Award Case Study. Gaithersburg, Md.: NIST, 1991.

————. National Institute of Standards and Technology. *Interim Report to the President and to the Congress on the Malcolm Baldrige National Quality Award*. National Technical Information Service, Springfield, Va.: 1991.

————. National Institute of Standards and Technology. *1990 Award Winner: Cadillac Motor Car Company General Motors.* Gaithersburg, Md.: NIST, 1990.

————. National Institute of Standards and Technology. *1990 Award Winner: Federal Express Corporation.* Gaithersburg, Md.: NIST, 1990.

————. National Institute of Standards and Technology. *1990 Award Winner: International Business Machines Corporation Rochester.* Gaithersburg, Md.: NIST, 1990.

————. National Institute of Standards and Technology. *1990 Award Winner: Wallace Company, Inc.* Gaithersburg, Md.: NIST, 1990.

————. National Institute of Standards and Technology. *1989 Award Winner: Milliken & Company.* Gaithersburg, Md.: NIST, 1989.

————. National Institute of Standards and Technology. *1989 Award Winner: Xerox Corporation Business Products and Systems.* Gaithersburg, Md.: NIST, 1989.

————. National Institute of Standards and Technology. *1988 Award Winner: Commercial Nuclear Fuel Division, Westinghouse Electric Corporation.* Gaithersburg, Md.: NIST, 1988.

————. National Institute of Standards and Technology. *1988 Award Winner: Globe Metallurgical Inc.* Gaithersburg, Md.: NIST, 1988.

————. National Institute of Standards and Technology. *1988 Award Winner: Motorola.* Gaithersburg, Md.: NIST, 1988.

Verity, C. William. "Quality–The Quest for Excellence." *Business America,* May 9, 1988, pp. 2–3.

Walton, Mary. *The Deming Management Method.* New York: Dodd, Mead, 1986.

Wilson, Bill. "Federal Express Delivers Pay for Knowledge." *Training,* June 1991, pp. 39–42.

Wood, Robert Chapman. "The Prophets of Quality." *The Quality Review,* Fall 1988, pp. 20–27.

Wriston, Walter B. "The State of American Management." *Harvard Business Review,* January–February 1990, pp. 78–83.

INDEX